W9-CDI-843

COMMUNITY
BUILDERS

Conflicts in Urban and Regional Development,
a series edited by John R. Logan and Todd Swanstrom

COMMUNITY
BUILDERS

*A Tale of Neighborhood Mobilization
in Two Cities*

GORDANA
RABRENOVIC

TEMPLE UNIVERSITY PRESS

PHILADELPHIA

Temple University Press, Philadelphia 19122
Copyright © 1996 by Temple University. All rights reserved
Published 1996
Printed in the United States of America

♾ The paper used in this book meets the requirements of the American National
Standard for Information Sciences—Permanence of Paper for Printed Library Materials,
ANSI Z39.48-1984

Text design by Will Boehm

Library of Congress Cataloging-in-Publication Data

Rabrenovic, Gordana, 1957–
    Community builders : a tale of neighborhood mobilization in two cities / Gordana
Rabrenovic.
        p.   cm. — (Conflicts in urban and regional development)
    Includes bibliographical references (p.   ) and index.
    ISBN 1-56639-409-0 (cloth : alk. paper). — ISBN 1-56639-410-4 (pbk. : alk. paper)
        1. Community organization—New York (State)—Albany.   2. Community organi-
zation—New York (State)—Schenectady.   3. Homeowners' associations—New York
(State)—Albany.   4. Homeowners' associations—New York (State)—Schenectady.
5. Community development, Urban—New York (State)—Albany.   6. Community
development, Urban—New York (State)—Schenectady.   7. Albany (N.Y.)—Social
conditions.   8. Schenectady (N.Y.)—Social conditions.   I. Title.   II. Series.
HN80.A33R33   1996
307.3′362—dc20   95-33292

The maps on pages 52, 67, 93, 138, 144, and 166 are by Alan Saiz. Used by permission of
Alan Saiz.

For my parents,
Ljiljana and Bozidar Rabrenovic,
who taught me to be persistent and
to believe in collective action

CONTENTS

TABLES AND MAPS

TABLES

ACKNOWLEDGMENTS

While researching and writing this book I had the support and encouragement of various communities. My academic community helped me clear my thoughts and sharpen my focus. Judith Blau, Nan Lin, Steve Siedman, Todd Swanstrom, and John Logan assisted me first as members of my dissertation committee and later as colleagues. My special thanks go to John Logan, who introduced me to the world of urban and community theories and research. He also generously shared his data and research, which helped supplement my own work, and made writing this book a less solitary process by willingly reading and discussing parts of the manuscript.

Other people read and commented on this work as well. Suggestions by colleagues and friends—Christine Gaily, Michael Blim, Will Holton, Maureen Kelleher, Glenn Jacobs, John Portz, Lori Rosenberg, Michelle Eayres, Alexander Thomas, and others—were very helpful and much appreciated.

People from the Albany and Schenectady neighborhoods were always ready to talk with me and to invite me to their community events and into their homes. Without their support, it would have been difficult, if not impossible, to complete my fieldwork.

I want to give special thanks to my friend Jeanne Winner for patiently editing this work. Jeanne, a political activist herself, shared with me her knowledge of labor history. Her consistent enthusiasm for this project was also a tremendous source of support.

Alan Saiz, who produced the maps for me, responded to my request on very short notice. His imaginative suggestions significantly improved the maps. I am grateful to Hannah Blake and Joseph Sluszka, from the Arbor Hill Development Corporation, for all their help and support in getting a photo for the front cover.

Michael Ames, editor-in-chief at Temple University Press, and anonymous reviewers offered valuable suggestions and strategies to strengthen the manuscript and its main theme: the connection between the city context and neighborhood mobilization. Bobbe Needham made the book much more readable, and Joan Vidal, the production editor, helped keep me on task.

I am especially grateful to my friends Tammis Groft, David Quinn, and Sally and Al Magid, who spent many hours with me discussing my research delights and dilemmas and taught me a great deal about the United States.

My family has grown over the years and has provided me with both emotional and intellectual support. My husband, Branislav Kovacic, read more versions of these chapters than he wishes to remember. My mother helped in two important ways: first by teaching me that rewriting is always worthwhile, and second by taking over my household responsibilities to give me time to rewrite. My sister, Olivera Vragovic, reminded me to take into account the business point of view and introduced me to Harvard Graphics.

My children, Boyan and Sonya Kovacic, helped by understanding the importance of this project to me and by giving me the time to complete it. Together with their cousins Boris and Sandra Vragovic, they provided welcome diversion from the sometimes frustrating process of writing.

COMMUNITY
BUILDERS

1

Introduction:
Economic Restructuring, Urban Change, and Neighborhoods in Crisis

Every day drug trafficking, street violence, and inadequate city services threaten the quality of life in thousands of American residential neighborhoods, while ongoing ethnic conflict and land-use battles polarize them. That cities have problems is not news, but the current deterioration of life in urban communities has a new cause: economic restructuring. The increase in jobs in the service sector and high-tech industry in the 1970s and 1980s and the decrease in manufacturing jobs have wounded America's cities (Bluestone and Harrison 1982; Stanback and Noyelle 1982; Mollenkopf 1983): That the jobs now available are fewer in number and lower in pay has meant a reduced tax base and fewer services for city residents. During those same decades, federal and state government cut their contributions to public services and social spending and increased funds for private entrepreneurship by offering tax breaks and a range of concessions to businesses. Because cities were forced to compete among themselves for money and for jobs for their residents, their local political administrations often catered to the interests of business coalitions (Peterson 1981; Logan and Molotch 1987). But there is a cost associated with such decisions. The cities that chose to use local resources for economic development did so at the expense of preserving or enhancing the quality of urban life.

What can be done to protect neighborhoods from further deterioration?

In earlier times residents of urban communities survived economic hardships by banding together and taking care of one other. They formed ethnic and labor organizations to provide services and support for their members, or to demand concessions from businesses and government. Although some ethnic organizations continue to provide help and support for their compatriots, it is much more difficult for labor organizations to influence the decisions of large corporations because capital is more mobile and corporations can easily move to places that offer more profitable opportunities. Most business decisions are made not on the local or plant level, but at a distance, at corporate headquarters. In addition, plant closings often force residents to move out of their communities to seek jobs. Residential mobility and the widening dependence on government to provide life-supporting services have also weakened ethnic and labor organizations.

Settlement houses, community development organizations, and social service organizations make up another kind of local organization that has existed and operated in cities, often formed and supported by federal, state, and local governments. The goals of such groups were to provide a sense of community, support, and services to urban residents. But over time many of these social-service agencies have become weak or ineffectual because of lack of money, poor coordination, and a limited, crisis-management orientation. Others became tools for social change and empowerment for minority and poor neighborhoods and lost government funding when, in due course, they started to challenge the social order.

A third type of local organization, neighborhood associations, is my focus in this book. I define neighborhood associations as place-based collective organizations formed to address local interests that residents share. The least radical and most parochial of all community organizations, they are also the most enduring. The neighborhood may foster a sense of togetherness against more powerful external forces. Residents of a geographical area enjoy or suffer the same quality of municipal services and public facilities. They are affected by each other's actions and those of public authorities and have an interest in improving their neighborhood. By pooling resources and sharing costs through a neighborhood association, they seek to solve common problems and secure collective benefits (Rich 1980b; Davis 1991). These lobbying organizations, although not new in form, gained popularity in the 1970s and 1980s precisely because they emphasized place-related interests.

The importance of these organizations has grown, according to some theorists, because many of the new conflicts and popular demands are seen as place related and stress the importance of territory and services (Ley and Mercer 1980; Castells 1983). Neighborhood associations' goals range from preserving and beautifying neighborhoods to securing better municipal services to keeping out "undesirable people"—often drug dealers, hustlers, and the homeless. Rarely do these organizations have extralocal goals. They seldom address major urban issues, such as the lack of affordable housing and employment opportunities. But, as organizations struggling to gain the power to define their place-based interests, they must be counted among the new social movements on which theorists of social change have focused in the past decade.

The central challenge in analyzing community-based organizations is that their record on social change is extremely varied. Neighborhood associations define their own boundaries, goals, and agendas, attempting to deal with larger political forces and partisan organizations while maintaining their independence. Groups are often divided by different economic interests, or by differences in how they perceive their homes and neighborhoods (see, for instance, Davis 1991). Some residents place the highest priority on protecting their economic investment in the neighborhood, usually the homes they own. Because the value of domestic property is determined by market forces, homes become commodities. Residents who want the houses they own to increase in value are often in conflict with residents who are more interested in being able to stay in the neighborhood, in neighborhood quality of life, or privacy—being able to make autonomous decisions about the use of personal living space. Because people can have different relationships with and within their place of residence, different group interests emerge.

People who join neighborhood associations, often aware that their power is limited, believe that together they can minimize problems and improve conditions in their neighborhoods. Members of "radical housing groups," by contrast, are often aware that marginal improvement of conditions in their communities cannot last without structural change and look toward developing new property relations and building alternatives to individual home ownership, such as community land cooperatives and tenant cooperatives.

Can alliances develop between residents who want to preserve their economic investment in the neighborhood and residents who want residential security and stability? Because these two groups have different class interests, one view holds out little hope for cooperation, a view that contradicts the notion that place-based movements offer opportunities for cross-class alliances, that residents of urban communities can be united by a shared interest in improving collective consumption in the cities, in creating and maintaining the specific cultural identity of their cities, and in promoting political self-management. According to this view, a social movement that combines these three themes can bring about social change, but if local organizations separate these goals or define them narrowly, the organizations turn into interest groups and lose most of their identity and impact (Castells 1983).

Whether their members take a larger view or not, not all neighborhood associations can influence social and political events at the local level, even in the limited areas in which they try to operate. In this book, I emphasize that neighborhood associations are embedded in and limited by their environment. Even if they do everything right—choose a successful model of organizational structure, create and maintain social ties with other organizations in their environment, and have committed membership and able leadership—the strategies and outcomes of their action depend on the social, economic, and political characteristics of their cities. Cities' fiscal and budgetary problems, the ideology of privatization, tax-limitation policies, and suburban flight combine to make generating resources locally more difficult every year. These aspects of economic restructuring have had important effects on neighborhood activism.

The City Context: Local Development Models

The debate about local development centers on two questions: What type of development is beneficial for cities? And who are the key players in decision making? To answer these questions, urban theorists analyze three forces that shape cities—economic development, political regimes, and neighborhood mobilization—often choosing one set of factors as predominant.

Pro-growth-oriented theorists argue that a city's future primarily depends on its economic development. In their view economic factors shape local politics (Peterson 1981). If a city wants to maintain its housing stock, have a low crime rate, and provide services, it has to address economic development first. But because the restructuring of the U.S. and world economies has profoundly harmed the economic life of most cities, they are finding this goal increasingly difficult. Multilocational corporations have been able to force cities to com-- pete to attract business; for corporate managers, cities are interchangeable. Acceding to such pressure makes cities economically dependent on the decisions of corporate headquarters (Kantor 1987).

Contesting the primacy of economic factors, political economists maintain that the political strategies of elected officials shape local development. Some believe that the politics of local development is based on agreement among a wide range of elite groups to heighten the exchange value of land. The issue of growth creates alliances among politicians, media, cultural institutions, utility companies, real-estate developers, local land and business owners, and organized labor. These actors—the growth elites—share a view of the city and its land as a market commodity and are able to reach consensus about growth, even when they do not agree on other issues. Competition between cities also can be explained as the competition between growth elites (Logan and Molotch 1987).

Other theorists argue that both the market and the state (defined as local, state, and federal government) influence development policy and that economic and political factors should be more broadly interpreted. "The market represents a substantial concentration of resources and economic activities in private hands, whereas the democratic state is based upon the principle of popular control through election" (Stone 1987:282; see also Elkin 1987). To generate economic growth and taxes, local officials must construct winning electoral coalitions while also forging alliances or "governing regimes" with market actors. Public officials have some autonomy in how they balance these imperatives. Based on the city's specific political economies, three types of political regime are: pro-growth coalitions, which concentrate on downtown development and intensifying land use; progressive or social-reform coalitions, which emphasize community development and more balanced growth; and caretaker coalitions, which stress fiscal conservatism and avoid development issues (Stone 1987).

Pierre Clavel and Nancy Kleniewski (1990) contrast progressive with pro-growth approaches in two economic contexts: manufacturing and service-sector cities. Progressive local elites or regimes in manufacturing cities promote a "build on the basics" approach that uses the city's infrastructure and skilled labor but reorganizes them to attract new investors, new markets, and new products. Pro-growth regimes in manufacturing cities, in contrast, adopt a "bidding down" approach that seeks to create a good business climate and to retain manufacturing production by cutting workers' wages, discouraging unionization, and giving businesses tax abatements, tax breaks, or free land. By cutting businesses' costs for land, labor, and taxes, these regimes expect their policies to persuade businesses to remain.

The response in service-sector cities is somewhat different. Pro-growth regimes promote corporate interests by using a "bail-out" strategy that further reduces investment in the manufacturing sector, increases investment in office construction and inner-city gentrification, and develops local policies in conjunction with private-sector financial institutions and public-private partnerships. Cities run by pro-growth regimes hope to support the conversion of their economies from manufacturing based to business and financial-service based, as well as to sustain profits and investment in downtown real-estate development.

Progressive coalitions in service-sector cities have more choices than do their counterparts in declining industrial cities. They make a greater effort to include the interests of labor and community groups when negotiating with the corporate sector about economic development. The role of local government then is to encourage private-sector participation in the pursuit of social goals defined by the whole community. In the economic life of the city, alternative forms of production and investment emerge, such as public companies, cooperatives, and worker-managed enterprises. Instead of a public-private partnership that defines the city's role as facilitating private profits, cities can adopt policies that promote social goals and create public profit, for example, linkage programs that require that high-profit projects subsidize some of the costs of low-profit projects, such as low-income housing and day-care centers.

The characteristics of cities—the city context—influence which strategy a city will pursue. Different types of cities have different development outcomes and foster different forms of political and neighborhood mobilization. Cities that do well pay attention to local needs, opportunities, and vulnerabilities and coordinate efforts among different actors (Gittell 1992). Even declining industrial cities can overcome their economic constraints. But they need a new vision, an action plan, strong local leadership, and the organizational capacity to use inside and outside resources effectively.

Types of Neighborhood Activism

I have found that the success of neighborhood associations depends more on the city in which the neighborhood is located than on the neighborhood itself. Neighborhood associations in healthy service-sector cities have more opportunities for improving and maintaining their neighborhoods than those in deindustrialized cities. Such cities can offer more resources for private and public investment, have more municipal resources, and have an easier time lobbying for federal or state programs. Deindustrialized cities lack the economic means to increase jobs or to raise more revenues locally. Place-based interests in such cities represent a limited number of shared concerns. In deindustrialized cities, therefore, local organizations—including neighborhood associations—have to be more active in seeking solutions to their problems than do organizations in healthy service-sector cities.

Another consequence of urban restructuring is a deepening of the disparities between neighborhoods. Urban-studies literature already includes extensive discussions about rich versus poor neighborhoods. In this book, my comparison of neighborhood associations in gentrifying and low-income neighborhoods in different cities points up the importance of the city context— its economic, political, and social characteristics—for defining a neighborhood association's goals and strategies, allies and enemies, successes and failures.

Looking at four neighborhoods and their associations in two upstate New York cities can help us see in practice what mobilization and access to resources mean for urban communities. Albany, a healthy service-sector city, and Schenectady, a declining industrial city, differ in both their economic resources (such as private and public investment, municipal resources, and the use of federal or state programs) and their institutional environments (such as local political regimes and networks of political organizations). Based on my study of these two cities, I distinguish four types of neighborhood mobilization: (1) a gentrified neighborhood in a healthy service-sector city, (2) a gentrified neighborhood in a declining industrial city, (3) a low-income neighborhood in a healthy service-sector city, and (4) a low-income neighborhood in a declining industrial city (see Table 1). Although in each city important differences show up between gentrified and low-income neighborhoods, consistent with the literature on community inequality and social mobilization, my central thesis is that these differences are overshadowed by disparities between the cities in which they are located.

Several important social forces shape urban political struggles and play a part in how groups operate and how successful they are, among them the degree and type of government intervention, and race and class inequalities. For example, through the movement for neighborhood historic preservation, government intervention has made some inner-city neighborhoods desirable places to live. Good housing stock, close proximity to the city's amenities, and funds for restoring historic houses have attracted middle-class residents and investors. The neighborhoods' considerable physical improvement has led to higher tax assessments and rents. These changes have had a dual effect: First, low-income people were displaced from the neighborhoods because they

Table 1: Models of Neighborhood Mobilization

Type of City/ Neighborhood	Service-Sector (Albany)	Declining Industrial (Schenectady)
Gentrified	Center Square	The Stockade
Low-Income	Arbor Hill	Hamilton Hill

could not afford to pay higher rents; second, residential change improved a neighborhood's position in the city's stratification of neighborhoods. Through their neighborhood associations, better-educated and more well connected residents have become influential in city politics and consequently able to improve conditions in their neighborhoods even more.

Gentrified neighborhoods in both types of city that I studied also benefit from federal programs designed to assist historical preservation. However, the gentrified neighborhoods in healthy service-sector cities also benefit from middle-class jobs that constantly attract new residents, and from the city's solid fiscal base that provides resources for neighborhood improvement. Neighborhood associations in such a setting are able to mobilize financial and political resources, have an easier time organizing residents around place-based interests, and are more likely to succeed in collective efforts.

Residents of gentrified neighborhoods in declining industrial cities contend with deteriorating city services and often have to use their own resources to improve neighborhood conditions. In poor cities resources for neighborhood improvement are limited, so that neighborhood associations' lobbying strategies have little influence on city governments. This model of collective action fits what Norman Fainstein and Susan Fainstein (1986b) expected to find in capitalist cities: When city administrations respond to the needs of residents, they are more likely to protect the residential interests of middle-class residents (and their neighborhoods), because they are important constituents. Also, if conditions of cities deteriorate even further, such residents can move out of their neighborhoods. However, the lack of investment in such cities also means that neighborhood associations will have fewer battles with "undesirable projects."

Low-income neighborhoods in both types of cities face problems of poverty, crime, unemployment, and deteriorated housing. As we have learned, even in cities with healthy and growing economies, not everyone benefits from economic development (Osterman 1989). Residents facing long-term obstacles, such as disabling illness, overwhelming family responsibilities, or lack of skills, or those hindered because of racial or gender discrimination often remain poor. Poor neighborhoods are also more likely to have "undesirable" private and public developments (incinerators, halfway houses, toxic-waste dumps) proposed or located in their territory.

Not only does economic development not help poor neighborhoods, it further isolates them by widening the social inequalities among city residents, polarizing them even more by income and race. New York City's Commission on the Year 2000 offers a good illustration of this process: "Today's poor live in neighborhoods segregated by class with few connections to jobs. . . . A city that was accustomed to viewing poverty as a phase in assimilation to the larger society now sees a seemingly rigid cycle of poverty and a permanent underclass divorced from the rest of society" (Mollenkopf and Castells 1991:4). Apparent in large U.S. cities, these trends can also be seen in medium-size cities such as Albany and Schenectady.

For poor residents, race and ethnicity are powerful divisive forces. Their neighborhood becomes a contested terrain not just between property owners and those without real-estate holdings, but also between one "propertyless" group and another. Low-income neighborhoods need organizations, coalitions, and alliances that simultaneously address multiple interests of residents across ethnic, racial, class, and gender divides. However, the success of these collective actions depends not only on residents' ability to organize and overcome fragmentation, but also on political opportunities made available by local and national governments.

Low-income neighborhoods in healthy service-sector cities have a greater potential to influence local decision making. They can use neighborhood associations to lobby local governments to redirect some of the city resources to improve conditions in their neighborhoods. But these place-based concerns are not the only problems that residents of low-income neighborhoods have, nor are they the most important. The policies of racial segregation and discrimination kept minority residents in the most deteriorated neighborhoods and the lowest paying jobs long before economic restructuring transformed cities (Massey 1990). Neighborhoods with a high proportion of minority residents are the most dependent on city bureaucracies, lack independent economic ventures, and need collective organizations the most, but, precisely because of these conditions, they are the least likely to create and sustain them (Logan and Molotch 1987:136). Because neighborhood associations do not represent the unemployed and working poor, these neighborhoods need other community, labor, and religious organizations to force local governments to address questions of affordable housing, unemployment, and poverty.

The problem for low-income neighborhoods is that, while they have to create organizations with more appropriate strategies, how to do it is not at all obvious. If urban residents and their neighborhoods are to address urban issues in a meaningful way, they need to work toward changing the social structure, either through "radical" organizations (Davis 1991) or through cross-class alliances formed around residents' common desire to make cities better places for everyone (Castells 1983). In Albany and Schenectady, both approaches were used, but neither was very successful. Although the "radical" organizations addressed important issues for all neighborhood residents, they were ethnically homogeneous and did not receive wide support. At the same time, black and white home owners were able to create joint neighborhood associations to protect their neighborhoods, but not across class lines—poor white and black residents were not active in these organizations.

Residents of low-income neighborhoods in declining cities are in the most desperate situation. They have lost their jobs and income and witnessed the deterioration of their neighborhoods and local services. The economic decline of the city and the increase in the neighborhood's racial and ethnic diversity have contributed to further social fragmentation. Lobbying strategies, which pit one group against the other, do not address their needs, and residents face problems not easily solved by municipal government, even if the city leadership is sympathetic. They need activities that build a sense of community and organizations capable of reaching beyond the city to demand services and resources from state and federal governments.

A Tale of Two Cities and Four Neighborhoods

In Chapter 2, I place neighborhood associations in the context of the economic and political changes that cities in the United States underwent between the last decade of the nineteenth century and 1990. Since the issues faced by the four neighborhoods in the book are fairly typical, this is a story not just about Albany and Schenectady, but also about other cities and neighborhoods reacting to the same national economic stimulus of deindustrialization, with mixed and often conflicting results.

The history of neighborhood movements in the United States points up the differences between these organizations and other locally based collective actions. Neighborhood associations have traditionally addressed issues that people share as residents of one community. I argue that stressing issues of residential life (residential land use, services, beautification) is more beneficial for residents who are home owners with a concomitant higher socioeconomic status than for non–home owners. I specifically examine the two issues that urban neighborhoods find the most urgent: land-use control and crime.

Neighborhood associations reflect the economic, political, and cultural characteristics of their environments, which in turn are changed and shaped by organizational activities. In Albany, the neighborhood movement developed in reaction to two forces: a political machine that shaped residents' political participation, and the state government that influenced the city's economic transformation. In Schenectady, neighborhood associations emerged because of a decline in the city's industrial base and the weakening of ethnic and labor organizations.

Some of the land-use characteristics of the four low-income and gentrified neighborhoods in Schenectady and Albany show that all share some common physical characteristics: old housing stock, a high density of buildings, a prevalence of attached multiunit structures, and (except the Stockade) a high percentage of rental units (see Table 2).

A comparison of gentrified and low-income neighborhoods shows that they differ markedly in the socio-economic characteristics of their residents. In Albany, for example, the gentrified neighborhood of Center Square in 1980 had twice as many high-income residents as Arbor Hill, a low-income neighborhood, had (see Table 3). Arbor Hill had nearly three times as many households receiving public assistance as did Center Square, whose residents were three times as likely to have college degrees and more than twice as likely to work in managerial or professional jobs than Arbor Hill's residents. The unemployment rate is three times higher in Arbor Hill. Center Square has more single households, and Arbor Hill has more households with children. A comparison between Schenectady's gentrified Stockade and low-income Hamilton Hill neighborhoods reveals similar differences.

By the same token, Center Square and Stockade have much in common. Most residents of these gentrified neighborhoods in different cities are affluent but not rich. They have professional jobs and are well educated and dedicated to urban life. Some residents have lived in these neighborhoods for years, are attached to neighborhood amenities, and participate in neighborhood social and political life. Other residents (perhaps the majority) are more transient and less likely to own homes in the neighborhood—and even if they do, this is not an obstacle to their residential mobility. They live in the neighborhood to be close to their workplaces, or because they like the diversity of urban life. Both neighborhoods have a percentage of low-income residents who are not very visible, often the elderly who lived in the neighborhood be-

Table 2. Land-Use Characteristics of Neighborhoods in Albany and Schenectady

Housing	Center Square (%)	Arbor Hill (%)	The Stockade (%)	Hamilton Hill (%)
Occupancy	77.9	69.2	83.8	82.3
Rental units	83.0	83.3	27.0	66.0
Multi-units	82.0	70.0	4.0	23.2
Built before 1950	99.0	70.1	98.0	99.4

Source: U.S. Bureau of the Census, Census of Population and Housing, 1981.

Table 3. Socioeconomic Characteristics of Neighborhoods in Albany and Schenectady

Residents	Center Square (%)	Arbor Hill (%)	The Stockade (%)	Hamilton Hill (%)
Black	11.2	72.9	2.0	26.1
Single	61.7	39.2	61.0	30.1
College degree	61.9	19.1	52.6	13.4
Work for government	38.9	38.7	25.3	22.7
High family income	15.3	8.0	19.2	6.2
Unemployed	4.4	12.1	5.6	15.6
On public assistance	11.6	32.4	19.5	33.4
Same house 5+ years	21.8	40.9	50.2	39.5

Source: U.S. Bureau of the Census, Census of Population and Housing, 1981.

fore it was gentrified. The fact that they are mostly home owners who rent out part of their homes explains how they can afford to live there. Also, some low-income people are clustered on the fringes of each neighborhood, which further contributes to their invisibility.

A close look at neighborhood organizations in the two cities helps us see the impact of city context on the effectiveness of locally based initiatives. In Albany (which I discuss in Chapter 3), "restructuring" has created a healthy service-sector city. Such a city provides a large number of well-paid professional jobs, has a sound fiscal policy, and is seen as a "good place for business." However, Albany also harbors deteriorated and crime-ridden neighborhoods.

This is the kind of setting where the concept of a local growth machine best applies, and where proponents of more intensive development are most clearly in conflict with neighborhood activists.

Chapter 4 offers a profile of a gentrified neighborhood in Albany, Center Square. Its neighborhood association, which represents primarily the interests of neighborhood home owners, mobilizes its resources and participates in cross-class alliances with organizations outside the neighborhood to fight common enemies, in this case city hall and real-estate developers, to preserve the historic value of the neighborhood and to oppose zoning changes that would intensify land use. At the same time, residents are anxious about safety, burglaries, and the drug trade.

In Chapter 5 I compare Center Square with a low-income neighborhood in the same city, Arbor Hill, whose neighborhood association seeks to stop neighborhood deterioration by attracting more home owners and by reducing the number of low-income residents. In this effort, developers are seen as allies, while low-income residents who want more low-income housing are viewed as enemies. In dealing with safety issues, residents rely on their own Neighborhood Watch and on helping each other. This group illustrates the "paradox of community organizations" (Logan and Molotch 1987:134–139)—those more in need can't organize effectively on their own behalf, and the organizations that do survive in their neighborhood will not represent them.

These Albany neighborhoods contrast in important ways with those I studied in Schenectady. The evolution of these two cities shows that uneven urban development exists not only along the Sunbelt-Frostbelt divide, but also among cities within the same region. In the last twenty years Schenectady has experienced a devastating economic transformation: Disinvestment of General Electric, the major employer in the city, drove residents out of the city and the region, depressed wages, raised unemployment rates, and reduced income for the residents who stayed. The city's response to its economic decline, urban poverty, and inner-city decay was to adopt corporate strategies to revitalize the local economy, a choice I evaluate in Chapter 6.

Chapter 7 presents the case of Stockade, a gentrified, historical neighborhood seen locally as the best thing that urban life in Schenectady can offer. Neighborhood-association members actively work to preserve the historical significance of the neighborhood and to improve the quality of residential life, with little pressure from developers. But the deterioration of the city exacerbates the problem of security, and the major issue for residents has become a search for a defensible and safe space.

In Chapter 8 I look at Hamilton Hill, synonymous for residents of Schenectady with decay and deterioration. A neighborhood with the worst problems and the fewest financial and political resources to address them. Out of necessity the Hamilton Hill Neighborhood Association has begun to change its strategy from lobbying to forming alliances around community-development issues and crime prevention, building consensus around the issues that all residents care about.

What can be done to defend urban neighborhoods? In the concluding chapter I compare the four neighborhood associations to illustrate how the city context supports or inhibits collective action. By examining how these organizations operate, we can see what they can and cannot accomplish.

2

Neighborhood Associations as Place-Based Collective Actors

Most people in the United States today find moving from town to town an unrealistic strategy for establishing a private haven from the problems of the public world. Inflated housing prices, limited transportation systems, and the lack of attractive alternatives to are leading many of us to make change happen in a different way: by staying where we are and organizing to overcome problems facing our communities (Hirschman 1970). Contrary to the models of public-choice theorists (Tiebout 1956; Peterson 1981), residents of contemporary U.S. cities no longer engage in a constant quest for a new community with better shopping areas, schools, parks, and other services. Instead, we opt to make our voices and choices heard in our present neighborhoods.

When rapid urbanization and industrialization in the nineteenth century made cities more diverse and harder to manage, neighborhood associations emerged to lobby for improving the quality of urban life. Today their goals are not much different. But today neighborhood associations are responding to different sets of economic and political factors: deindustrialization, decreasing government expenditures, and widespread privatizing of city services.

Economic restructuring in the 1970s and 1980s added these new pressures to those cities were already coping with. Central cities have been transformed by the expansion of service-sector jobs and of high-tech industries, and by the decrease in manufacturing jobs. In addition, as the suburbs have grown and attracted more middle-class residents and businesses, central cities' tax bases have eroded, as has their ability to provide services to their residents. With little to offer in the way of investment inducements, declining industrial cities have been forced to compete among themselves for businesses and developers. In contrast, economic restructuring enabled some cities to use the service sector to foster development; these "restructuring cities" (Fainstein and Fainstein 1986a, b) had comparative advantages in their location, aesthetic appeal, and the position of local industries in national corporate hierarchies (Mollenkopf 1983). They were also able to offer investment inducements to foster their development based on their current economies and their labor-force composition.

Although changes in urban economies constrain what cities can do, there is still room for local action (Gittell 1992). Political institutions such as local governments, political parties, labor and ethnic organizations, and community and neighborhood organizations can influence the economic development of their cities. As the activities of zoning boards, school committees, and policy-planning bodies demonstrate, they do that by adapting or linking a city's economic policies to its needs and the needs of its residents (Ley and Mercer 1980; Logan and Rabrenovic 1990).

Neighborhoods and Collective Action

Ample evidence has shown that neighborhoods can be a source of cooperation and a base for social mobilization (Henig 1982; Fisher 1984; Thomas 1986; Davis 1991; Heskin 1991). They organize against attempts by city officials, businesses, and developers to alter the local scene (Taub and Surgeon 1977; Susser 1982); they organize for better city services for their residents. Place-bound communities "do act—sometimes out of a common interest in improving local safety, services, or amenities; sometimes out of a special interest in protecting local property values; sometimes because not to act is to acquiesce in the community's own destruction" (Davis 1991:7). This process of mobilization and confrontation creates a sense of togetherness and helps establish a base for internal unity and cohesion. Neighborhood organizations can knit a community together and help to turn an aggregation of people living in the same area into a cohesive moral unit (Milofsky 1987). They also give members a sense of purpose and identity. The actions of neighborhood organizations help to promote communal values, maintain social order, or develop sentimental or emotional attachments to neighborhoods (Susser 1982).

People develop social ties and emotional feelings about the place where they live. Recognizing the contribution of a place to the social well-being of its residents as a group has a long tradition in sociology (Park and Burgess 1925; Burgess 1929). Positive feelings influence mental and physical well-being, make residents less fearful of crime, decrease residential mobility, and increase local political involvement (Gans 1962; Hunter 1974; Fischer 1982).

The significance of neighborhoods in people's lives has been challenged by urban theorists who argue that emotional attachment has become less important, in part because of residential mobility and our ability to satisfy our daily needs in larger geographical areas (Janowitz 1952; Greer 1962). However, more recent research suggests that neighborhoods remain important for our everyday lives. Logan and Molotch (1987) find that we draw upon our emotional and social resources to build lives and entrepreneurial schemes based on community opportunities. Chatting with neighbors and having a large proportion of friends and relatives in an area are important sources of social support in a neighborhood (Lin et al. 1978; Wellman 1979; Sampson 1988). For people living in poverty, sharing and support networks are a major means of economic survival (Stack 1974; Susser 1982; Sacks 1988). Our neighbors often serve as informal agents of social control, influence the socialization of our children, and help promote neighborhood safety. Particularly for families, the neighborhood proves an important place for satisfying social and emotional needs. Finally, neighborhood connections also provide economic assistance and opportunities for political mobilization.

The Importance of Place-Based Interests

The neighborhood movement in the United States emerged in response to new types of conflict related to place. In the nineteenth century, the issues that captured neighborhood attention were still determined by class. In lower- and working-class neighborhoods, socially and politically oriented organizations responded to social disorganization, powerlessness, exploitation, and neighborhood destruction brought about by the emerging urban-industrial order (Arnold 1979; Fisher 1984). Neighborhood-maintenance organizations in upper- and middle-class neighborhoods were concerned with problems that threatened property values or neighborhood homogeneity, or that were triggered by insufficient services (Fisher 1984; Jackson 1985). Through these organizations, neighbors learned about problems, formulated opinions, and sought to intervene in the political process to protect their local interests.

In the twentieth century, however, these class divisions have been mediated by a range of political and economic forces and so are a less obvious basis for mobilization. In the 1980s and 1990s, residents frequently organize neighborhood associations because of a specific issue, often related to a land-use change in the neighborhood. Various industrial, commercial, or residential development proposals, such as the planned construction of a shopping mall, office complex, or multifamily unit, can mobilize a community and lead to the formation of a neighborhood association. Once organized, an association may address other issues, such as traffic congestion and parking, police and fire protection, the level and kind of services provided to the community, or other quality-of-life issues in the neighborhood (Logan and Rabrenovic 1990).

How class affects and defines community formation is unclear. Some urbanists feel that an issue such as loyalty to place can transcend class boundaries (e.g., Castells 1983), while others believe that community issues are in fact class based (e.g., Davis 1991). The importance of place-based interests, according to Castells, can be explained by the fact that "the condition of living in the city became a crucial part of the social wage, and is itself a component of the welfare state. While these developments released pressure on demands over direct wages and created a framework of relative social peace between capital and labor, they also led to the formation of a new type of demand movement dealing with the standards, prices, and ways of living as conditioned by urban services." In that respect, neighborhood associations represent the common interests of people of all classes, for they all demand good-quality services. Mobilization to improve collective consumption is thus, "in contradiction to the notion of the city for profit, in which the desirability of space and urban services are distributed according to levels of income" (Castells 1983:316, 319).

Though neighborhood residents are interested in preserving or improving the residential quality of life, they do not always have a shared vision of what it should look like. Some issues, often referred to as "safe," generate no conflict in the neighborhood and frequently result in success for neighborhood associations (Bachrach and Baratz 1962). Putting flower boxes on window ledges, planting trees, or cleaning up the streets are the kinds of beautifying efforts by neighborhood groups that often garner undivided support. But class-based issues are sources of conflict within and between neighborhoods: "So many resources are tied to location: access to schools, to jobs, to social services, and to networks of sociability that depend partly upon where you live. Space is, then, a resource, and, therefore, is not only an arena but also a reason for conflicts between social groups. Protecting 'turf' means protecting capital, prestige, and power" (Logan 1988:352–353). It is not surprising that gentrification of a neighborhood, for example, enhances the interests of new middle-class residents at the expense of previous low-income residents.

Neighborhood associations differ from other community organizations in the ways their members identify what constitutes a locally based interest. Not every neighborhood problem becomes an issue for a neighborhood association. Those that capture the group's attention are ones that the most active members of the association perceive as threats to their quality of life in the neighborhood. And because the most active members are middle-class home owners within the neighborhood, their interests become the neighborhood's interests. Therefore, urban issues that neighborhood associations address are still class based, not cross-class issues as some contend (Castells 1983).

In addition, neighborhood associations' localism influences which issues are selected. Issues of local education, economic development, and poverty are left to citywide organizations like political parties and issue-specific groups like PTAs. It is not that such issues are considered unimportant; it is rather that neighborhood associations feel they cannot successfully address them. Why do neighborhood associations choose not to lobby more vigorously for these issues? Perhaps the "significant" or more prosperous groups in the neighborhood are not directly affected by them, and see no connection between, for example, employment programs or affordable housing and the safety of their neighborhood. Out of their own private resources they can afford to buy a home or pay higher rents; they can send their children to private schools if they think the city schools are inadequate.

The Formation of Neighborhood Associations in the United States

During the last years of the nineteenth century and the early years of the twentieth, every large city in the United States developed neighborhood associations. In Baltimore, middle-income residents organized to gain better local facilities and services and to insure that city funds were used for their neighborhood's benefit. Each association was a special-interest group seeking to advance its own interests over those of other neighborhoods. Such early political contests revealed the dichotomous nature of local reform, divided between the "urban-island" concept and a cooperative philosophy. The former was an argument for urban segregation, to protect middle- and upper-class residential neighborhoods from general urban development. The latter was a plea for neighborhood cooperation, based in part on the argument that neighborhoods could not escape urban problems by isolating themselves from the city at large (Arnold 1979:17–22).

The desire to establish an urban island may not have been the sole reason prosperous residents of nineteenth-century cities organized neighborhood associations. Perhaps they were also prompted by their loss of political control in expanding cities: The system of ward representation had been deflected and confused by partisan politics (Taub and Surgeon 1977). The political machines that dominated the political life of many cities generally sought to channel resources, legitimate the activities of outsiders, and provide information for decisions within and outside the neighborhood through allegiances based on traditional ties and informal relationships. Local business leaders and property owners organized neighborhood associations to reassert the original purpose of the local system of municipal representation and to reassure independent citizens of their control over local government. Neighborhood associations represented political pressure groups outside the regular party structure, and they made citizens aware of exactly how public goods were distributed in the city. They were thus useful agencies of local public opinion.

When the first suburban neighborhoods were built in the 1880s, their new residents formed neighborhood improvement associations to enhance or maintain their communities, successfully organizing to pressure city officials to provide basic urban services to their neighborhoods. Some of the most successful organized in the suburbs of Cincinnati, Baltimore, Columbus, and Chicago (Fisher 1984:74).

Around World War I, improvement associations in outer-city neighborhoods in the North began to shift their attention from securing services to neighborhood protection. This often translated into excluding lower classes and racial minorities, especially blacks, from neighborhoods (Fisher 1984:76). Land-use restrictions in effect at the time acted to protect both residential interests in the suburbs and commercial interests in the cities. Residents of the inner city usually lived on land owned by absentee landholders who were mainly interested in financial returns from their property and did not view the preservation of residential quality as a priority (Jackson 1985:242).

After 1948, most neighborhood improvement associations were organized in suburban areas far from the central city. As civic clubs, home-owner or property-owner associations, or neighborhood-protection organizations, they shared common objectives: to protect property values and community homogeneity by opposing commercial development, and to exclude members of the lower classes and racial minorities.

For decades suburban development was guided only by minimal standards, so it is not surprising that in the 1980s the accelerated growth of suburbs fostered a new wave of neighborhood groups concerned with the social and fiscal costs of this growth. On their agendas were more open spaces, and recreational facilities, higher environmental quality, and less traffic congestion.

Meanwhile, poor neighborhoods at the turn of the century responded to urban problems with two brands of organizations: those made up of socially conscious people who stressed the need for social change and for delivering services to the community, and those headed by political activists who sought to organize poor neighborhoods so they could represent the community's interests. Neighborhood associations oriented toward social change were engaged in building a sense of community, gathering together social-service organizations, or lobbying for and delivering social resources (Fisher 1984: 154). Organized by socially conscious activists who sought to address local problems by working face-to-face with urban residents, they included neighborhood settlement houses, community centers, adult-education schools, and health clinics, institutions viewed as promoting community spirit or trying to create a just and compassionate society.

In contrast, political activists regarded the community as a political entity or potential power base. They were focused on obtaining, maintaining, or restructuring power in the community for the community. As defined by these organizers, the problem was the absence of power needed to defend the neighborhood or give people more control over their lives. Their groups were generally composed of the working and lower classes, with a middle-class organizer intent first on helping the community understand its problems and its potential power, and then on mobilizing it to determine and implement solutions (Fisher 1984:155).

From the end of World War II through the 1950s, in central cities nationwide, Blacks, other minorities, and poor Whites reacted to urban-renewal programs by reviving the old form of neighborhood associations. The main purpose of these organizations was to find a place for the urban poor and minority groups—themselves—in decision making. Besides opposing the urban-renewal projects that were displacing them, often demolishing their homes, and sometimes obliterating their neighborhoods, they addressed more comprehensive socioeconomic problems, such as race relations, the rebuilding of the urban environment, and the pursuit of both individual and communal conceptions of the good life (Arnold 1979).

By the 1960s more communities were adopting the model of these organizations. But it took, for example, "the community-action revolution" and the federal government's War on Poverty (1965–1966) for twenty new neighborhood groups to mobilize in the first two years of Cincinnati's community-action programs, almost twice as many as had formed during the previous ten. The new stake in the poverty programs created neighborhood organizations in low-income, predominantly Black areas where the earlier devastation of urban renewal could not (Thomas 1986:33, 41).

The decline of inner-city neighborhoods created the real problems that these organizations faced and still face. The flight of jobs from the city to the suburbs has made it difficult, if not impossible, for inner-city dwellers with modest means to obtain them. The resulting concentration of poor people has been followed by the deterioration of the inner cities and a decline in the quality of city services. Their local organizations failed to force local authorities to improve services or conditions until the gentrification of inner-city neighborhoods brought middle-class professionals back to the city. Attracted by inexpensive brownstones and the potential amenities of urban life, these new "urban pioneers" embarked on the difficult task of improving the residential life of their communities. As they were a century ago, neighborhood associations have become a tool for concerned middle-class citizens to press for the improvement of local urban life.

Federal Intervention and Neighborhood Mobilization

Government intervention in the twentieth century gave both poor and well-to-do neighborhoods greater influence and required more public participation from them. From the initial federal involvement in housing programs during the Depression and postwar years to the antipoverty programs of the 1960s and the renewed interest in neighborhood conservation in the late 1960s and 1970s, government housing policies and highway construction have allowed suburbs to expand, increased home ownership, and provided more urban services.

By 1976, the concept of neighborhood revitalization had become an important part of political rhetoric. At the federal level, the concept was legitimated by the appointment of the National Commission on Neighborhoods. Federally sponsored community-development programs gave citizens the right to comment at public hearings. However, residents still had a limited impact on program implementation. These programs were nevertheless seen as tools of power for residents, especially the National Environmental Protection Act in 1969 and the Historic Preservation Act in 1966. New programs also gave the neighborhoods economic resources. The Better Community Act of 1974 provided cities over a period of three years with $8.4 billion for neighborhood programs and permitted some funds to go directly to local governments to be used for redevelopment at their discretion (Shoenberg and Rosenbaum 1980). In addition, the concept of "neighborhood" grew in value after 1974 as more and more neighborhood groups worked to improve, or at least maintain, local services (Goering 1979).

Even though the recent spread and consolidation of the neighborhood movement has occurred because residents perceive neighborhood organizations as successful tools for stabilizing their neighborhoods and attracting federal funds (Thomas 1986), government intervention has not benefited everyone. For example, urban renewal did not improve residential life in poor neighborhoods. Downs's study of 130 large cities showed that urban renewal was carried out in cities where large corporations had their headquarters and the central business district was already being revitalized. Moreover, the corporations exerted their influence on city policymakers to help them expand into adjacent areas by using urban-renewal funds to clear the land, often of low-income housing (Black 1975; Downs 1981:5). The low-income housing programs intended to provide shelter to those unable to purchase it on the private market were not funded sufficiently to replace the housing that was destroyed, let alone to provide housing for all who needed it. In subsequent years, redevelopment policy has emphasized the improvement of places rather than assistance to people. Community-development block-grant funds, distributed by formula rather than to specific projects, could not be used for constructing low-income housing. Renters were offered only a few benefits, for rehabilitation funds were generally limited to owner-occupied housing. Most unfortunate of all, redevelopment carries no guarantee that residents will not be displaced from "upgraded" neighborhoods (Fainstein and Fainstein 1986a:16).

City Context and Neighborhood Associations

The future of a neighborhood depends on the future of the city of which it is a part. For example, a lobbying strategy helps neighborhoods in poor cities much less than those in prosperous ones. In that respect the success or failure of neighborhood associations depends more on the characteristics of the city in which the neighborhood is located than on the neighborhood itself. Each city has its own tradition and history that prescribe to a large extent how organizations, businesses, and public officials may negotiate with each other. These ways are known to local organizations and individuals, who adopt them to insure success in their struggles (Granovetter 1973; Meyer and Rowan 1977, 1983). This city context—in other words, its environment—is a complex combination of economic, cultural, and political characteristics that define what is economically and socially possible for an organization within its boundaries (Zald 1970; Wamsley and Zald 1973; Hasenfeld 1983).

Organizations are especially influenced by institutional environments

(Meyer and Rowan 1977; DiMaggio and Powell 1983; Scott 1987), and we can expect different cities to offer different institutional resources to their neighborhood organizations, such as rules and beliefs about the development and operation of organizations as well as existing networks of organizations at work. Since organizations gain the legitimacy and resources they need to survive and grow if their structures and operations reflect the requirements and expectations of the institutions they deal with (Meyer and Rowan 1977), it is important to examine relationships between neighborhood organizations and their city environments (Granovetter 1992). The political environment determines the type of formal organizing favored for dealing with neighborhood problems. Not only do local governments and networks of local organizations influence the organizational values and norms of neighborhood associations, (although these values are also affected by public opinion), they also have a decisive, practical impact: They can arrange favorable institutional conditions for neighborhood associations by furnishing them with resources or structured access to decision making. Both the strategy a neighborhood chooses to pursue and its outcome thus depend on the social, economic, and political characteristics of its environment, the city.

Even though neighborhood organizations are influenced and constrained by their environments, they are not powerless, for they help shape those environments. Specific constituencies use organizations to articulate their values, to redefine prevailing norms, and to legitimate issues by putting them on public agendas.

I explain the successes and failures of local collective actions by building on two theoretical traditions. The first, supported by urban and organizational theorists, stresses that successful local action requires the mobilizing of resources. The second, drawn from the literature on community organizing and from the new social movements, says that, in resource-scarce environments, organizations emphasize the importance of grass roots tactics, protest, and changing social meaning and the "control of the symbolic realm of information and culture, which . . . is increasingly contested in postindustrial societies" (Čapek and Gilderbloom 1992:42).

Resources and Neighborhood Action

By pooling neighborhood and community resources, neighborhood associations want to address member-defined issues and solve common problems threatening the residents' quality of life. Typical financial and political resources include money, access to information, knowledge, expertise, and sociopolitical support, but the characteristics of each city influence the amount and kind of resources associations can acquire. Some urban political economists root the success of locally based residential efforts in the relationship among the city's economy, its government (political regime), and national policies (Mollenkopf 1983; Fainstein and Fainstein 1986a, b). Economic policies in a capitalist society are shaped by the activity of profit-driven, pro-growth entrepreneurs, whose interests in turn rely on political forces in each city—local government, political parties, and citizen participation. (Of course, sometimes these actors are the same individuals or organizations.)

In the 1960s and 1970s national policies provided resources to locally based organizations to influence urban development and to challenge the interests of economic elites (Mollenkopf 1983). But the increased competition among cities for economic development and the fiscal conservatism practiced by local regimes to protect and enhance their city's solvency hinder successful neighborhood mobilization. Dependent on private economic institutions for employment and for the built environment, cities present business interests as the cities' interests (Fainstein and Fainstein 1986b). Even when city administrations want to do something about urban problems, they can do little alone. The problems of cities are caused by the failure of national policy and have to be addressed at that level.

Still, economic restructuring is an uneven process that has in fact benefited some cities. In such cities, old-style neighborhood movements may still be effective, proving that "in a democratic society, political action can make a difference in people's lives" (Čapek and Gilderbloom 1992:xiii). Neighborhood associations can challenge local administrations and business alliances, pursue residents' concerns and issues by making them part of local political agendas, and develop network ties and organizational structures able to mobilize resources within and outside the neighborhood—that is, actively seek the resources available in their environments. They succeed by becoming part of organizational social networks (Obershall 1973; Gamson 1975; McCarthy and Zald 1977) and by making strategic decisions about adapting to the environment (Aldrich and Pfeffer 1976).

Mobilizing resources and choosing effective strategies and tactics to address local issues requires two sets of organizational resources: internal ones such as degree of formalization, membership commitment, importance of leadership, and legitimacy patterns, and external ones, environmental variables. These environmental characteristics—the complex combination of economic, cultural, and political characteristics of a city—influence the issues that organizations pursue, the state of public opinion, resources available to organizations, and so on. Whether or not a neighborhood association can continue to function in a competitive, resource-scarce environment depends on its ability to develop an appropriate internal structure and to establish interorganizational relations that sustain a steady flow of resources (Knoke and Wood 1981:17).

Stressing the importance of economic and political resources limits neighborhood activism to a narrow list of possible goals strictly defined by the characteristics of the environment. What are neighborhoods in poor cities to do? How can they mobilize local economic resources where there are none? A different approach asks questions such as: How can organizers provide opportunities for grass roots participation? How can they frame issues in a member's own terms? How can they choose the right tactics? Of course, it is reasonable to assume that answers to these questions will depend on the environment of a local organization. But even if a poor neighborhood and a poor city limit what a local organization can do, its scope may broaden if it can see its own potential members as one of its resources.

Community Organizing and Neighborhood Activism

Social activists and practitioners debate the effectiveness of using protest strategies to fight for social justice and social change, or community-development strategies that concentrate on building the economic and social infrastructure of a neighborhood. The argument for protest strategy lies in the fact that class influences how neighborhood residents participate and how much influence they have (Piven and Cloward 1979): Lower-class groups who abide by the norms governing the electoral representative system have little influence. To achieve political power, they have to defy political norms, change the rules of the game. The ability to mobilize and to protest is the only resource the poor have. Indeed, when poor residents concentrate on developing formally structured organizations with a mass membership, they are often co-opted by the elite.

Protest strategies range from marches, rent strikes, and nonviolent demonstrations to riots. Riots occur because economic and racial inequality in the cities trap the poor into neighborhoods that provide them with few options for mobility (Conant 1973; Downs 1976). Unable to make changes using "legitimate" political means, some urban residents turn to violence. Although some theorists reject such an explanation (Banfield 1974), empirical studies of urban riots in the 1960s and 1970s show that many residents of Black communities viewed the riots as a form of political protest (Sears and McConahay 1973). However, riots also increased fear among White residents and discouraged economic development within the neighborhood. Also, the fear of crime and disturbances pressured urban social services to increase social control of the poor.

Nevertheless, a study of community organizations in Cleveland shows that groups that never used confrontation or protest strategies rarely succeeded in achieving any social change (Reidy 1975). To address their problems, low-income neighborhoods must deal with the distribution of power in the community. The important question becomes this: How can an organization force a city to address neighborhood issues without alienating more moderate supporters?

In cities where economic resources are scarce, neighborhoods can most usefully forgo protest strategies and instead direct action toward gaining control over the delivery of services, or over programs and development projects that will directly serve their members (see Davidson 1979; Burnett 1983; Mayer 1984). A large number of communities and neighborhoods have formed at least three types of development corporations to do exactly that: community-development corporations (for economic, physical, and housing development), community-based organizations (for employment and training), and neighborhood service centers (health-care centers, child-care centers, or multiservice centers) (Hallman 1984). These various nonprofit corporations have been funded by the federal government (a major resource from 1965 to 1980), and then by local and state governments, by foundations and corporate grants, and by fees for services. Their purpose is to provide a comprehensive approach to problems of poverty by addressing simultaneously the economic, social, and physical development of a neighborhood (Zdenek 1987).

Today, most neighborhood corporations concentrate on housing activities and are often known as nonprofit housing corporations. Most have strong, talented executive directors with some level of experience with development projects and good support from neighborhood residents and board members (Mayer 1984). But they are also limited by small staff, or by the restriction of their project experience to a particular housing-rehabilitation area. Consequently, many are forced to seek technical assistance from beyond the neighborhood. Two potential problem areas can undermine community-development corporations' success (Bruyn 1987). The first challenge is to maintain local autonomy by insuring that local residents have control over economic resources. With corporation success and growth, citizen involvement often decreases, or the focus shifts from community needs to individual and group interests (Blakely and

Aparicio 1990; Stoecker 1991). The second challenge is to develop and to maintain economic viability, which means developing and managing resources and creating a surplus that can be reinvested in the community. The success of community development depends on how well communities meet both these challenges.

Critics of the neighborhood movement's reliance on providing social services point out that service provision often comes at the expense of political advocacy (Mollenkopf 1983; Stoecker 1994). Organizational constituents become clients and consequently lose their power to frame issues and articulate solutions. The problem with social-service activities, say such critics, is that they "attempt to clean up the social damage after it has already been done rather than address its structural sources" (Mollenkopf 1983:293).

Others take issue with this viewpoint, arguing that the essence of community organizing is community building and that community organizations encourage people in a neighborhood to interact. "While many of us would like to see those relationships result in collective action that will end inequality and oppression, there are many intermediate goals that are much less threatening and more easily funded" (Stoecker 1991:35). Carol Hardy-Fanta's study of Latina women in Boston illustrates this point well. She shows how immigrants use their ethnically based personal connections, collective organizations, and political consciousness to mobilize their communities. Her definition of political participation is the ability to make "connections between people, connections between private troubles and public issues, and connections that lead to political awareness and political action" (Hardy-Fanta 1993:3). The women use these ties not to create an ethnic enclave, but to connect their ethnic community with the larger society. For a minority or immigrant community that suffers a lack of political power and is most vulnerable to economic changes, such connections can have an important bearing on the success of locally based collective action.

Women and Collective Action

Women are at the core of much local organizing. And this is not a new phenomenon. As early as the beginning of the nineteenth century, women were active members of place-based local voluntary associations formed to increase the public provision of social services. Because of their association with the home and family, women faced fewer cultural barriers and role conflicts in community organizations than they did in political parties. Because caring for children and family were seen as legitimate concerns for women, and because women had

little opportunity to participate in other areas of public life, they typically organized around family-related issues (Wolfe and Stracham 1988)—the domestic,
family, and environmental aspects of urban life. When women participated in
movements that addressed political and economic concerns, they were more
likely to campaign within their own communities or to support actions taken by
local men. Although they frequently initiated collective actions, organized support, and held leadership roles, their success, visibility, and recognition often attracted men who took over the leadership (Lawson and Barton 1990).

Woman began in the 1960s and 1970s to legitimize their demands and to
overcome the artificial separation between public and private spheres (Ackelsberg 1988) by declaring women issues's public issues. Likewise, feminists
studying women's participation in local struggles are challenging the assumption that women's "traditional concerns" are just domestic, to be sharply distinguished from the traditional male concerns of politics and the economy. Instead, they point out that when women have organized around the need to
improve education, health care, neighborhood safety, and social services, they
have been addressing issues that are public and closely connected, affecting at
the same time the family, work, and community roles and responsibilities
(Susser 1982; Morgen 1988).

Women in low-income neighborhoods in particular are reacting to political and economic changes that have created instability in employment opportunities, and that have increased residents' dependence on the state to provide
life-maintaining services. When the state, as often happens, fails to respond or
to provide adequately, low-income women mobilize communities to fight for
resources and services and in the process become involved in formulating political demands and organizing for them. Beginning in the 1960s, "they took
leadership roles. They became presidents of local block associations; they made
speeches, coordinated demonstrations, organized food distribution, and dealt
with politicians—both local and national" (Susser 1988:267).

Women draw upon their personal networks as resources by bringing close
friends, neighbors, co-workers, and family members into their political struggles (Hardy-Fanta 1993). In the workplace, women's participation in friendship and ethnic networks, their sharing of common churches, schools, and
neighborhoods, have proven instrumental in their fights for work-based concerns (Zavella 1987; Bookman 1988). We must view such gendered networks
as resources because women do not necessarily enter local struggles as isolated
individuals, "but as women strongly rooted in their class, ethnic, or cultural
communities" (Ackelsberg 1988:303); the same holds true for ethnic and
racial minorities.

Participating in local struggles has a positive effect on one's feelings of neighborhood attachment, one's sense of community, and one's political consciousness (McCourt 1977; Susser 1982; Bookman and Morgen 1988; Gilkes 1988; Hardy-Fanta 1993). Through their efforts, community residents can meet other people from their neighborhoods, cement friendships, and act, rather than feel paralyzed by frustration. They also become aware of how their problems are related to the political and economic conditions of their communities. Local struggle then becomes oriented toward changing these conditions.

Neighborhood Associations in Albany and Schenectady

The neighborhoods I looked at in Albany and Schenectady are part of a larger region, the Capital District, which has about 700,000 people and is located in northeastern New York State. Historically, this has been an important transportation and trade center: in the nineteenth century, because of the superior water transportation on the Hudson and Mohawk Rivers, the Erie Canal (which facilitated travel west to the Great Lakes and beyond), and the Champlain Canal to the north; in the 1860s, as a hub for rail traffic; and in the twentieth century, when a complex system of interstate highways was built. The area's three major cities, Albany, Schenectady, and Troy, important industrial centers in the nineteenth century, developed over the next hundred years under contrasting economic, social, and political conditions.

Albany, the seat of New York State's government since 1797, is one of the oldest chartered cities in the United States. After the Civil War it grew in population and commerce, but it remained what it had become by the early nineteenth century—a political and financial rather than an industrial center. Schenectady and Troy, by contrast, were more important as industrial cities. The region was rich in natural resources, with mountain streams generating power for the mills, while the adjoining canal and river network provided cheap, convenient transportation for raw materials and for the distribution of finished products to other markets. With the advent of steam-engine manufacturing in 1848, Schenectady became an industrial center. Two industrial giants, the American Locomotive Company (founded in 1854) and General Electric (1886) made this city famous as "the city that lights and hauls the world" (Hart 1975).

In the twentieth century, however, Albany, Schenectady, and Troy have all suffered a continuing economic decline and an exodus to the suburbs, as have many older cities in the northeastern and central United States. The transition from an industrial to a postindustrial economy was easiest for Albany, a capital city with a strong service economy. As a result of the national expansion of government in both scope and size, Albany County now has a relatively stable economic base and considers itself insulated against national and regional economic slowdowns or recessions (Albany County Planning Board 1986:3); professional services associated with the managerial functions of business and government, based in Albany's downtown area, have made its surrounding neighborhoods desirable places to live. But a stable economy also can adversely affect neighborhood residential land use. Precisely because Albany neighborhoods are desirable for both residential and commercial development, they have constantly to watch zoning regulations and have to work to keep pressures for growth at bay. Neighborhoods like Arbor Hill, where the poor and black residents are concentrated, gain little from Albany's economic stability.

Schenectady and Troy went into a steady economic decline after the 1970s. Schenectady's General Electric plant reduced its operations drastically, the tax base declined, and the city has failed to draw more people or to create attractive opportunities for business, becoming more socially and spatially polarized. High-tech experts working for research laboratories and living in the Reality Plot neighborhood or in the Stockade section, Schenectady's historic neighborhoods, which were able to survive the overall decline. With both public and private capital scarce today, such gentrified neighborhoods usually have fewer "undesirable projects" to fight against, and developers are more careful to build projects architecturally in keeping with the neighborhood's historic look—to sell or rent them faster. But most of Schenectady's neighborhoods are like Hamilton Hill, developed at the time of industrial expansion in the nineteenth and early twentieth century. These more traditional working-class and ethnic neighborhoods have lost the young population that characterized them, and declining property values have drawn the poor, who cannot afford to live anywhere else.

The economic conditions of Albany, Schenectady, and Troy have influenced their political responses. In Albany, political and social life has long been dominated by a political machine, the Albany County Democratic Party, which has governed the city and county continuously since 1921, the longest surviving political machine in U.S. history (Swanstrom and Ward 1987). It operates through precinct leaders, responsible both for securing the Democratic vote and for monitoring local issues. Only in the 1960s and 1970s, when the machine started to weaken, was the independent neighborhood movement able to emerge.

As an industrial city with a large working-class population, Schenectady differs from Albany politically. In Albany at the end of the nineteenth and beginning of the twentieth century, one political machine succeeded another; in Schenectady the mayor was a reform-oriented, antiboss Socialist. With its working class concentrated in big enterprises, the city administration had to pay attention to working class needs. "Between 1911 and 1914, the Socialist Party, under George Lynn, paved the streets, installed good sewers, bought land for parks and started public garbage collection" (Barhydt 1948:49). The city's trade unions fought for better working conditions and demanded better living conditions. Ethnic and religious organizations helped the workers adapt to an industrial city by providing a system of support networks. Through these organizations residents of Schenectady participated in local politics.

In all three cities, "churches and association activities, such as picnics or parades, were available to all, and religious and ethnic charities constituted one of the major forms of mid-century urban welfare. The church was the primary non-familial institution around which immigrant neighborhoods organized" (Walkowitz 1978:121).

Though the population in the Capital District at the end of the nineteenth century increased rapidly, the political machine in Albany, labor unions in Schenectady and Troy, and ethnic and religious organizations in all three cities made the problems of urban life less severe. There was enough land to build separate ethnic and working-class communities, as well as space for housing for an emerging middle class at a distance from the working class and the central business district. The working-class neighborhoods, not yet merely residential, were seen as ethnic communities as well as power bases for the political machine or for the unions. Only a few neighborhood-maintenance organizations had come into being, an indication that the Capital District's cities were changing more gradually than other U.S. cities, a result of their relatively modest size the tradition of union organizing in Schenectady and Troy, and machine responsiveness to urban problems in Albany.

The Emergence of a Neighborhood Movement

After the World War II, the Capital District had a harder time responding to change. Suburbanization destroyed some middle-class residential neighborhoods. The growth of state employment, although it benefited the area as a whole, was detrimental to Albany's downtown area. The pressure for office development in Albany was so great that even the machine could not control it. Placing the large state office complex downtown changed the appearance of the city, destroyed the downtown section as the traditional commercial center of town, and brought new populations into downtown neighborhoods. These more middle-class residents had less need for protection by the machine; as state workers, they knew how the system operated. Their knowledge, connections, and experience would prove assets to neighborhood organizations when more federal money was available for restructuring and improving residential communities.

In comparison with Albany, Schenectady and Troy were slow to react to postwar economic and organizational changes; working-class and lower-class neighborhoods were much less prepared to deal with their new problems. Traditional means—ethnic, labor, and religious organizations—continued to seem more appropriate for addressing the challenges of urban living. In the 1960s and 1970s, with no independent neighborhood group yet in existence, these organizations applied for and received federal money. Only in the late 1970s and early 1980s, when the economic bases of these cities had shifted and these traditional organizations weakened, were neighborhood associations founded in large numbers. (By 1988 General Electric had eliminated more than 50 percent of its blue-collar jobs in Schenectady by opening plants in other parts of the world.) The survey of neighborhood associations conducted in mid-1986 shows that in the six years between 1980 and 1985, twenty-six neighborhood associations were established in the three cities (Logan and Rabrenovic 1990:74).

The poorer neighborhoods in Albany and Schenectady, it could be argued, started their associations inspired by the success of early neighborhood associations of prosperous residents like Albany's Center Square Neighborhood Association and Schenectady's Stockade Neighborhood Association. They represented good examples of the possibilities of residents' influence and paved the way for other city neighborhood associations. In Albany, several neighborhood associations joined to form the Neighborhood Resource Center in 1975 to encourage the formation of new neighborhood associations. The next year they created a formal coalition, the Council of Albany Neighborhood Associations (CANA). Not that it was easy for neighborhood associations to establish their area of influence. In Albany, where neighborhood development depended on political-machine interests, the machine was not sympathetic to these groups. The absence of any independent political force apart from the machine, residents believed, accounted for weak code enforcement, favoritism, and city-government inefficiency and corruption, which they considered the major causes of neighborhood problems. Only when political conditions changed, due partly to the neighborhood-association movement, did the neighborhoods begin to exercise more power over decision making. In that respect, neighborhood associations were part of a broader coalition with reform Democrats, who had also organized against machine politics. Most low-income residents who had organized and participated in active neighborhood associations, however, benefited little from the changes in machine politics. The root of their problems lay less in corrupt government than in the absence of jobs. Most of Albany's Arbor Hill residents were and are so poor that they cannot afford the rent to maintain their buildings in code compliance; if city officials had enforced the housing code, many of them would have been forced to leave.

The rise of neighborhood associations in Albany can be explained in terms of organizational theory: Organizations gain the legitimacy and resources needed to survive and grow if their structures and operations reflect the requirements and expectations of the institutional environment (Meyer and Rowan 1977) and if they manipulate that environment to their own advantage (Zald 1970; Wamsley and Zald 1973; Hasenfeld 1983). In Albany, the Council of Albany Neighborhood Associations was an important force in making neighborhood associations a dominant organizational form for dealing with neighborhood problems. The council provided favorable institutional conditions for neighborhood associations, using the media and the reform Democratic Party to gain favorable public opinion for neighborhood associations and to provide easier access to local resources and decision making. Consequently, neighborhood associations gained some power and made the city administration more responsive to residents' needs. Now they are routinely called to attend important meetings and participate in special committees and task forces. They have become more predictable. The city knows their major concerns and the issues that mobilize them. And if the city avoids direct conflict with them, they can work on solutions together.

After 1975, federal redevelopment programs also helped neighborhood movements in both Albany and Schenectady. In Albany, from the mid 1970s to the 1980s, twelve new organizations were founded. The Community Development Block Grant program distributed its first funds there in 1975 (about $2 million per year, increasing to about $4 million per year in 1979), and the South End Neighborhood Association was formed in 1978 to promote the construction of moderate-income housing in that neighborhood, using federal community-development funding.

In Schenectady, where the local government encouraged the formation of neighborhood associations, between 1975 and 1978, six new organizations were founded. Schenectady's neighborhood associations are less unified than

Albany's. The city's political climate is shaped by the conflict between the Republican and Democratic Parties, whose members primarily disagree over development policies and the distribution of the city's scarce resources. Schenectady always was more divided by class than was Albany, and even today the higher-income neighborhoods have fewer problems. The few citywide community organizations were disbanded for lack of support from city residents—some neighborhood associations from wealthier neighborhoods found that they could gain an advantage over other neighborhoods by establishing direct contact with the city government. Poor neighborhoods' limited resources have forced their organizations to look for allies outside the neighborhoods, although, reaching across neighborhood lines, social and religious organizations play a more important role in improving this city's living conditions than they do in Albany. Over the years, for instance, the Schenectady Inner-City Ministry has established itself as the city's most vocal organization. Its primary goal is to provide services for residents, but it also joins neighborhood associations to lobby for neighborhood improvements.

Neighborhood Associations and Their Issues

Neighborhood associations attract and keep members by addressing issues of concern to them. Although some neighborhood associations spring up as single-issue political actors, usually in response to specific changes or proposed changes in land use, once created they discuss a variety of issues. In the Capital District, issues of concern relate to safety, collective consumption, lifestyle, and development (Logan and Rabrenovic 1990).

Among questions of personal and property safety, it is not surprising that issues of police and fire protection are high on neighborhood-association agendas. In that respect the security of domestic property and of the surrounding place and neighborhood are interrelated (Davis 1991:50). Urban renewal and highway construction, for example, changed the physical appearance of neighborhoods and made them less safe, as did the decline in public expenditures for city services. Neighborhood quality of life is also influenced by the services available or conditions in the neighborhood—parks and playgrounds, streets and sidewalks, garbage collection, traffic, shopping and health-care facilities. Like police and fire protection, these services are delivered neighborhood by neighborhood, so neighborhoods have to act collectively to address them. Life-style issues deal with how attractive a neighborhood is: the condition of its housing, its reputation, its cleanliness, the noise level, its appearance and architectural standards, and the types of people who live there.

Development issues are those most consistently on the agendas of neighborhood associations in the Capital District: the impact of commercial, industrial, and institutional activities on residential land use, and residential land-use changes, such as construction of new housing developments and condominium conversion. The well-established neighborhood associations with good zoning ordinances and little pressure for growth succeeded in protecting their neighborhoods from unwelcome development. But, especially in Albany, residents still have to be alert to changes in zoning ordinances or in the economic plans of local government.

Missing from the agendas of neighborhood associations in the Capital District are issues such as affordable housing, rent control, teenage pregnancy, unemployment, and AIDS. Also missing are discussions of candidates for local office. Representatives of neighborhood associations in Albany and Schenectady explain that their organizations were nonpartisan and not committed to any candidate, but rather to specific issues.

The Effectiveness of Neighborhood Associations

Neighborhood associations in Albany and Schenectady have been locally based and have addressed local issues. Some neighborhoods have acted to preserve home-owners' property values; others have reacted to threats to neighborhood safety, services, aesthetics, or amenities. Since many of these threats originated outside the neighborhood, solidarity among the residents developed as they responded to a common enemy. However, though some place-based interests bring unity to a neighborhood, others create conflict. Many economic, social, and political differences exist between people that share a common territory. These conflicting interests over the use and meaning of space are reflected in the goals and activity of neighborhood associations. Stressing primarily the residential quality of life will most benefit home owners with an interest in maintaining or improving their investments. Similarly, residents of higher socioeconomic status are more likely to have other resources or avenues to meet their nonresidential needs. Therefore, they tend to limit the agendas of neighborhood associations to specific residential concerns.

The same concerns and characteristics typify associations in other cities. In Grand Rapids, Michigan some middle-class neighborhoods have organized to keep subsidized housing or homelike institutions for the mentally ill out of their areas. Considerable physical improvement in other sections has led to higher tax assessments that have forced out fixed- and low-income residents (Williams 1985). In gentrified neighborhoods in other states, the rising value of housing likewise drives out tenants and fixed-income residents and reduces the amount of affordable housing. Some urbanists suggest that conflicts develop in gentrifying neighborhoods because residents have different interests. Because renters have significantly lower incomes than homeowners (DeGiovanni and Paulson 1984), for example, a gulf may develop between these groups when neighborhood associations pursue improvement strategies that encourage property owners to raise rents (Zukin 1987). Gentrifiers who buy and maintain multifamily dwellings are torn between an owner's interest in getting higher rents and a resident's desire to keep the neighborhood unpretentious, affordable, and somewhat socially diverse (McDonald 1983). These different interests often tear a community apart.

Even if lower-income residents do not have such conflicts, they have other problems that are not primarily place based. To improve their residential quality of life, they need to improve their socioeconomic position. Better and more secure incomes, for example, will give them resources that they can use to fund their own improvement and to share the costs of collective action. Their interconnected, class- and place-based interests need to be addressed simultaneously. Neighborhood associations can thus be effective instruments for achieving the goals of lower-income neighborhoods if they address issues that also enhance residents' class position.

The description of neighborhood movements in Albany and Schenectady explains why neighborhood associations are embedded in their environments. The associations' characters were influenced by (1) sociodemographic characteristics—residents' age, race, ethnicity, and social class; (2) changes in urban economic activities—the growth of government and service-sector jobs in Albany, and the decline of the industrial base in Schenectady; (3) the local political context—a political machine and neighborhood coalitions in Albany, and the decline of labor and religious organizations in Schenectady; and (4) external agencies—federal social and redevelopment programs. Despite the differences in their environments, neighborhood associations in these two cities have formulated their concerns in similar ways and addressed the same sets of issues: urban services, residential quality of life, and neighborhood safety. Neighborhood associations in different cities and neighborhoods thus appear to be members of the same "category" of organizations, and to represent the interests of similar memberships. In the following chapters, as we look at specific neighborhoods and their associations, however, we will find that differences in their organizational environments are what makes the difference in the ability of these associations to take action on place-based issues.

3

Albany, the Restructured City: State Government,
Its Political Machine, and Neighborhood Politics

The best way to approach Albany is along the east bank of the Hudson River. After miles and miles of low-rise towns and countryside, a beautiful urban skyline appears, dominated by the Governor Nelson A. Rockefeller Empire State Plaza, a complex of tall government buildings, a museum, and a theater. It is the symbol of the new postindustrial city.

Albany has a long tradition of being an important place. Grand old structures like the state capitol and the court-house point to the long presence of the state government, just as new buildings testify to the city's significance as a financial and service-sector center. Both reflect Albany's ability to adapt to changes in the national economy. In the last fifty years, as Albany transformed itself from an industrial to a postindustrial city, it changed not only its physical appearance but the composition of its residents. Some of the changes were products of outside forces—suburban development, a shift to a service economy, and the greater role of federal and state government in political and economic life. The others were caused by local forces—the presence of state government, the power of the local political machine, and the composition and characteristics of the city's residents and local organizations.

Urban Restructuring

After World War II, the nature of urban development changed because the economic role of government, nonprofit, and producer services was growing as the economic significance of agriculture and manufacturing declined (Stanback and

Noyelle 1982). Most new jobs were in information-processing industries, service industries where more than half the employees are executives, managers, professionals, and clerical workers (Kasarda 1983:23). The number of government jobs also increased, especially in state and local government. Currently 12 million of the 15.1 million full-time civilian public employees in the country work for state or local governments (Osborne and Gaebler 1992:xvii). The magnitude of the change is shown by the jump in service-sector jobs from 48.6 percent (Bell 1976); to 75 percent in the late 1980s (U.S. Department of Commerce, 1988).

Changes in the employment structure reflected national and global economic trends and were caused by technological, organizational, and political factors that affected how people work and live. As employment became more diversified, new inequalities emerged. In restructured service-sector cities, for example, a gap developed between highly skilled professional workers and low-paid service workers. In the 1950s the federal government made it possible for better-paid urban residents and businesses to move to the suburbs; in the 1970s it helped them again, this time to move back and gentrify historic neighborhoods in inner cities. Low-paid service-sector workers, meanwhile, continued to live in ungentrified city neighborhoods where the rents were lower than in the suburbs. They worked in the city or commuted to suburbs where the jobs had moved. Their neighborhoods deteriorated because of the lack of investment in maintaining the urban center.

Apart from postwar changes resulting from the new service economy, improvements in the production of steel, metal products, automobiles and the introduction of automation increased productivity after World War II drained even more jobs from the cities, for most companies, instead of upgrading or expanding existing facilities, decided to relocate. The development of truck transportation and the increased use of oil, natural gas, and electricity as a fuel for production freed industries to locate their plants anywhere. Looking for cheaper labor and land and for lower taxes, businesses left the industrial cities of the northeastern and central United States for the suburbs, the South, Mexico, or overseas.

The flight of businesses from cities was not a new phenomenon. Industries began relocating in the 1920s, when companies producing shoes, textiles, and apparel left the Northeast for the lower-wage, nonunionized South. After World War II, industries began moving overseas as well (Bluestone and Harrison 1982). The larger, older industrial cities, most affected by these changes, lost their industrial base and could not attract "new" industries—electronics, defense, and high tech. From the beginning, these located in the suburbs or in new cities in the West or Southwest. The jobs in these new industries were often not available to those who had lost jobs in the older industries that had moved out of the cities; they required different skills or were not accessible to industrial workers living in central cities. The factory, a symbol of the industrial city, was displaced by corporate headquarters and office buildings (Mollenkopf 1983), by research and development facilities, distribution centers, commercial and investment banks, or accounts-processing centers. These new information-processing industries and the expanding old ones like banks were the beneficiaries of federal policies and federal money that promoted their expansion and profits. Their growth and mobility gave them a kind of independence from local political administrations that their predecessors had not known.

Cities that had a mixed economy—remaining production centers, combined with strong corporate, banking, and third-sector activities—emerged stronger than before (Mollenkopf 1983). Albany was such a city, with cultural, commercial, and government institutions that had flourished since the Revolutionary War. Its transformation from an industrial to a service economy was facilitated by the presence of state government and by its history as a center for trade and commerce.

Characteristics of Albany

At the end of the American Revolution, Albany was the sixth-largest city in the United States and growing rapidly. The capital of New York State, a regional center of commerce and manufacturing on the Hudson River near the junction of the Hudson and the Mohawk, it was a natural center of transportation. "By 1815, every major valley in the state had one [turnpike], and virtually all of them eventually fed into a turnpike leading to Albany" (McEneny 1981:75). Albany entrepreneurs pressed for the construction of the Champlain (1823) and Erie (1825) Canals, which made the city a water-transportation center; in 1853, after consolidating ten state railroads into the New York Central system, Albany became a center of rail transportation.

By the late 1880s downtown Albany had developed into a banking and retail center as well as a transportation, manufacturing, and political center. One observer described how in the nineteenth century the city displayed its urban wealth in its "public buildings and private residences, [and] in the large capital of the different banking institutions" (Weise 1884:458). The state government had helped Albany to develop these transportation systems, to become prosperous and important.

The original long-term residents of Albany, descendants of Dutch and English settlers, began to give way to new immigrants who established their own distinct neighborhoods, close to the river and the commercial center of the city. Like residents of ethnic neighborhoods in other growing U.S. cities, they reestablished and drew upon the institutions and resources of their native culture: churches, cultural and benevolent associations, and local restaurants and shops. The Irish were the most numerous immigrants, arriving in numbers in the 1840s, finding jobs building and maintaining the turnpikes, canals, and railroads. By the end of the nineteenth century, every city ward had its Irish neighborhood. Lacking economic power, the Irish used their numbers and location to gain political power, joining a political machine, forming a voting block. Political machines, with a long tradition in running U.S. cities, often helped immigrants gain a political voice and adapt to urban living (Merton 1957). Usually Democratic, they were run by "bosses" and ward leaders and controlled access to jobs and services. In hard times, like the Depression, they created public-work projects and helped the unemployed by distributing food and fuel. In return, they expected people to vote for their candidates in local elections.

German immigrants, arriving in Albany in the early nineteenth century, maintained ties with each other and with their cultural heritage through local German-language newspapers, and by offering church services and Sunday school in German. Newspapers and publications in German served as important sources of information about local politics; "of 7,000 copies of the 'Albany City Record,' detailing the proceedings of the Common Council and city government, published every week at the turn of the century, 3,000 were printed in German." During World War I, in the face of anti-German feelings, Albany's German Americans identified themselves as Dutch. "German was dropped from the curriculum of Albany High School, books were banned from the library, and the colorful German street bands were heard no more" (McEneny 1981:106).

The city's Black population also grew. Blacks had been in Albany almost since the city's founding. In the nineteenth century, most worked in unskilled and low-paying jobs, lived in substandard housing, and had limited employment opportunities. A small number were members of the clergy, doctors for the Black community, hotel owners, hairdressers, musicians, or blacksmiths. The poor lived in the South End neighborhood, and the more prosperous in the Arbor Hill neighborhood (McEneny 1981:108–111).

Because racial segregation excluded all Black people from public life, poor and affluent Blacks joined to create various benevolent organizations, churches, and schools to insure adequate education for Black children, and to lobby for more justice and better community services and recreation. Albany's Black Literary Round Table, for example, was a popular group that sponsored readings and literary discussions, like other Black community organizations providing "a sense of belonging and . . . spiritual uplift" (Sorin, Buckley, and Kloppot 1989:15).

Albany's Growth and Decline

The influx of immigrants in the late nineteenth century not only changed housing patterns in Albany but created a housing shortage. While the spread of rooming houses eased the shortage, it created overcrowding that led some well-established families, who looked with disdain at the culture and manners of the new immigrants, to consider relocating. Some moved to newly extended residential neighborhoods in nearby Capitol Hill and Arbor Hill, which offered larger houses with gardens and still allowed residents to walk to work and shop in the downtown retail district. Capitol Hill became more desirable than Arbor Hill when Washington Park was built there, "about 81 acres of land, decorated with large ubrageous trees, pretty parterres of beautiful flowers, extensive lawns, numerous walks and long drives" (Weise 1884:482).

The introduction of the streetcar in the 1890s and automobiles after 1915 gave residents the opportunity to move even further from the downtown. New neighborhoods in the uptown section of Albany were primarily characterized by single-family homes with gardens. Downtown continued to be a busy place, attracting working-class immigrants who lived in their own ethnic neighborhoods and worked nearby.

Albany began to change in earnest after World War II. Following the national trend of suburbanization, White residents began to leave the city in 1950, and the Black population grew from 3 percent in 1950 to more than 12 percent by the 1970s (McEneny 1981:111). Blacks lived in downtown neighborhoods such as Arbor Hill, by the 1970s a predominantly Black neighborhood. Government policies, such as funding for highway construction and tax deductions for mortgages, continued to encourage investments in housing construction in the suburbs and to promote ownership of single-family homes. By 1960, 62 percent of U.S. families owned their own homes, compared to 43 percent in 1940. And 85 percent of new homes went up in the suburbs "where the [White, middle-class] nuclear family found new possibilities for privacy and togetherness" (Coontz 1992:24). The investment in suburbs came at the expense of public housing and public transportation for the urban population. Middle-income and affluent working-class families from Capitol Hill and Arbor Hill could more easily move to the new suburbs than obtain loans to repair their old houses.

The suburbs offered better services, such as new elementary and high schools; houses with modern amenities; more space and land. They were seen as better places to raise children, and they offered affordable housing and employment. By the early 1970s, more Americans lived in suburbs than anywhere else, and by the mid-1980s, twice as many worked in manufacturing jobs in the suburbs as in the central cities (Coontz 1992:88).

Suburban flight left behind the less affluent, the less educated, and the elderly with fixed incomes. Racism excluded Blacks from the surburban housing market. In Albany, absentee property owners converted large homes into boardinghouses for low-income residents. Because these inner-city neighborhoods were not granted government and bank loans—a discriminatory practice known as redlining—owners had little incentive to improve or maintain them. The lack of investment in public amenities and neighborhood services contributed to their further deterioration.

The departure from the city to the suburbs did not immediately affect the city administration, which still had the support of the White, mostly working-class residents who had remained in the city, and it often responded helpfully to their individual demands. At the same time, the police kept an eye on the Black population and discouraged any attempt on their part to protest the deterioration of their living conditions. But in the 1960s Albany would undergo changes that would end the political alliance between the White working class and Albany's administration, until then retained in office by Albany's very successful political machine.

Albany's Political Machine

Albany has long been managed by a political machine. Following thirty years of Republican Party rule, the Democratic Party controlled the city from 1921 until 1983, first under political boss Dan O'Connell and, after his death in 1977, under his hand-picked successor Erastus Corning, Mayor of Albany from 1941 until he died in 1983. What was unusual about this political machine was its basis in a Catholic-Protestant coalition: The Irish Catholics controlled the party, the Protestants the city government. The party was in charge of patronage, police, and the city's night life. The Protestants contributed financially to the party and ran the city. This tradition of shared power ended in 1977 when Mayor Corning, who ran city government, gained control of the party too.

Albany's machine has enjoyed the longest period of domination of any party apparatus in the country (Brown 1986:69–70). Like many others, it operated through precinct leaders, who were responsible for securing the Democratic vote and for keeping an eye on local issues. A charismatic leader, Mayor Corning had a reputation for being responsive to residents' needs and encouraging people to approach him directly with their problems. He must not have been untypical, for Richard Kendall, the historian and professor at the State University of New York (SUNY) at Albany who studied Albany's political machine, wrote of the loyalty people felt for it; the men and women "who held elective offices and posts in the Democratic party, were enthusiastically and inseparably part of the community. All the stories about the five dollar vote, 'registering the graveyard,' peeking in the voting booth to insure party loyalty, and intimidating the odd independent-minded stray do not account for the consistent and crushing majorities in all the elections for local offices" (Kendall 1986:89).

The machine relied on more than loyalty, maintaining its power through corruption and election manipulation, for which it was notorious, and using the local police force to punish opponents. Whenever New York elected a Republican governor, the new administration would initiate an investigation of Albany's government, compile evidence of its criminal actions, and almost always fail to prosecute anyone. Party and city officials were well connected and loyal to the state and national chapters of the Democratic Party, campaigning and delivering votes during state and national elections. In return they expected to be left alone to run the city. But the machine's control of the city also effectively protected it from national organized crime; criminals from outside Albany were unable to survive there (Kenney 1985:161). Crime did exist in Albany: The state police closed down the city's open gambling in the 1940s. One of Albany's legends about the power of its political machine is that even prostitutes paid their dues by "voluntarily" contributing to the party to avoid harassment by the police.

How could the machine have been corrupt and vicious and at the same time command genuine loyalty among its working-class supporters? It provided some tangible benefits to its constituency—jobs, party and city appointments, services—operating on the principle of "the exchange of favors; loyalty to the boss, to the party, and to the vote determined the recipient of benefits" (Hardy-Fanta 1993:71). But the patronage system excluded some racial and ethnic groups from receiving benefits. The political machine had "its roots in the local community and the neighborhood" (Merton 1957:74) and in Albany "local community" meant White working-class neighborhoods. The losers were Black residents and their neighborhoods, and White middle-class reformers who opposed machine politics. The harsh treatment of opposition and racial minorities, and the economic benefits that individual ward leaders garnered for themselves, challenged the image of the machine as a "good thing" for ethnic communities and disadvantaged people of Albany.

The Catholic-Protestant coalition controlled not only political and "criminal" life in the city but also its business community, channeling its influence through the Albany Chamber of Commerce. In the 1950s, with suburbanization in full swing, younger members of the chamber, unhappy with machine control of the city, split from the Albany chamber and formed the Greater Colonie Chamber of Commerce in a nearby suburb. There, they were able to benefit from the presence of state, financial, and banking institutions in Albany free from the interference of the city's political leaders. Consequently, the Town of Colonie became one of the most developed residential and industrial suburbs in Albany County. Today, most suburban neighborhoods surrounding Albany have Republican administrations. One explanation for such a trend is the unpopularity of Albany's machine politics.

With no strong corporate presence to bolster urban growth, Albany's machine could successfully manipulate the city's business leaders. In exchange for their loyalty, the machine controlled or crushed unions and made it easier to conduct business, helped business leaders obtain city contracts by relaxing local rules and regulations, and routinely used tax assessment to reward supporters and punish enemies and critics. But the machine had little power over national trends in urban and economic development. In the 1960s, declining the city's offer to build downtown, the Sears Corporation opened a store in Colonie and started the first shopping mall in Albany County. Sears based its decision on the movement of residents, employment, and commercial activities from the cities to the suburbs. Why locate downtown, even with the incentives the city offered, when economic opportunity lay elsewhere? National forces, in this case, overrode local conditions.

Construction of Empire State Plaza

Local legend, attributes the inspiration for constructing the Empire State Plaza to the 1962 visit of Princess Beatrix of the Netherlands to Albany. Republican governor Nelson Rockefeller, her host, was embarrassed because "the city appeared to be in a state of decay, many of its downtown neighborhoods were slums, and all in all the governor considered it an unfit capital for the state of New York"; he decided to make Albany "the most beautiful capital city in the world" (McEneny 1981:171, 174), one that would reflect "our generation's vision of what the capital of a great state should be" (Kennedy 1983:304).

In 1962, the state expropriated 98.5 acres in the city's center for building the Plaza, which would include the state office complex. It destroyed 1,150 structures (mostly private dwellings) and displaced 9,000 people (3,600 households), of whom 17 percent were Black (Kennedy, 1983:307). New York State had chosen a working-class neighborhood where residents lived in rental properties and rooming houses. The project also destroyed some of the city's finest nineteenth-century buildings and churches, wiped out some small Franco-American and Italian neighborhoods, and destroyed the downtown as a central shopping area for the neighborhood (McEneny 1981:174). Only two prominent buildings survived: the Roman Catholic cathedral and the governor's mansion.

With most residents loyal to the Democratic Party and counting on the political machine to protect their interests, very few organized to oppose this project, for in the beginning the city seemed to be on their side. The land was expropriated without the consent of the city administration. The mayor called the move "a ruthless takeover" and the future construction "sterile monuments" (Kennedy 1983:309) before he understood that the project would be a great opportunity for economic gain for city officials. These economic interests overshadowed the city's obligation to residential interests.

Nelson Rockefeller needed the city's cooperation. He did not intend to use his private fortune to build his "dream capital city," and he knew that he would never convince the voters of New York State to approve the projected cost, $480 million (the final cost was about $2 billion). The relationship between Republican governor and Democratic city administration had never been good. Rockefeller himself had proposed and built the new campus of the University of Albany on Mayor Corning's favorite golf course. But city officials set their old animosities aside for the opportunity to raise funds for themselves, to rebuild Albany, and to gain some political favors from an unsympathetic administration. To help Governor Rockefeller secure funds for construction they offered to make Albany County a nominal owner of the Plaza.

"Albany County floated the bonds for the project, and New York State [rented] the complex from the County. Included in the deal [was] a bond-marketing fee paid to the County and the city ($570,000 in 1986). Furthermore, the State agreed to provide funds for relocating residents and for building public housing" (Swanstrom and Ward, 1987:26). Local contractors, business leaders, banks, and other service industries in the area negotiated lucrative contracts and benefited from the construction and ultimate use of the complex. The mayor also revised his opinion of the new construction, calling it "a magnificent and breathtaking reality . . . and the greatest single governmental complex history has ever known" (Kennedy 1983:315). (When he died in 1983, the tallest building of this government complex was named Mayor Erastus Corning Tower.)

For the design of the Plaza the governor was inspired by the hilltop palace in Lhasa, Tibet. The Plaza's eleven buildings of Italian white marble and glass include office towers; a performing-arts center known as the Egg, which houses a theater and recital hall; a cultural education center that is part of the state museum; the state library; and the state archives. The buildings are connected by an underground concourse that houses the largest public art exhibition in the United States, its paintings and sculptures, created in the late 1950s and early 1960s, all examples of the New York School. This exhibition is controversial not only because it represents the personal taste of Rockefeller, who passed on the purchase of each piece, but also because Albany's own distinctive Hudson Valley School is not represented.

The urban redevelopment triggered by the construction of the Plaza marked the beginning of a new era for Albany and its residents. In the 1970s and 1980s governors and city officials used urban-renewal and state-development funds to further change and rehabilitate the downtown, renovating old buildings and constructing new ones. The city-state partnership persuaded the machine that the old view that federal programs were a threat to their power had been mistaken.

> Albany was among the last major cities to take advantage of federal programs. The Albany County Urban Renewal Agency was not established until 1960, and its first housing project did not break ground until 1967. It was the Republican Party, not the Democrats, who promoted greater participation in the "War on Poverty" (an issue in the 1965 mayoral election). The city's first application for anti-poverty funds was denied because local officials failed to sign it; the next, because the city's three-person "community representative" advisory board was understood even by the Federal bureaucracy to be unrepresentative of the community. (Logan and Rabrenovic, 1990:15)

The machine became more entrepreneurial, offering to help developers and real-estate agents interested in intensifying land use in Albany and abandoning the interests of its loyal downtown residents, intent on transforming Albany's downtown from a residential and retail district into a central business district. This departure from the traditional role of political machines is the primary reason that the Albany machine has survived.

The economic revitalization of downtown helped neighborhoods that were gentrified in the 1970s and 1980s and offered employment that favored a better-educated labor force. But other neighborhoods became overcrowded and deteriorated even faster, and for residents without the new skills, the only jobs available were in low-paid services.

The Transformation of the Machine

Although the construction of Empire State Plaza, completed in 1973, made city and party officials wealthier, it weakened the machine's grip on the city, for it removed a great part of the downtown residential area, taking with it much of the machine's political base as longtime residents were forced to move out of the city. The neighborhoods that did survive attracted new residents; not only were they not loyal to the machine, but they were part of the new reform forces gaining power, and they wanted to reclaim the political process.

By the late 1960s the machine had begun to lose control of the elections, and so of city and state offices and agencies. From 1966 until 1970, a Republican represented the district in Congress, and in 1968 the Republican Party elected a state senator, two state assembly members, and a county district attorney—a position critical to the operation of a political machine (McEneny 1981). Although these losses were later recovered through redistricting, they introduced a new level of competition into local politics (Swanstrom and Ward 1987). But the alarm sounded when the mayor's position was threatened. In 1969 Mayor Corning won reelection by a landslide (37,896 to 15,212); in 1973 he won by his smallest margin ever (25,390 to 21,838). In the same election, an insurgent Democratic candidate lost by only fourteen votes in her bid to represent a downtown residential neighborhood in the city council (Logan and Rabrenovic 1990).

To machine leaders, the election results sent a clear message: If the machine was to survive, they would have to find another power base. They found it among uptown middle-class residents and neighborhoods where city workers lived, and in the business community. The political machine transformed itself into a growth machine. Although Tom Whalen, mayor from 1983 to 1993, had risen to power through the support of the machine, he lacked the personal charisma Mayor Corning had counted on to insure popular support.

Instead, he stressed the importance of the city's sound fiscal policy. His administration supported projects that brought more tax revenues to the city. He still used the party and the machine to gain electoral support, but the party favors, jobs, and appointments went not to White working-class but to loyal middle-class residents. The practice of using tax assessment for political purposes continued.

What happened in Albany, although unusual for a political machine, was not unique. Urban researchers have found that local administrations or political regimes in cities are the most powerful shapers of the institutional environment (Elkin 1985; Fainstein and Fainstein 1986b; Stone 1989; Vogel 1992). In a pro-growth economic environment, these regimes keep themselves in power by becoming brokers for business; they directly translate the program of powerful interest groups into local policy. Different city administrations support different sets of interests. In some cities, administrations pursue the interest of their growth machines, notably the local property-owning elite, of business leaders, landowners, real-estate developers, and bankers (Molotch 1976). Scarce development funds force localities and their elites to compete with each other, and city governments take the upper hand in attracting development. Consequently, members of the elite become interested in joining the local government in order at least to influence the city's decisions, at most to help make them. This economic process is often considered by politicians, business leaders, and many social scientists as one that a city must follow if it is not to become destitute.

In this view, economic prosperity is necessary to protect the fiscal base of local government. Good government has to pursue development policies that will attract investment to the city. Otherwise, "local business will suffer, workers will lose employment opportunities, cultural life will decline, and city land values will fall" (Peterson 1981:29). A local government intent on attracting investment to its city must compete relentlessly with other cities for scarce resources for development. Albany followed such a policy; judged by this economic view, its program is a success story.

The Restructured City

By the 1990s, city officials were happy to pronounce Albany a city with a healthy service-sector economy, able to attract public investment and increase the number of state-government functions. It also benefits from the presence of a large state university. Although public institutions and nonprofit organizations are exempt from local property taxes, the city gains from the jobs that they provide. Albany and its suburbs have a well-educated work force, good housing stock, ample cultural and educational institutions, and a good transportation system that connects with the other major cities in the region such as New York, Boston, and Montreal. Lake George, Saratoga, and the Adirondack and Catskill Mountains provide residents with the opportunity to enjoy a variety of summer and winter sports.

These amenities are touted to promote the city as a good place to conduct business, to work, and to live. Major employers cover the public, private, and nonprofit sectors and include the state of New York, the city and the county of Albany, the New York Telephone Company, the Niagara-Mohawk and Power Corporation, and the Albany Medical Center. *Fortune* magazine in 1991 ranked the city seven on a scale of fifty in its access to quality labor, and twenty-eight in its probusiness attitude. Both rankings were higher than those of other cities in the region notably Boston, Buffalo, and New York City (Huey 1991:73).

In the late 1980s when I was gathering material for this book, Albany had approximately 100,000 permanent residents and 20,000 students resident from September to May (Bruce and Swanstrom 1986). Most who came after World War II were drawn to Albany because of the prospects for government employment, which grew 32 percent between 1956 and 1961 in Albany County. By the end of 1985, over 382,100 people were employed in Albany's metropolitan area, and the unemployment rate was a low 5 percent. Approximately one in four residents in the region worked for the government, with state employment exceeding local and federal employment combined, about 39,000 and 9,500 respectively (Albany County Planning Board 1986:3).

Governor Rockefeller contributed to Albany's development by enlarging the local university, part of the state university system. SUNY at Albany, founded in 1844 as New York's first normal school for the training of teachers, is now one of the largest universities in the state. Together with nine other colleges and universities, it makes Albany an important center of higher education. The large numbers of students maintain a high demand for off-campus housing and so have mitigated the effect on the housing market of the flight to the suburbs.

A generous gathering of medical facilities and hospitals makes Albany a regional medical center as well. Among these, Albany Medical Center is a teaching hospital with an excellent reputation, one of the most modern facilities between New York City and Montreal, whose patients come from throughout eastern New York and western New England for specialized treatments such as open heart surgery, kidney transplants, and premature infant care. The medical industry is supported by many nursing homes, public-health agencies, and research facilities.

With more than twenty commercial and savings banks, Albany also serves as an important financial center. Two superregional banks, KeyCorp and Fleet Norstar Financial Group had their headquarters in Albany until 1993, when KeyCorp moved to Cleveland. Brokerage firms and Fleet Norstar provide a variety of local and regional services in underwriting, commercial, and investment banking. Most of the financial institutions have headquarters and offices downtown, some in their original turn-of-the-century locations, some in grand, renovated buildings, like Union Station. In the 1990s, enough financial institutions had been merged, absorbed, consolidated, and relocated to cause office vacancies in Albany's downtown area to rise by the end of 1994.

For Albany residents, urban renewal has been a mixed blessing. When whole neighborhoods are sacrificed to redevelop city centers and attract and retain business, the pursuit of economic development creates urban problems and inflicts more hardship on the poor. Although the city's poorer residents failed to mobilize against the construction of the Plaza in the early 1960s, wealthier residents who replaced them in the gentrified neighborhoods would organize to protect their investment in the neighborhood and to preserve Albany as a "livable" city. Neighborhood associations would emerge to fight for a place-based interest—the preservation of the quality of their life (see Map 1). Together with other reform forces in the city, they would, by the 1970s, occasionally challenge city government, businesses, and developers.

Investment and plans for expansion in Albany continue to make land use the most important issue for the city's neighborhoods and their organizations. Land issues differ from issues about services or amenities. Land value depends on its uses (residential, commercial, or industrial), on the availability of public services (the infrastructure of streets, water supply, sewers, community facilities) and on the social and physical environment (Davis 1991).

Land-use issues are sources of conflict because land has two distinct values: use value and exchange value (Logan and Molotch 1987). For home owners, the house has primarily a use value—it is where they live. However, the house is also an investment and therefore has exchange value. For landowners, the exchange value of land is more important. This value will be realized when it is sold. When landowners and home owners view the future of the community differently, that is, when the primary values that they are protecting (use value and exchange value) are at odds, they may come into conflict. This is less likely to occur in wealthier neighborhoods because both landown-

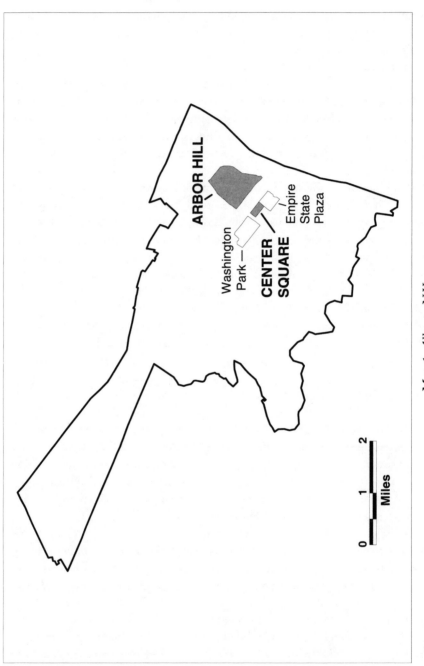

Map 1: Albany, N.Y.

ers and home owners want to maintain high rents or housing prices and neighborhood amenities.

Probably because they are concerned with protecting their investment in the neighborhood, home owners are more active in local politics than are renters (Harvey 1973; Agnew 1978), although this interest may be only part of a more complex motive. If people have only an economic interest in a neighborhood, we would expect them to move out when that interest is threatened; however, home ownership may make people less mobile, and because relocation is not always possible, they may thus become more active in neighborhood groups (Cox 1981). This would explain the activism of residents in Albany's downtown gentrified neighborhoods who invested personal resources, time, and energy in renovating their houses, aware that the amenities they have now are rare.

Over the years neighborhood associations in Albany had opposed proposals for commercial developments that would have changed the use of buildings from residential to commercial, increased the traffic in the area, and contributed to parking problems. Some residential developments are also perceived as a threat to the quality of life in a neighborhood. Neighborhood associations have organized against multiunit housing, group homes, and low-income housing, opposed to any development they feared would increase the population density in the neighborhood, strain local services, introduce crime into the neighborhood, and consequently lower local property values.

The existence of different use values can create splits within a neighborhood. When a neighborhood association must choose between whose daily round, neighborhood sentiment, or identity it will pursue, the values of middle-class residents and home owners often prevail. Political regimes are also more likely to protect the interests of middle-class residents (and their neighborhoods) because they are important constituents (Fainstein and Fainstein 1986b); they frequently have easier access to local government officials (Gamson 1975; Davidson 1979; Gittell 1980; Guest 1985). They understand how the system works, and predominant values and institutional procedures benefit them (Bachrach and Baratz 1962). Their neighborhoods are thus often protected by officials, whereas residents of low-income neighborhoods have to agitate publicly (Suttles 1972).

In Albany, neighborhood associations first arose in the neighborhoods close to downtown. Their members were well educated, owned homes, and were committed to urban life. Some lived downtown because they worked for the government and liked walking to work. Many were state workers, familiar with how the government operates; they knew how to reach city or state officials, and how to find information. These early neighborhood associations benefited from their members' knowledge of city and state government, and the success of their campaigns apparently inspired residents in other neighborhoods to establish their own associations.

But all neighborhood associations were not equally successful. While middle-class neighborhoods took advantage of national policies that encouraged and financed urban renovation, poor neighborhoods had to deal with the negative consequences of urban renewal, which had created more problems for them than it solved: available but not affordable housing, crime, inadequate services, and few well-paid nonprofessional jobs.

Historic Preservation and Neighborhood Mobilization

The Empire State Plaza profoundly affected Albany's inner-city neighborhoods. It upgraded Center Square (part of the old Capitol Hill neighborhood) at the expense of displacing the poor and the elderly, and physically separated the neighborhood from the less-affluent southern parts of the city. The Plaza and other state buildings became buffers, creating a quiet residential area in the midst of the central business district.

The Plaza was built during the years of nationwide interest in old neighborhoods, when some young professionals wanted to live downtown near their workplace. In the 1970s, every salvageable townhouse or row house in Center Square became a target for rehabilitation. The new residents, most of whom were either professionals or state employees, had resources to invest in housing: First, they used their own capital, then money from federally sponsored programs. Although the Community Development Block Grant program was designed to assist low- and moderate-income households and their neighborhoods, in Albany, as in other cities, gentrified neighborhoods received generous assistance. Additional money came from historic-preservation tax credits, offered to residents who bought and renovated buildings in historic districts.

Center Square was the first neighborhood in Albany to benefit from these new policies. The new movement helped promote neighborhood viability in urban areas, as the interest of preservationists shifted from single structures and sites to whole districts and neighborhoods. The Historic Preservation Act of 1966 prevented the demolition of particular structures in central cities and encouraged the channeling of funds into neighborhood rehabilitation and reconstruction (Schoenberg and Rosenbaum 1980). Residents of neighborhoods with historic buildings used this change in national policy to change zoning ordinances and give their neighborhoods a special status as historic-preservation districts.

The "historic" designation made it easier for neighborhoods to fight for renovation rather than the demolition of buildings. The new laws protected designated historical buildings as national treasures. In most cities where historic preservation was adopted, city administrations offered subsidies, grants, and loans to the district's homeowners for facade improvement and structural rehabilitation. In 1974, 65 percent of cities in one national survey had undertaken renovation in their historic areas (Black 1975). The new policies also encouraged landowners and realtors to join home owners in investing in neighborhoods. Neighborhood associations nationwide were formed to preserve the gains of residents' investment, to work toward improving their neighborhood image, and to promote investment in the area by financial institutions, city agencies, and new home buyers (Davis 1991:182).

Albany has a strong network of organizations formed to lobby for historic preservation and to protect neighborhoods from demolition. The Capitol Hill Architectural Review Commission, a nonpartisan body, was appointed in 1974 to keep an eye on developments in the area surrounding the newly built Plaza. Neighborhood-improvement corporations provided housing rehabilitation services to neighborhoods, while the Neighborhood Resource Center helped neighborhoods interested in starting neighborhood associations. The city's neighborhood movement became more formalized when in 1976 the Historic Albany Foundation and the Council of Albany Neighborhood Associations (CANA) were founded.

Coalition building allows organizations to exchange information and resources, especially vital for organizations of lower-income groups because they can gain access to the resources of middle-class organizations. Organizations that fail to build coalitions have little hope of remaining on an equal footing with city agencies (Hunter 1974). Broad-based coalitions of community organizations have the potential to become the keystone of new social movements (Gittell 1980:117; Castells 1983). CANA is just such an active neighborhood coalition, an asset to other local organizations in the city. One of the earliest coalitions of neighborhood associations in the Capital District, CANA grew out of the Coalition for Effective Code Enforcement and consists of representatives from fourteen neighborhood associations, who meet on a regular basis and use a variety of means to achieve their goals. The coalition lobbies for community-development funds and annually provides an analysis of and commentary on Albany's budget. It fought city proposals that endangered the lives and property of residents such as propane-storage tanks in residential neighborhoods and new hospital incinerators. The coalition also sponsors annual neighborhood conventions, where specific issues are addressed.

Between 1970 and 1980 fifteen more neighborhood associations were formed. The strong organizational network not only helped neighborhoods fight for their place-based interests but made Albany a leader in the historic-preservation movement. In the 1980s Albany had the most projects in New York and was among the top twenty of all major cities in the United States.

Unfortunately, the positive consequences of historic preservation in Center Square are overshadowed—as they are nationwide—by the displacement of residents from the neighborhood; people who left because they could not afford the higher rents or taxes or the cost of a house in their old neighborhood. It did not help that displaced residents were often active members of neighborhood organizations and participated in clean-ups and promotion efforts. They were replaced by wealthier residents. In Center Square, the May 1984 *Capitol Newsletter* reported, urban revitalization converted ninety-one rental units into luxury condominiums. Some cities tried to soften the blow of gentrification by introducing rent control and subsidized housing, but overall these policies had limited results because they were underfunded, hard to implement, and difficult to maintain politically. United Tenants, a citywide tenant organization, has tried to address these issues, seeking to persuade neighborhood associations and home owners to keep rents moderately high and arguing that the stability of neighborhoods depends on the stability of the tenants.

Because historic preservation did not mandate that entire neighborhoods be restored, in effect it divided neighborhoods into restored and neglected sections, as happened in Arbor Hill in the 1970s. A mix of poor and middle-class residents had lived in Arbor Hill until the early 1950s; by the 1960s, it had become ghetto. The overcrowded conditions caused by the construction of the Plaza and further deterioration of the buildings contributed to social instability, crime, and racial tensions. But Arbor Hill's good location and historic buildings made part of it a target for gentrification. The residents of that section were moderate-income home owners who, because they were black or because of strong ties to the neighborhood, had not left in the 1950s. They worked downtown and supported the city's political machine. Their houses were well maintained, but because their neighborhood was not, they had to struggle with the consequences of poverty.

The success of the Center Square Neighborhood Association, earlier in the decade moved them in the late 1970s to use their own neighborhood association to pressure the city for help. At the same time, the Albany Urban Renewal Agency (which later became the Albany Community Development Agency) sponsored auctions for foreclosed buildings in the neighborhood, with starting prices of $5 to $10,000; new owners would be awarded grants of $70,000 and $80,000 loans at 3 percent interest. The neighborhood association was given the power to rank qualified bidders, and to participate in choosing future residents. Consequently, lower parts of Arbor Hill were gentrified. The city government again was able to reward its supporters, this time with federal resources.

Coalition Building and Neighborhood Preservation

In 1970, the president of the Center Square Neighborhood Association (CSNA), Harold Rubin, wrote a letter to Governor Rockefeller urging him to take action to improve conditions in the area surrounding the Empire State Plaza's (also known as the South Mall):

> Our neighborhood has been improving because of self-help, but self-help alone cannot withstand the pressures arising from the South Mall project. Some buildings are deserted and boarded up; more are overcrowded and deteriorating. Albany's zoning ordinance, enacted in 1968, has been inadequately enforced. This neglect of zoning, building and housing regulations can lead to the paradox of the nation's finest capital surrounded by a slum. The solution lies not with traditional urban renewal with its emphasis on the bulldozer, leading to a new "development." The need is for intelligent laws, fairly enforced, to encourage preservation and rehabilitation of an important part of old Albany.

He asked the state to take measures to prevent further deterioration, to avoid wholesale redevelopment, and to protect and enhance the historic environment of the new capitol area.

The letter lay dormant for two years until McDonald's announced plans to build a restaurant across from the Empire State Plaza's southeast corner. The *New York Times* wrote in 1974 that "state officials were privately appalled at the prospect of a hamburger stand framing the entrance to their 'Acropolis.'" (Greenhouse 1974).

The Hudson River Valley Commission, which had jurisdiction, organized a public hearing for a zoning change. More than a hundred attended—representatives of neighborhood and community groups, Mayor Corning, and city officials. People from the neighborhood and community groups came prepared to oppose a fast-food restaurant being built near the state capitol; they agreed with the statement put forward by the representative of Center Square Neighborhood Association (made available to me from a private collection) that "the area does not need grandeur. The Mall provides that. What it needs is a modest scale, a quiet and peaceful atmosphere, cleanliness and beauty that will be preserved in part, renewed in part, and protected in its whole. There may well be a need for additional low-cost eating facilities in the area, but these should be established after there is a plan for the area's architectural standards. Otherwise the South Mall will be framed by hamburger stands, pizza huts and fish fries, all emblazoned by neon lights." The Sierra Club's Hudson-Mohawk group representative urged "the State to find a handle to control those forces and give historical and community values the recognition they deserve in making urban land-use decisions." A representative of the Eastern New York chapter of the American Institute of Architects used his turn to plead for "more concern for the physical, social, cultural, and economic fabric of the community at large."

On January 16, 1973, according to a New York State Park and Recreation news release, the commission concluded that "the project will have an unreasonably adverse effect on the scenic and historical resources of the area and that the commercial and economic benefits to be derived are not sufficient to outweigh the resulting impairment to such resources."

Although the restaurant would not have been built in the neighborhood association's formal boundaries, the Center Square Neighborhood Association felt that this case was so important for its own future that it could not let it pass: The association's members did not want further commercialization of the area. If they could win this case, they could win the war. The proposed construction of an elevated highway gave them the chance to test their new strength in marshaling diverse organizations to press for collective benefits.

Fighting the Highway

The National Environmental Protection Act in 1969 required that every federally funded program that significantly affected the human environment had to file an environmental-impact statement specifying those effects. Consequently, the environmental-impact statement has become a useful weapon in the cause of preserving the nation's urban neighborhoods, as the opposition to constructing an arterial highway through the Empire State Plaza illustrates.

Governor Rockefeller wanted to reap the benefits of the 1956 Federal Aid Highway Act, which promised to provide 90 percent federal funding for interstate highways, to build the Lark-Dove arterial to connect two interstates.

The state had already bought most of the properties between Swan and Lake Streets, where the highway would be built, and the remaining private owners saw no need to maintain their buildings in an area that had deteriorated; many felt that it was best to sell the property and leave.

The CSNA took a different position. Its members opposed the project because they felt that the highway was unnecessary: It was a short drive to the Plaza from existing roads. The project, they argued, would disrupt the neighborhoods, mar the tranquillity and ecology of Washington Park, and cost far too much. The neighborhood association formed a coalition with other neighborhood organizations in the city and organized people to attend the hearings. Those harmed by the proposal protested loudly, while there was no noticeable overt public support for the highway. In addition, the neighborhood association was able to "rid[e] the crest of a wave, because in 1969 over 20 urban segments of interstates were in dispute." Three years later, "the Governor's $3.5 billion Transportation Bond issue was defeated, and this seemed to put an end to the South Mall arterial. Soon after that, Rockefeller left Albany to take over as Vice President, and with him went any vestige of real support for the highways" (Cohen 1983:14, 15).

In response to the well-organized opposition, a joint city-state commission was formed, primarily to develop a plan for the South Mall environs. The commission recommended that the area around the Empire State Plaza needed special preservation zoning and that the city establish a special nine-member, nonpartisan Capitol Hill Architectural Review Commission to oversee plans and construction for the neighborhood. Four members were to be appointed by the mayor and four by the governor with a city planner as secretary to the commission, all to serve without compensation. In October 1974, Albany enacted Article 13 to its zoning ordinance to establish the commission, and two months later Governor Malcolm Wilson appointed four people to the group, all from a list submitted by the downtown neighborhood associations.

The successes of CSNA consolidated its power as a legitimate representative of the neighborhood. Its history of success supports the idea that without political and economic influence and power, communities can do very little (Gans 1962). Especially since the 1960s, citizen involvement in community programs has been encouraged or required. Now residents participate in developing neighborhood plans and implementing various programs to the point, it has been argued, that some neighborhoods have developed "political partnership[s]" with some city representatives (Davidson 1979:186). Neighborhoods that have not been able to establish such longstanding political partnerships are sometimes able to revive them, as CSNA did; the group has not had consistently good relations with city officials but has restored them over serious issues.

CSNA was also able to remain an important voice in city politics and real-estate development for a number of reasons. It offered structured citizen participation, which makes communication easier from and to the neighborhood. Its members sat on advisory committees, so the neighborhood had the chance to influence public policy and gain what it needed. It had continuous internal support from its members, essential if an organization is to continue its activity after neighborhood problems have been resolved.

Community Development in Poor Neighborhoods

The Arbor Hill residents who were not forced out through urban renewal, like residents of other predominantly black and poor neighborhoods, benefited very little from Albany's urban restructuring, from the weakening of machine control of the city, or from federal and state programs. The move to the suburbs and urban decline had driven most Whites out of Arbor Hill, and the neighborhood began to be known as a ghetto. Although the civil-rights movement was weak in Albany due to machine politics—Arbor Hill had Black party ward leaders who were loyal to the machine—some groups tried to address the problems of Black residents. One of the most influential formed during this time, the Brothers, consisted solely of Black men but received help and support from area churches and universities.

To improve the quality of life in Arbor Hill, to fight against racism, unemployment, and political corruption, the Brothers organized free clinics, voter registration drives, day-care centers, and an antiheroin campaign. One of the most influential groups in the neighborhood, they publicized their causes and protested against city politics in memorable ways: They once brought jars of live cockroaches to an award ceremony for Mayor Corning to dramatize housing conditions in Arbor Hill. Their actions brought mixed results. They succeeded in improving some conditions in Arbor Hill, but they could never win over the machine politicians, who first opposed them with disruption and manipulation and, when that failed, sent the police to harass, attack, and jail them. (I discuss this organization and its impact on Arbor Hill in more detail in Chapter 5.)

By not applying for funds from federal programs, the machine also refused to help poor neighborhoods rehabilitate their houses. In Albany in the mid-1960s, independent community organizers, backed by voluntary social-service agencies, attempted to promote socially active community organizations, most tellingly in the South End. There, a church-backed settlement house, Trinity Institution, encouraged the formation of four small community-action organizations—the Progressive Community Betterment Association, the Catherine Street Civic Association, the Grand Community Association, and the Better Homes and Community Organization. But precisely at the time that these groups began to agitate vocally for improved city services, the city government retaliated by cutting off Trinity Institution funds—about $13,000 per year. None of the four action groups survived beyond the 1960s.

Once downtown redevelopment got under way, and machine leaders and city officials became more entrepreneurial, they showed much more interest in tapping federal programs. In the late 1970s Albany used urban-renewal money to clear some parts of Arbor Hill, displacing 572 families, 316 of whom were Black (Kennedy 1983:264). Urban-renewal money also helped construct the downtown Albany Hilton Hotel (now the Omni Hotel). City officials justified this use of funds by claiming that the hotel would provide jobs for residents of poor neighborhoods—but they proved to be low-paying, service-sector jobs.

The Community Development Block Grant (CDBG) initiated by the Housing and Community Development Act of 1974 was part of the federal government's effort to give local governments more control over distributing funds, primarily to develop "viable urban communities, by providing decent housing and a suitable living environment and expanding economic opportunities, principally for persons of low and moderate income" (Housing and Community Development Act of 1974, 88 Stat. 634, 42 U.S.C. 5301). Across the country most funds from this act went toward housing rehabilitation and preservation and local economic development, with minimal amounts spent on clearing slums and rebuilding housing, or on providing direct social services to the poor.

The discretionary power of local officials over CDBG funds allowed them to pursue their own economic and political agendas, aided by the ambiguity of national urban priorities. It was never clear if CDBG was "the program to physically eliminate slums or a program to aid the people who live in them" (Swanstrom 1985:181). The loose federal control over local government decision making and its use of funds made CDBG, like previous programs, unsuccessful in addressing the needs of poor neighborhoods.

The allocation of CDBG funds in Albany between 1982 and 1987 is a good example. Most of the funds went for housing rehabilitation and preservation (around 45 percent), public improvement programs (25 percent), and economic development programs (20 percent). Public services that include some social services for low-income people accounted for only 2 percent of the funds. Lower-middle-class home owners received the most help, and the poor—mostly low-income Blacks and the elderly, disabled, and mentally ill—received the least. Too poor to become home owners, they were paying rents too high for their income. According to the Albany Strategic Planning Committee, in 1985 almost 32 percent of Albany renters spent more than 35 percent of their income on housing expenses.

The Future of a Service-Sector City

The goals of the current economic policy in Albany are to further develop and invest in the service-sector economy. Predictions are that the need for skilled professionals will increase, a demand that city officials hope will attract more middle-class residents to downtown neighborhoods, where they can live close to work and enjoy the advantages of the nearby Plaza, with all its activities. However, as McEneny writes, "it is important to remember that they [the Plaza and neighborhoods around it] were built at a cost—a cost measured both in material and in human terms" (1981:175).

Low-income people in Albany have little hope that their situation will improve. They have neither the skills nor the education for the jobs created locally. The city's emphasis on developmental policies denies them proper social services. What they desire is security of tenure in the neighborhood and physical safety, both constantly undermined by the city's policies. In the 1950s and 1960s city administration and landowner abandonment and redlining of their neighborhoods threatened these interests; in the 1970s and 1980s office buildings, gentrification, and condominium conversion deprived some of them of their homes and forced others to pay higher rents or live in worsening conditions. Public investment and disinvestment in a neighborhood, forces that shape a neighborhood's future, are also forces over which low-income residents often have very little control (Davis 1991).

The neighborhood associations that stress gentrification as a way to improve their neighborhoods can do little to address the interests of low-income residents or to help them secure their tenure in the neighborhood. Changes in the local political climate however, may create favorable conditions for community- or ethnicity-based groups to emerge and address such interests. By challenging their limited access to economic resources and political power, these organizations can gain more say in defining urban development and in articulating solutions to urban problems.

This is exactly what happened in Santa Monica, California, when residents elected a "progressive majority to a city council that was committed to the democratization of urban decision-making, redistributive economic policies, a 'human-scale' environment, and local control of resources" (Čapek and Gilderbloom 1992:8). The council introduced policies on rent regulation, laws against speculation, assistance for tenant ownership, and moderate-cost housing for low-income people. Consequently, housing became more affordable, and more people were able to continue to live in the city.

In the struggle between the residents who want to preserve the urban space as a community and developers who want to turn it into a commodity, new alliances are possible (Castells 1983; Gottdiener 1985; Boyte, Booth, and Max 1986; Čapek and Gilderbloom 1992). Cities like Albany, with solid economic bases, have the resources to make these alliances even stronger. Democratic, inclusive decision making increases the participation in local political life of marginalized groups, such as low-income residents, members of ethnic and racial minorities, and women. It also provides them with opportunities to put their issues (like tenants rights, well-paid jobs, and quality health care and education) on local agendas, defined in terms of their own interests.

4

Center Square and Its Neighborhood Association:
Organizing for Success

What can we learn about community organizing from a neighborhood association in a gentrified neighborhood in a healthy service-sector city? The Center Square Neighborhood Association (CSNA) in Albany fits Castells's criteria for a successful urban movement: It expresses its interests clearly, and its members know what their goals are; it uses the media and the advice of experts, forms connections with officials in the local government structure, and still remains relatively autonomous (1983: 328).

With CSNA's long history of successful fights with city officials and real-estate developers, members have learned to use the media well and are not afraid to go to court to enforce the city's zoning ordinances. CSNA defines itself as a nonpartisan group that tries to stay out of party politics. The conflict between reform Democrats and party Democrats sometimes makes it difficult for CSNA to maintain true independence, however, because it gained its strength and importance as a part of reform forces in the city. During the 1989 campaign for the Albany Common Council, the June 15–21 issue of *Metroland* reported, some residents of Center Square raised the issue of organizational neutrality, complaining that the old guard of the CSNA were reform Democrats with "a standing policy of cutting residents dead who run against their candidates." CSNA leaders denied the accusations and argued that the organization does not take part in partisan politics, *Metroland* reported in its June 22–28 issue: "The association neither backs nor opposes candidates. We deal with elected officials, those supported by our taxpayer dollars (not those aspiring for office)." But their relationship with city officials—demanding services as taxpayers, not as rewards for electoral support—reflects the reform view on political participation.

After thirty years of neighborhood activity CSNA members enjoy a sense of accomplishment and success. They are keenly aware that an important resource of the neighborhood is the education and expertise of its residents, who in large numbers are lawyers, state workers, professors, and other professionals. Most moved to the neighborhood in the 1970s and 1980s, after the construction of Empire State Plaza, to work in the expanded service-sector economy. They were attracted by the beauty and historic value of the neighborhood buildings, and by its amenities: Washington Park, the cultural institutions, the variety of restaurants and specialty stores, and proximity to the central business district, making it possible for many to walk to work. CSNA's goals—to preserve the historic value of the neighborhood and to oppose the land-intensifying interests of real-estate developers—are defined by the interests of its active members, neighborhood home owners. Their allies are the agencies and individuals that help them protect the residential use of the neighborhood, and their enemies are those who want to raise the exchange value of land there.

In 1968, CSNA played a prominent role in developing and implementing new zoning and code-enforcement ordinances, besides helping other neighborhoods start their own neighborhood associations and helping establish neighborhood improvement corporations, historical and preservation societies, and intereighborhood coalitions. In Albany, neighborhood associations are an accepted way for residents to present their interests. Neighborhood and community organizations share resources, confront officials as a bloc, and often address city problems as collective problems.

CSNA established its reputation by well-publicized and successful actions during the 1970s. In 1971, residents defeated efforts to demolish four structurally sound historic buildings to build a parking garage. In one year, 1972, CSNA successfully opposed McDonald's effort to open a restaurant in the neighborhood and, as part of a coalition of neighborhood and community groups, was instrumental in forcing the city to abandon the construction of an elevated highway. At least two forces lay behind these successes: the neighborhood association's active work to reshape the organizational environment, and nationwide support for preserving the architectural heritage of cities.

Consolidation of Center Square Neighborhood Association

Center Square is a part of Capitol Hill, a neighborhood that grew up on the high grounds that surround "old" Albany. Known as Pinkster Hill in the eighteenth century, this land was used by the slaves, freedmen and freedwomen of the city for their yearly Pinkster Festival. "Though these fetes were occasions for merriment, the tradition was of religious origin and was connected with the city's Dutch heritage. By a city ordinance of 1811, the further erection of booths for the sale of 'liquors, mead, sweetmeats' and the like was prohibited" (Roseberry 1964:101). The last Pinkster Parade took place in 1822, homes were built on the land, and Pinkster Hill became a White residential neighborhood.

The new residents came from important old Albany families. Quality Row, "a row of perfectly beautiful houses with gardens" (Kennedy 1983:107) was built along Washington Avenue. But around 1905, after Washington Park was built on the opposite side of the Hill, Quality Row began to decline; then it was colonized by new property owners, who converted the large homes into boardinghouses. Washington Avenue below Swan had grown into a row of small stores and farmers' hotels, which in time gave way to public buildings and the emerging central business district, "sleek banks and office buildings, . . . and the grand old homes [became] headquarters for clubs and societies, doctors' and dentists' offices, coffee shops, nightclubs, and apartments" (113). Yet some of Quality Row, much altered, survives as part of Center Square and is considered a segment of Albany's great historic heritage.

When CSNA was founded in 1957, it defined the boundaries of a small, new neighborhood now known as Center Square that occupies four streets—State, Chestnut, Lancaster, and Jay—on one side bordered by Washington Park, on the other by Empire State Plaza (see Map 2). To the east lie low-income houses and a slum area. On the west, Washington Street separates the neighborhood from Arbor Hill.

According to 1980 census data, Center Square has 1,980 residents and 1,545 housing units, most of which are brick, with 99 percent built before 1950. Most of the housing units are part of attached, multiple-unit town houses, and 82 percent are occupied (see Table 4). Most residents of Center Square are renters (83 percent). Though in the last ten years the number of home owners has increased, most still rent part of the house, since the majority of buildings in the neighborhood have two or more apartments.

Most of the residents were White in 1980 (only 11 percent were Black). Half worked in managerial, professional, or technician jobs, and 40 percent work for the government. In 1980 the neighborhood was still economically mixed, with 40 percent of family incomes under $7,500 (in 1980 considered "low income") and only 15 percent over $25,000 (in 1980 considered "high income") (Table 5). However, by 1990, the highest rents in Albany were in this neighborhood, with some one-bedroom apartments renting for $600. A two-

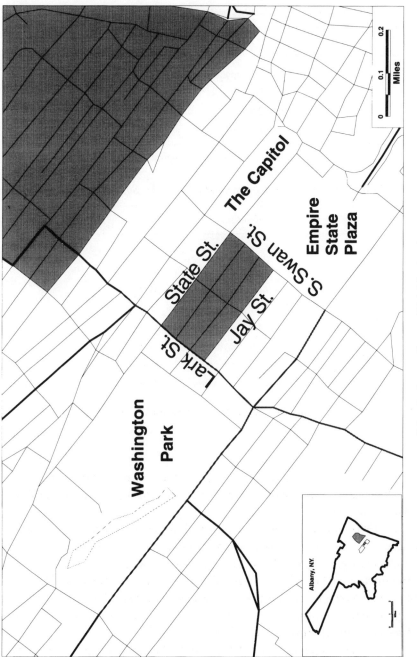

Map 2: Center Square Neighborhood

Table 4: Land-Use Characteristics of Center Square Neighborhood

Housing	%
Occupancy	77.9
Rental units	83
Multi-units	82
Built before 1950	99

Source: *U.S. Bureau of the Census,* Census of Population and Housing, *1981.*

Table 5: Socioeconomic Characteristics of Center Square Neighborhood

Residents	%
Black	11.2
Single	61.7
College degree	61.9
Work for government	38.9
High family income	15.3
Unemployed	4.4
Public assistance	11.6
Same house 5+ years	21.8

Source: *U.S. Bureau of the Census,* Census of Population and Housing, *1981.*

story building, according to the *Albany Times Union* real-estate section, June 18, 1989, can cost from $140,000 to $180,000 or $200,000. In short, this is a relatively affluent neighborhood.

By 1990 only two vacant lots remained in the neighborhood, one on the corner of Lancaster and Dove, and another at the end of Lancaster Street, and developers were eager to build town houses on these. The area has several prominent churches: Trinity Methodist at Lancaster, Emmanuel Baptist at State, and Westminster Presbyterian at Chestnut. Used for community and neighborhood meetings, the churches also draw worshipers from other parts of the city and suburban neighborhoods.

In 1957, CSNA was founded to promote the inner-city area as an attractive place to live and, according to an early CSNA leaflet dated March 26,

1958, "to boost each other's morale, to discuss ways of living in this district so that other desirable families who appreciate such living will buy into this neighborhood and maintain the quality that we value. The neighborhood association's meetings could discuss programs to improve our streets, and such topics as parking, planting of trees, clean-up and paint-up activities" (Corning Papers). Today the neighborhood association has the same goal, although the rhetoric in a 1989 CSNA leaflet among my own papers is somewhat different: "The purpose of the association is to promote the quality of residential living in the city environment, and the preservation of the historic 19th-century housing stock."

What has changed are the association's strategies for achieving these goals. During the late 1950s and early 1960s, when the well-organized Democratic machine was in power, neighborhood negotiations with the city were friendly. For example, a March 1958 letter from CSNA to Mayor Corning, who was born on Chestnut Street, noted that he "properly valued the neighborhood" (Corning Papers). The neighborhood association counted on his support for projects such as installing window boxes and planting trees, and for the more broadly defined goal of maintaining the neighborhood's stability. Today, to achieve its organizational goals, CSNA relies on the advantages of a pluralist political system. As an interest-based organization that lobbies city officials for what it wants, it has adopted interest-group tactics and favors neighborhood advocacy for its community-organizing efforts, exactly what many urbanists believe neighborhood associations in a pluralist society should do to be successful (O'Brien 1975; Henig 1982; Hallman 1984). They theorize that in a pluralist society power is dispersed among a wide range of interest groups (Dahl 1961). In this approach, each neighborhood has the chance to organize around common interests, and the decision-making process involves much coalition building and bargaining among different interests. Specifically, neighborhood associations function as advocates of the neighborhood in dealing with the city, county, and state, as well as with private businesses, non-profit institutions, and other groups that have an impact upon neighborhood conditions (Verba and Nie 1972).

To successfully present their interests, however, groups need political resources: the willingness of their members to invest time; information; solidarity; and access to external funding, credit, or members' own money. Although political resources are limited, they are not fixed. Each group can struggle to obtain them and to influence the decision making of city and state officials and agencies as a strategy to protect its interests. To do this, neighborhood associations may circulate petitions, threaten legal action, give evidence at public inquiries, attend council and committee meetings, withhold payments, demonstrate, contact councilors and officials, write letters to newspapers, and forge coalitions with other organizations (Verba and Nie 1972; Hallman 1984).

CSNA has used all these tactics and extended them, establishing its reputation as a successful organization by building coalitions with other groups and by acting collectively with them. Early on, its active members realized that they shared interests with other groups, and that by pooling their resources they could obtain a common objective. When association members organized coalitions to help them campaign for city regulations to preserve the historic character of their neighborhood and to oppose the construction of a highway, they not only won their campaigns but strengthened their own position. They consolidated their own organizational power and gained greater political power when the city passed ordinances that enabled them to defeat plans for any future development in their neighborhood that would threaten its historic nature.

Organizational Characteristics of CSNA

Like any organization, CSNA's internal characteristics—how formalized its structure, how committed its membership, the style of its leadership, and how it gains legitimacy in the community—influence its effectiveness. Specifically, an organization's functioning in a competitive, resource-scarce environment depends on "its ability to select an appropriate internal structure and to establish inter-organizational relations that sustain a steady flow of resources." Committed members also must work to keep the organization functional. The more committed members are to an association, the more resources (energy, skills, time, money, support, or grants) they can bring in (Knoke and Wood 1981:170).

Over the years, the Center Square Neighborhood Association has developed a formal structure, moving from an informal group of residents interested in beautification to a well-established organization with a reputation for being tough on city agencies, developers, and absentee landowners. The organization remains small, its president told me in March 1989, because "that way we can more easily mobilize residents and have face-to-face contact with each other. Fifteen years ago, it was proposed to incorporate part of the Hudson/Park Association, but it was rejected because we thought that the association would become too big. Also we did not want to incorporate the Washington Park Neighborhood Association, because of its different interests.

Their central focus is on the park. They also have many large buildings with absentee landlords. Our neighborhood has more long-term residents who are property owners."

Although the neighborhood association was formed in the 1950s, it did not have a legal title until its incorporation in 1974. Incorporation is important, association members believe, for court and legal purposes. The association has seven active committees to address specific issues; four liaison committees for maintaining an interorganizational relationship with specific organizations; and sixteen block captains to cover all parts of the neighborhood and to keep an eye on potential issues. One block captain, a woman in her late thirties, explained to me in February 1990 that "as a block captain, you have to look for what is going on in your block . . . people often know who I am, and they let me know whenever they see something as a problem. . . . I am a neighborhood busybody, I go around delivering fliers for the meetings, I talk with residents, and in that way keep a continuity of the organization between neighborhood meetings." In some ways, the block captains resemble ward leaders, but unlike ward leaders they support collective goals rather than pursue individual economic and political power.

The association maintains a membership list of nearly 250 (as of 1989), collects dues from its members, and publishes a regular newsletter prior to membership meetings. These characteristics make it a more formal organization and give greater legitimacy to its claims to represent the neighborhood. The membership list, for example, is "official proof" of how many members an organization has. The newsletter informs members and community residents about the activities of the neighborhood association and shows that the organization is doing something vital for the community's well-being.

The financial resources of the organization are solid enough to cover the expenses of publishing the newsletter and agendas for board meetings. For larger projects, the organization relies on fundraising and on volunteer time and expertise. Residents' characteristics, such as their racial composition, income, education, and types of employment, are often considered very significant in community literature for explaining what a neighborhood association can do. Studies have shown that residents' income, education, and occupation have a positive impact on organizational effectiveness (Gittell 1980:68; Burnett 1983). Although neighborhood associations have modest budgets, in emergencies (such as money needed for legal-action campaigns) those with a higher percentage of prosperous residents can organize fundraising drives, and association coffers grow rapidly.

Cultural resources, also crucial to organizing success, are reflected in a neighborhood's acceptance of the values and norms of the larger society, such as organized democratic participation. Members need to know how institutions operate, and be able to use institutional structures to their advantage. Center Square residents who worked for the local government enhanced these cultural resources for the association. Their employment endows them with some prestige, so they command respect and service from others. Neighborhoods where a high proportion of residents are administrators in public agencies have been found to make more demands on local government, most likely because they provide information about local issues to other residents and thus stimulate participation (Davidson 1979). Therefore, neighborhood associations with a high percentage of public employees (even those with low socioeconomic status) will probably have more personal and potentially collective resources than neighborhoods with similar socioeconomic characteristics but few public employees.

Closely tied to cultural resources are social resources, such as the internal and external ties and connections of residents of a neighborhood. People with high socioeconomic status are generally better adapted to the cultural and political system and have more ties with influential people, multiple networks, and higher positions in the networks (Fischer 1982; Marsden and Hurbert 1988). For neighborhood associations like CSNA engaged in constant interaction with the local government, a high percentage of public employees among residents makes direct contact with government agencies more likely. Neighborhood associations can tap into residents' professional networks to gain access to money, information, and sociopolitical support for the organization.

Another way to measure social resources is to examine the commitment of residents to the neighborhood, which some researchers cite as an important component of organizational activity. For example, buying a house in a particular neighborhood represents a major commitment. One active member with long involvement in CSNA illustrates this point well: "I lived in this neighborhood as a tenant first. At that time, although I knew about the neighborhood association, I was not involved. We [she and her husband] were in school then and busy with other things. When we bought the house, we got involved. We just invested all that we have in this neighborhood, and we wanted to know what was going on. Also we wanted to meet people from the neighborhood."

People who own their homes, have children, and live for a long time in a particular neighborhood are expected to be more committed to it and consequently more engaged in preserving it through neighborhood organizations (Verba and Nie 1972; Arnold 1979; Davidson 1979; Cox and McCarthy

1980; Guest and Oropesa 1984). In gentrified inner-city neighborhoods, however, having children is often an obstacle to a strong commitment to the neighborhood, for inner cities often lack good education opportunities and residents with children often move to areas with better schools. A better explanation for the higher participation of home owners in local organizations is that their investment (money, effort, time) in the neighborhood and the changing real-estate market, especially for condominiums, makes them less mobile (Čapek and Gilderbloom 1992).

CSNA has another resource: a number of lawyers, previous or current neighborhood residents, who have agreed to provide legal advice and services to the organization, or even to represent neighborhood interests in court at low cost or pro bono. When a judge who lived in Colonie used a building in the neighborhood for his law practice in violation of the zoning law, for example, the neighborhood association challenged him. A lawyer, George Carpinello, one of the association's former presidents, continued to represent the association's interests in the case for several years after he moved out of the neighborhood, according to CSNA's fall 1988 newsletter. As organizational resources, these pro bono services are not easily measured. Connected with the high status of gentrified neighborhoods, they provide a degree of credibility and clout that other neighborhood associations find difficult or impossible to achieve.

The Importance of the Neighborhood Association Board

As voluntary organizations, neighborhood associations need a permanent body, such as a board, to provide stability. According to the formal documents of Albany neighborhood associations, in most of them boards make the decisions. In practice, boards are even more important in decision making than the formal procedures indicate. Usually they shape the policy of an organization, set its agenda, and prepare motions to be voted on. Board members are often the most committed members, the ones who pour time and skills into the organization and who can address obstacles to organizational health.

I was able to interview eleven of Center Square Neighborhood Association's nineteen board members, some of whom are also block captains. Board meetings are open to the public and held on the last Tuesday of every month. All the board members I spoke with are prosperous and have significant social resources. Nine have master's or doctoral degrees, and ten had family incomes higher than $40,000 (comfortably middle class at the time); nine have paid jobs, and two are housewives. All but one are home owners, and all are white. Seven are married; six of these have children. All eleven households have members who work outside the home: six work for government, two for universities, and three in other professional occupations. Most of the eleven board members have lived in the neighborhood more than five years: five for more than twenty years, four for between five and fifteen years, and two for less than five years. Also, most joined the association more than five years ago (the distribution is similar to the length of residence in the neighborhood). Six have been board members for less than five years, and five for more than eleven years.

Most of the board members I spoke with have extended personal networks and are active in other organizations. All said they use their professional and private ties for organizational purposes. Nine are active in three to five other voluntary organizations, and two are members of more than five other voluntary organizations. Some of these organizations are professional or religious, but others have a strong social and political orientation. One of the most vocal members of the association is a woman who has challenged the city's establishment for twenty-five years. "I got involved in 1964," she told me, "when other residents and I tried to convince Mayor Corning to participate in a federal jobs and housing program. We failed, but I continued to be interested in local and national matters. Now I'm active in the reform Democrat movement, the Save the Pine Bush organization, the Social Justice Center, and the Albany Coalition for Housing. I'm active in the neighborhood association because I see it as an advocate for the residents against the city administration." By being members of other organizations, board members have extended their local networks and brought more information, experience, and connections to the neighborhood association. Resource mobilization (Obershall 1973; Gamson 1975; McCarthy and Zald 1977) and network theorists (Granovetter 1973; Galaskiewicz 1979; Lin 1982) agree that successful collective action depends not only on resources available to a group (a function of the characteristics of residents), but also on the position of individuals and organizations in social networks. Aware of the benefits of networks, CSNA makes an effort to choose board members involved in local organizations.

The association also has a very well developed interorganizational network. It has a permanent liaison committee with four organizations: the Capitol Hill Improvement Corporation, the Historic Resource Commission, the Coalition of Albany Neighborhood Associations, and the Lark Street Merchants Association. CNSA helped to establish three of these organizations, so its members are especially interested in their activities and often sit on their boards. Neighborhood association representatives believe in sharing some of their organizational resources and experience with these other organizations, and they do not hesitate to meet with surrounding neighborhood associations for issue-related purposes.

Interest-Based Community versus Expressive Community

The Center Square neighborhood, in many respects, is a *community of interest,* and it is an example of what is known as a community of limited liability (Janowitz 1952; Greer 1962). Individuals with limited investments in a neighborhood, such as home ownership and socialization of children, are likely to take a "functional" or "instrumental" interest in it. They participate in community organizations to know their neighborhood better and to protect their investment. In that respect residents relate to their community in only a partial, calculating, and selective way; they tend to come together for functionally specific, relatively well defined goals. This kind of community differs from an *expressive community,* which offers residents emotional support and is a source of security for them. One of the members who joined the organization recently, for example, told me in March 1990, "I had my dental practice in this neighborhood for the last twenty years, but I lived in the suburbs. It was better for the children. When the last child left, we decided to move here. I got involved in the neighborhood association because I like to see the neighborhood's desirability increased. Also, being professionally active in the neighborhood, I want other people to know me. . . . It's good for my practice."

People often enter into relationships through the exchange of resources like money, information, or sociopolitical support that help them meet functional needs (Galaskiewicz 1979). Strong ties characterize the intimate social circle of individuals with similar characteristics; when relied on only within a limited network, strong ties make individuals provincial about larger social events and trends. Weak ties characterize the infrequent interactions and peripheral relationships among dissimilar individuals (see also Lin, Ensel, and Vaughn 1981); to reach better social resources, individuals need to call on these weak ties (Granovetter 1973). Communities whose members have strong personal associations and few instrumental ones may remain unaware of the possible impact of public events and decisions on their lives and may have no access to policymakers who have some power over the circumstances affecting them.

How can individuals and their organizations extend their peripheral relationships and reach these better resources? Nan Lin (1982) theorizes that if reaching up the hierarchical structure means obtaining better social resources, then breaking out of one's intimate circle increases the likelihood of making a contact at a higher social position. People who have higher socioeconomic or political positions not only have access to better social resources themselves but can more easily reach people who can be helpful to them and their organizations. The access to and use of these better social resources enhances the effectiveness of collective actions, whatever the objective.

If this is the way individuals build networks, how are neighborhood networks created and maintained? Avery Guest (following Tönnies 1963), defines the social organization of communities along two dimensions—a Gesellschaft dimension and a Gemeinschaft dimension—each generating different types of ties (1985). The Gesellschaft dimension represents ties formed for functional purposes through such means as instrumental voluntary associations where members are organized for political or quasi-political purposes. Gemeinschaft ties, in contrast, connect people for emotional and socially supportive reasons and are reflected in activities like chatting with neighbors and having a high proportion of friends and relatives in the area. Although they are important for individual well-being, they do not protect the neighborhood as well as Gesellschaft ties do.

Ties can be further distinguished as external or extralocal, which are based in contacts outside the community, or as local or internal, based within the community. Thus every community, according to Guest, may have four major types of ties: internal Gemeinschaft, external Gemeinschaft, internal Gesellschaft, and external Gesellschaft.

Local and extralocal Gesellschaft ties are closely related, for both represent important means by which a community protects its interests. In a contemporary metropolis, real political action is focused around such instrumental ties (Goering 1979; Crenson 1983), which largely reinforce one another and are related to the common high-status origins of community residents. Extralocal ties especially are helpful in providing information about and contact with public officials. The more resources and network ties neighborhoods have, the more successful they can be (see also Lee et al. 1984).

The leadership of CSNA understands how important maintaining local and extralocal Gesellschaft ties is, one reason CSNA leaders stress the interest-based nature of their organization, such as protecting the residential nature of the neighborhood. They also use their network ties to achieve organizational goals. Harold Rubin, a CSNA board member and president in 1990, is a good example of an interest-based active member. To enhance the neighborhood's power within the city, he pushed the formation of the Coalition of Albany Neighborhood Associations, of which he is president. With a successful career in state government, he feels a special calling to preserve the beauty of city life. As he told me in November 1989:

> I continue to be involved because I'm very much interested in what we're doing. When I came here thirty years ago, I was appalled by the deterioration of the neighborhood and by the lack of attempts from the city to do something about it. Our biggest fights at that time were over code enforcement. It was terrible; houses were in such bad shape, and, instead of stabilizing them, they [the developers who bought them] wanted to demolish them. We used to guard some houses during the night, because we were afraid that they would demolish them. Our major concern was always buildings, not people . . . people come and go, but buildings are always here. We don't care who lives in the house, as long as he/she keeps it according to law. . . . I believe that we made, and still can make a difference. . . . We don't ask the city for favors; we tell them, this is your law, enforce it. Now I'm president again, because nobody was available to take the job. I just retired, and I have time.

Other active members of CSNA share his views. They like the neighborhood amenities and location--the proximity of work and downtown activities, its physical appeal, what they consider a diversity of residents, and the sense of community. In our February 1990 interview, another board member with long tenure in the neighborhood described living there. "Center Square is a real neighborhood. It's getting more expensive, but it's still a mixed neighborhood. I like its convenience, the proximity of the park and downtown. I don't think the neighborhood will change much. Nothing dramatic's going to happen in the city to bring more people. Also, here we have lots of committed people who will insure continuity of the organization. Now [during a campaign against a developer] more people are getting involved, but the Center Square Association always has had a core group of residents who persist in being active."

The association does not consistently represent the interests of everyone in the neighborhood. For instance, most residents are tenants. Some of them participate in the organization, but when they become board members they work to support organizational goals, that is, to preserve neighborhood amenities, not to fight for tenants' rights. Some members acknowledge that ignoring tenants' rights can be a problem. A member who joined the organization more than thirty years ago told me in November 1987:

> Personally, I would like to see more tenants getting involved [in the neighborhood association]. But I think we have been unwilling to address their problems because their issues are not clear-cut. Tenant-landlord conflicts often call for

judgment, and our association tries to minimize those areas that call for judgment. We are good at developing policy based on laws and long-established practices. . . . In the past, this neighborhood used to be more engaged in providing services to residents. We had the Neighborhood Walk-In Clinic, for example. At that time we were more mixed, had more people who needed help for drug-related problems . . . but not any more. We still make an effort to help older residents, check on them to see that they are okay and offer help if they need it, but this is not official neighborhood policy. When we detect such problems, we refer them to the Capitol Hill Improvement Corporation.

Commercial development in the neighborhood is another example of neighborhood conflict. The Lark Street Merchants Association and CSNA share an interest in the further development of Lark Street. Sometimes, however, they differ over what constitutes healthy neighborhood development. CSNA's position is to keep "desirable" businesses in this area—small specialty shops, antique shops, and the like. Restaurants that are open late and draw people from out of the neighborhood (especially students) are discouraged. Not all residents agree with this policy. *Metroland* for July 20–26, 1989, reported the plaint of one unhappy resident: "At times, the Neighborhood Association acts very repressively. The association maintains a policy which is against sidewalk cafes in this neighborhood, and was recently active in denying the opening of an art gallery/cafe. This is an urban neighborhood and needs more diversity." The association denies that it is repressive and claims that its main goal is to maintain quality of residential life for everyone. A sidewalk cafe may be good for most residents, but not for the person who lives next door to it. This is why the organization tries to develop formal policies and clearly defined structures that will allow it both to successfully address threats from the "outside" and to avoid conflict over what becomes an issue for the organization.

Beyond these instrumental, or interest-driven, goals, CSNA members wish to preserve their neighborhood as an expressive community, one that offers security and emotional support. The group sponsors several annual social events: a house tour, a Christmas party, and neighborhood clean-up days, with parties following. A board member who lived in the neighborhood for a time, moved out, and then returned, told me in 1989, "We know each other here. We talk, have parties, and care for the neighborhood. After living in Center Square for awhile I got much more social. Therefore, when I moved to Philadelphia [in a suburban neighborhood], I introduced myself to my neighbors. They were all surprised. They had lived there for years, but they didn't know who their neighbors were. When I came back to Albany, I rejoined the association to meet new people and to catch up on the latest news." Social reasons attracted others too. The organization's younger members seem to enjoy the same neighborhood qualities, as I learned speaking with a man in his mid-thirties: "I moved here from New York City. My wife and I heard about the Center Square neighborhood, and we rented an apartment here. Later we decided to purchase a house. I engaged myself in the association because I wanted to be of service to the community. I see the association's interests as my interests as well. The neighborhood is pleasant and physically attractive. It's close to my workplace [state government], and you don't need to use a car all the time. As a newcomer, I thought this was a good way to get to know the neighborhood."

Whatever induces people to join the association, they remain in it because of its success on a number of issues over the years. One long-term resident I spoke with in 1990 is, in some respects, typical of the "old-time" members: "Being active in the association is not that time consuming. I don't go to every meeting. I used to be president of the association, and now I am on the real-estate committee. When a hot issue comes up, I get involved . . . I like to see myself as an elder statesman. . . . When the organization needs my institutional knowledge [and connections], I get active and offer my help." Neighborhood-association board members are not only successful, influential people who care about the neighborhood, but also people who are deeply involved in shaping the neighborhood's destiny.

Neighborhood Survival Tactics

While many urbanists believe that contemporary neighborhoods are changing from social to political groups, what I have learned about CSNA shows that this is not necessarily true: Some organizations also want to preserve their neighborhoods as social communities. Social events like the Make Your Neighborhood Beautiful campaign, Christmas and spring parties, summer picnics, and receptions for new members have both an internal and an external purpose: internally, to foster support and to attract more members, and externally, to show other actors in local political life that the neighborhood association and its leaders are legitimate representatives of the community.

Similarly, other older neighborhood associations in the Capital District are more likely to stress social than political goals, although the majority of newly created neighborhood associations see themselves primarily as political organizations. Most neighborhood associations established before 1979 view

*Table 6: Characteristics of Neighborhood Associations in
Capital District by Year of Establishment (N = 72)*

Purpose	Before 1969 (%)	1970–1979 (%)	1980–1985 (%)
Social/civic	56.3	53.3	26.9
Address broad range of issues	50.0	48.1	22.7
Sponsor social events	43.8	33.3	19.2
Increased social orientation	25.0	26.9	10.0

themselves as both social and civic (political) organizations, but only one-third of the organizations established between 1980 and 1985 identify themselves as both social and political (Table 6). I suggest the reason for this difference is the maturity of an organization. During the first half of the 1980s a large number of neighborhood associations were formed to solve particular problems. As late as 1989, the existence of a common threat continued to bring members together, and as newly formed organizations they could continue to count on the support of founding members without making any special appeals to them. Older organizations have discovered that functional or instrumental interests alone are not sufficient to maintain an organization; they have had to generate other activities and are more likely to address a broad range of issues (50 percent compared with only 23 percent of young organizations) and to sponsor social events.

Social activities become more important as associations change what they ask their members to do and what level of participation they expect. The older the organization, the more likely it is to increase its social orientation. We can expect young organizations to follow this pattern, and in years to come to address more of the social needs of their residents. I am not suggesting that neighborhood associations will become social organizations, but that they do not survive without adopting expressive activities. They remain primarily interest-driven groups with strong instrumental goals.

Current Issues

Today, Center Square has a well-developed neighborhood association that addresses a broad range of issues and is known as one of the most successful in the Capital District. Association leaders still watch carefully for any change that might disturb Center Square's quality of life, for Albany has a strong pro-growth coalition. The goal of the city administration is to increase fiscal resources, and to use them to make the city a more attractive place for business and real-estate developers. But it is also aware of the growing power of reform forces in the city and the need to cooperate with neighborhood organizations. For this reason city leaders become allies of these groups on some issues. As the May 28, 1987, *Albany Times Union* reported, CSNA received the Mayor's Award that year for "its watchdog role in the eventual construction of housing at 70–78 Chestnut Street by developer Richard Gerrity. The association consistently notified the City Planning and Building Departments when Gerrity's contractors failed to meet design standards in keeping with the neighborhood's architectural requirements. Gerrity had to change several features before the Building Department would issue Certificates of Occupancy."

But that same year, 1987, the association had a bitter dispute with the city over tax assessments. Property taxes in Center Square were doubled and in some cases tripled; since uptown neighborhoods were not reassessed, residents believed that they had been singled out and punished for their active involvement in local matters. CSNA took the assessment issue to court, with the city clearly identified as the enemy. Legally, residents had to fight reassessment individually, but the association offered advice and kept members informed about individual lawsuits.

The role of local government in many U.S. cities is ambivalent. For some neighborhoods, it is a cooperative force promoting change that will enhance residential life, while for others it is a conflicting force undermining neighborhood efforts. Depending on the issue, elected city-council members can disagree both with elected board members and with each other, planning departments can be at odds with city engineers, developers can be challenged by store owners, and conservative and progressive community groups can oppose each other (specifically, over a development in the neighborhood they both claim to represent). Land-use change is often an explicitly political event, involving negotiations among alert neighborhood groups, private households, city hall, and entrepreneurial interests (Ley and Mercer 1980).

Over the years, CSNA has developed a working relationship with the city government. It does not hesitate to approach city officials and other actors in policy-making directly, either to offer help and expertise or to demand that neighborhood interests be taken into consideration. The members also know that the city's intentions can conflict with their neighborhood's interest, so they are unwilling to rely on local officials to solve neighborhood problems.

Experience has taught them never to assume that the city will acknowledge that the neighborhood-association position is right and always to remember that a fight may be necessary.

Fighting the Garage

Over the years, CSNA has been actively engaged in finding solutions for limited parking and for traffic congestion, has sponsored beautification efforts (planting trees and flowers, sweeping sidewalks, observing the "pooper-scooper" law), and has worked to improve neighborhood schools. Its major focus remains controlling land development. Business interests and real-estate developers typically are identified as opponents of the association on land-use issues, because CSNA wants to protect use value, which often means a low-density, residential development, while the developers want as large a return as possible from their investment and therefore favor higher-density land use, raising the exchange value of land.

When in 1989 the Brooklyn-based Benjosh Management Corporation bought buildings on 183–197 Jay Street (part of a historic brewery) and an empty lot at the corner of Lancaster and Dove, CSNA was concerned about plans for development. Soon the City Planning Department contacted the group for its input. The developer's intentions were to replace the buildings on Jay Street with a parking garage for approximately 250 vehicles and to turn the vacant lot into five two-family houses. To demolish the building in a historic neighborhood, the owner needed a building permit from the Historic Resource Commission; to build on the vacant lot, he needed a zoning variance from the city. CSNA saw the hearings as an opportunity to pursue its interests through legal means. Neighborhood members, who had engaged in similar battles before, also had legal knowledge and expertise and the will to fight for what they considered important. The existence of the Historic Resource Commission assured the CSNA's participation in the proceedings and gave its representatives an opportunity to lobby for organizational interests. The organization also sought and was given positive coverage by the media and gained the support of other organizations, such as the Historic Albany Foundation.

As with other land-use issues, CSNA had already discussed the future of the Jay Street buildings and the vacant lot, and they saw low-density residential uses as desirable for both. Low-density use would also help solve the parking problem. So when the developer reduced the capacity of the proposed garage from 250 to 125, anticipating neighborhood opposition, that was not enough. CSNA members suggested that the Jay Street buildings be turned into a handful of apartments and thirty nine parking spaces. For the Lancaster Street lot, they wanted a project in accord with the zoning ordinance (one- or two-family units) and developed in the spirit of the historic neighborhood.

When the City Planning Department and the Historic Resource Commission requested that CSNA review the projects, the president of the association called an emergency board meeting to inform residents and encourage them to participate in the review. The association also invited the developer and his architects to come to the meeting and present their projects and assigned the block captains to inform residents about the issue and the impact that a garage could have on the quality of life in the neighborhood. But it was not easy for all block captains to get the association's concerns across. A homeowner in her late thirties who works for the state and is a block captain for Jay Street told me:

> I went door-to-door to mobilize residents to come to the meeting. In the beginning, I didn't have much luck. Over the last fifteen years the residents of this street have changed. We used to have a lot of people who came in the 1970s and were interested in the historic value of this neighborhood. They were not rich, but they loved the houses. Some moved because they got jobs elsewhere, others got divorced, and even others could not resist the high price that they were offered for their houses. Since then the quality of life has deteriorated here. The new residents who came in the eighties are different; they're rich, have these fancy cars, and are less neighborly. They bought houses because they saw them primarily as good investments. . . . Well, I was telling them what impact the garage was going to have on the life on this street. All the fumes and noise . . . but they didn't care. Then I asked them, "What do you think is going to happen to the property value of your house? Do you think somebody is going to buy a house across the street from the garage?" Well, then I got them. Incredible, these people are just interested in their pockets.

Held on June 8, 1989, the meeting drew a large number of residents. The block captains had persuaded them to participate by addressing two concerns: quality-of-life issues and decreasing property values. The president of the association opened the meeting, which I attended, by defining the issue in legal terms: "According to the zoning ordinance, this neighborhood is a residential neighborhood. All apartment houses, garages, offices, et cetera in Center Square are nonconforming uses, which means that they will be terminated upon discontinuance." He introduced the developer and architects and acknowledged the presence of journalists from the *Albany Times Union* and the *Schenectady Gazette*. Then the architects of both projects showed drawings for the garden apartments; residents raised some minor complaints about the design of the project and suggested ways to improve it. In this discussion, the board members' technical knowledge came into play. One of the board members recommended specific changes: "The ground-level entrance should be located under the stoop, as is common throughout the neighborhood. . . . The sliding doors on the rear of the buildings are unacceptable for both reasons of security and historic district appropriateness. . . . For the parking lot, putting some trees along the edge of the property would be good. . . . Also I suggest a wall, preferably brick, at least six feet in height in order to effectively screen the cars and complement the neighborhood architecture." The developer and his architects took these comments gracefully, thanking the residents for their useful suggestions. Clearly they wanted to please.

But the second project, the plans for the new garage, raised many more substantive complaints from the floor. The architect, for his part, did not present the proposal well. He could not satisfactorily explain how the garage would accommodate the arrival of a large number of cars in a short space of time in the morning, and their departure in the evening. The residents were concerned about noise, fumes, and greater traffic congestion in the neighborhood. Some remarked that only state workers seeking parking spaces would benefit from the project. The president of the association rose to remind us "about the association's position on these issues in the past. The association's fundamental policy is to evaluate each proposal from the vantage point of whether or not it will improve the quality of living in our neighborhood, and we have followed this policy over the thirty-two years of the association's existence. We oppose any parking facility in residentially zoned areas to provide for those who do not live in the neighborhood. We don't want this neighborhood to become a parking lot."

But not everyone opposed the garage. For a long time, the neighborhood had been parking-space poor. Residents and state workers at the Empire State Plaza compete for a limited number of spaces. Several days after the meeting, one board member told me about some residents' frustrations:

> Parking is a very painful issue for older residents and mothers who stay home with their young children. If you leave during the morning, you cannot find a spot when you come back. I know a woman with two small children. Every morning she takes her older child to nursery school, but when she comes back she cannot find a parking space. And when she finally finds a spot, she has to

walk several blocks to her home with a child in one hand and a grocery bag in the other. Often she is so frustrated that she actually cries. This is not really a family neighborhood. Not that many people with children live here. And when she invites friends with small children to visit her, they only come once and never again—they spend more time looking for parking than actually visiting her. . . . Now they're thinking about moving to the suburbs.

Some residents from other streets, in fact, wanted to discuss how the garage could be designed to fit into their neighborhood. As one resident put it in a letter to the association dated July 14, 1989 (made available to me from a private collection), "I suggest that the Center Square Association take a much more rational and reasonable approach toward this garage. We should propose ideas and suggestions, as regards the facade of the building, to maintain the architectural integrity of the neighborhood, but we should not rule out the possibility of having a garage here."

As residents began to discuss their opinions of the proposal after the developer and architect left, the president repeated the organization's principles:

In this neighborhood we do not play one street against other. Think about this garage as being next door to your house. Would you like that? If you don't, neither would residents of Jay Street. Let me remind you, the Historic Resource Commission ordinance opposes demolition of the historic buildings unless the owners can demonstrate that they have met all the standards for demolition. They have to show that, due to structural deterioration, it is not economically feasible to save the building. And if they demolish the building, under the zoning ordinance the nonconforming use status would be terminated. Therefore, under such circumstances a new garage is not authorized under present zoning. What is authorized are row houses as a principal use, and garage apartments as a special use. If the buildings are torn down, then we can discuss the possibility of supporting row houses or garden apartments.

By the end of the meeting, the residents concluded that tearing down the historic buildings and replacing them with a garage would harm the neighborhood and its quality of life. Therefore, the association decided that at a public hearing they would oppose the proposal. This decision was consistent with their organizational goals, and the active involvement of the organization's members insured that the issue was framed in that way.

With a decision reached, the association's board members had to develop a strategy. They decided to begin by writing the association's statement clearly, to send some members to the City Planning Department to review the developer's proposal, and to have some residents with engineering degrees collect more information about similar projects in other places. Their main strategy, the organization decided, would be to oppose the garage project on legal grounds.

CSNA was well prepared for the public hearing organized by the Historic Resource Commission. The association invited representatives of the press and local television news programs, and it chose several of its members to testify against the project. The director of the Historic Albany Foundation testified against the plan to demolish the historic building. The association successfully turned the issue into a dispute over the demolition of a historic building: Those members who testified stressed over and over again the legal point that Albany's historic ordinance states that a developer should first try to rehabilitate a building, and if that can not be done the building should remain for sale until it can be. The Historic Resource Commission would approve demolition only if the building could not be rehabilitated. To this day, no developer has gotten a demolition permit.

CSNA's success in influencing city policies can be attributed to its participation in decision making, its well-established legal procedures, its members' class and social resources (expertise and knowledge), and the group's organizational resources: a clear organizational policy, experience with similar issues in the past, committed members, able leaders, and past successes. CSNA had allies in city government who provided timely information, and who sought its members' opinions.

Why did the city support the neighborhood association and not a developer, even when the garage would have increased tax revenues for the city? The explanation may be that the developer was a relative newcomer to the city, and that 1989 was an election year. By supporting a neighborhood association, city officials legitimized claims that they cared about neighborhood interests.

Neighborhood Watch

The residents' concern for personal safety and police protection has continued to mobilize the neighborhood and engage the attention of board members, even though most people stress that they feel very safe in the neighborhood. A long-term resident in her forties told me in January 1990, "Yes, I was burglarized three times in the last twenty years that I lived here, but I don't worry about crime. Having a security system would be good, but as a renter it's too expensive. If I had a house here, I would probably have a security system." To increase the residents' awareness of crime, the association periodically sponsors meetings with representatives of the Police Department, who tell them about measures to insure the safety of their property and lives. The *Neighborhood Resource Center News,* Winter 1987, informed residents that "the Albany Police Community Services Unit offers many resources to assist in crime prevention. It comes to your home and does a security survey, it helps install window pins to prevent break-ins, it will engrave your valuables to help recover items if they are stolen."

But more important, Center Square is the only downtown neighborhood to have a "beat cop," that is, one officer assigned to patrol the neighborhood on foot. Several years ago, when the Neighborhood Resource Center received an anticrime grant, the CNSA was eager to participate. At that time, several break-ins in basement apartments had occurred, and everyone was concerned. Center Square's policy was to maintain a close relationship with the police and the "cop on the beat." As the president explained the organization's point of view to me in 1990: "The police like to work with Center Square. We are cooperative, and we show how much we appreciate them. I am now on the board of the Albany Police Athletic League. . . . When we got the grant, the Hudson/Park Neighborhood Association participated with us. But they didn't like the police that much. . . . They had more of these young people who would smoke pot and were not thrilled with the idea of the police sniffing around." Today, Center Square does not maintain a formal Neighborhood Watch program, but this is a neighborhood with a high concentration of single people, and women especially worry about rape. Older residents are more concerned about safety than younger ones. An older woman told me in February 1990 that, when she moved in, "this neighborhood used to be safer. But now it isn't. Drugs are coming to this neighborhood. My friend saw some people dealing drugs outside in her parking lot. She immediately called the police, but it was scary. . . . The older residents know each other, but it is difficult to know tenants. They come and go."

CSNA adheres to its early practice of speaking directly with the police. To respond to residents' concerns, over the years police have worked with the association to improve street lighting and identify dangerous spots. Residents watch out for each other, make efforts to secure their apartments, and see their beat cop as an important person for maintaining the security of the neighborhood. When, for example, in the fall of 1989, a stabbing and a murder occurred in the neighborhood, all the residents were shocked. For some of them, this was a sign that the neighborhood was, in fact, urban and therefore dangerous. When the beat cop arrested both suspects in these crimes, they were reassured that violent crime was contained in their neighborhood, and that police on the streets protected them well. As one board member told me in November 1989, "We were so happy that Tom [the beat cop] found both guys. The board organized a breakfast to honor him, and to show our appreciation we gave him a plaque and a T-shirt with 'Center Square Neighborhood Association' written on it. We made him an honorary member." The beat cop, on his part, was glad of the neighborhood's reaction. At the CSNA meeting on October 25, 1989, thanking them for the plaque and the T-shirt, he said, "What I did was part of my job. But I'm very happy to know how much you appreciate me. It is not often that a policeman is appreciated. Thank you."

The residents of Lancaster Street, where the stabbing occurred, decided to form a block watch. They stressed the need for all neighbors to keep an eye out for one another, to learn to report incidents and suspicious activity accurately, and to act as liaisons with the police to learn about patterns of criminal activity. At the next neighborhood meeting, they discussed starting a more efficient Neighborhood Watch in the whole neighborhood. Once again, representatives of the police came to offer their help, but to date a Neighborhood Watch has not been organized. I was told by a board member that "this is an urban environment, and accidents sometimes happen. We cannot keep a police officer in each resident's back yard. If you take precautions, know your neighbors, and watch out for each other, you are fairly safe here." A Neighborhood Watch's major contribution to safety is to increase awareness among the residents and to help them establish contact with one another. However, in this neighborhood, people already know their neighbors fairly well and are aware of potential dangers, and risks are relatively low, so they have little need for a more structured Neighborhood Watch program.

More annoying to residents are the noise and disturbance that come from the Knickerbockers Apartment Building, considered the neighborhood eyesore. Its rents are low or moderate, and in some ways the Knickerbockers resembles a rooming house. Most of the tenants in this five-story building of ninety apartments are single men and women and the elderly. The place has changed hands a number of times over the last several years, and neighbors view the tenants, changing owners and condition of the building all as disruptive. A resident who lives next to the Knickerbockers told me in 1990:

> The tenants of this building behave in a way which is not acceptable in
> residential areas. Honking of cabs, loud music, and noise make life miserable
> here. The building does not have an intercom; therefore whoever comes to visit

has to shout. Because we have a good relationship with the police, we have discussed this problem with them and with the building code inspectors. They told us to write down all incidents and to call every time an incident happens. They would record our calls, and then we can build our case against the building's owner for disturbance of the peace and order. Then the building inspector can charge them with violations and they would be forced to improve the building [put in an intercom, hire a door attendant], or they'd lose the right to rent apartments.

The goal of the CSNA, although no one will openly admit it, appears to be to force residents whose behavior disturbs the "residential quality of life" of the association's members to move away. The organization also tries to frame nuisance—drug activity, loud music, and a landowner's failure to maintain a building or clean up garbage in the street or backyard—as a land-use issue that can be regulated by zoning ordinances. However, Albany's zoning board sees this as a low-enforcement issue rather than a land-use issue and repeatedly refuses to bow to neighborhood demands.

It is hard for residents of any community to eliminate crime and nuisance behavior from their neighborhood. While CSNA was successful in gaining support for its interest-based concerns, and in disassociating itself from other inner-city neighborhoods, Center Square remains part of a city where poverty and unemployment, both associated with crime, persist. Residents indicated to me that they know crime is a difficult issue. Resigned to the idea that crime cannot be stopped, they are satisfied with the responses from city officials and the police, even though they still worry about crime. They see the police as providing them with adequate protection. Also, they are not giving up on challenging the way neighborhood buildings are used and zoning-board decisions.

CSNA as a Class-Based Organization

In pursuing their residential quality of life, neighborhoods have to deal with land-use issues, public-safety concerns, and the distribution of local services. For Center Square and other gentrified neighborhoods, the major question is how to keep land developers and real-estate agents from intensifying land use by creating apartments and projects that lead to higher density. The Center Square Neighborhood Association shows us that one successful strategy is to influence zoning ordinances and city regulations by becoming part of the structural decision making. Resources were obtained by mobilizing residents around shared interests—protecting the property values of their houses and preventing a deterioration in the quality of life in the neighborhood.

The CSNA experience demonstrates that neighborhood associations can be successful in protecting interests that people share locally. Key to CSNA's success, however, is that this is an organization of powerful people, in an affluent neighborhood, who are willing to use their money, time, expertise, and knowledge for common goals. Where they exerted an effort also made a difference. A less obvious reason for CSNA's success is that Albany is a healthy service-sector city with resources to spare for neighborhood improvements. Members of CSNA reshaped the organizational environment, made their interests part of local land-use policies, and, in addition, took advantage of nationwide interest and support for neighborhood preservation.

In that respect, CSNA is an example of the organizations described better by community and new social-movements literature than by the pluralist approach to local political action. It did what Castells (1983:278) argues urban social movements have to do: produce qualitative changes in the urban system, local culture, and political institutions. To do that CSNA had to contest the power of the prevailing institutionalized interests in the city, that is, real-estate developers and the city administration. CSNA succeeded in getting neighborhood rehabilitation and historic preservation defined as desirable land uses, and it successfully prevented real-estate interests from intensifying the neighborhood's exchange value. CSNA made alliances with the reform forces in the city: By opening up the political process, it paved the way for community and neighborhood organizations to take part in city decision making. The zoning and historic-preservation ordinances that were passed were used as tools to protect resident interests.

The neighborhood association also successfully built coalitions within and outside the neighborhood. While its members belong to a range of political organizations and have varying political views, CSNA's limited goals allow its active members to disregard political differences and mobilize most of the residents when they believe the interests of the whole neighborhood have been threatened or require support. The combination of a stable economy in Albany (which makes its neighborhoods desirable for both residential and commercial development) and a city administration that supports pro-growth interests creates a political environment that forces neighborhoods and their organizations to work together. CSNA not only provides leadership for these coalitions, but also shares its resources with other local organizations

A good example of such a coalition is the neighborhood response to Lark

Street deterioration. In the early 1990s, as economic recession hit the city, some shops on Lark Street were closed, and some signs of urban ill-health like graffiti and panhandling appeared. Merchants and neighborhood activists got together, formed the Lark Street Revitalization Committee, and applied for and in 1994 were awarded about $500,000 in planning and rehabilitation grants and loans. The money came from both public and private sources: $160,000 from the Urban Development Corporation and $50,000 from the city and its federally funded community-development program to fund physical improvements to residential buildings in the neighborhood. Another $50,000 is expected to come from designating Lark Street a special tax district. The money will be used to fund marketing, security, and clean-up work. Two other grants—$15,000 from the New York Department of State and the Historic Albany Foundation, and $125,000 in low-interest loans from the Albany Local Development Corporation—will be awarded to building owners who participate in the improvement programs to cover their portion of the projects' costs.

CSNA does not represent the interests of all residents in the neighborhood, nor is it an example of a cross-class alliance. It is an organization of home owners that addresses their interests and depends upon their resources. The organization uses neighborhood amenities to attract similar people to the neighborhood, and higher rents and property values to discourage those who cannot afford to pay them. CSNA began as a class-based organization and remains one.

5

Arbor Hill: Revitalizing
an Inner-City Neighborhood

The Arbor Hill Neighborhood Association shares organizational characteristics with the Center Square Neighborhood Association, which created a model for collective action widely emulated in Albany.

Arbor Hill's problems differ from Center Square's, however. As is typical of poor neighborhoods, its association plays a far more limited role than those in middle-class neighborhoods and is not the most successful way of mobilizing a community. Arbor Hill thus has a much richer history of neighborhood mobilization than Center Square does. Its residents have formed a wider range of neighborhood-based organizations and have used not only advocacy but also protest and community development to improve housing, to empower themselves, and to build a sense of community.

Characteristics of Arbor Hill Neighborhood

The Arbor Hill neighborhood was named for its multitude of grape arbors and its lofty position on a hillside. In 1850, it was known as one of the most delightful locations in the city. The famous Ten Broeck mansion was there, and Arbor Hill was "the most mercurial of Albany neighborhoods, a place of Arcadian wealth, gentility and beauty" (Kennedy 1983:96). Although its early residents were wealthy merchants and bankers, the neighborhood soon expanded to the north, and these sections became primarily working-class areas bounded by heavy industry (see Map 3). Some of these workers had come to Albany to build the Erie Canal during the 1820s; others were employed in the thriving lumber industry.

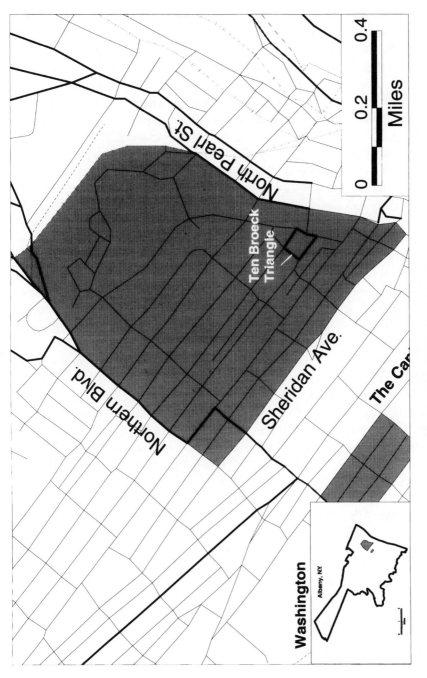

Map 3: Arbor Hill Neighborhood

By the end of the nineteenth century, the neighborhood had started to decline. The decision to build Washington Park (1869–1882) on Capitol Hill made that neighborhood the more desirable. When trolleys replaced horsecars in 1890, they did not travel to Arbor Hill but stopped at Clinton Avenue. Two decades of frustrating protest by residents began, and "not until 1911 was the trolley to be seen on Livingston Avenue, and its journey then was not always a blessing. Livingston is a steep hill and on slick and icy days, despite sanding, the downhill car would sometimes jump the tracks and crash into Grace Methodist Episcopal Church at Ten Broeck, or sometimes into the home of the Sixth Ward's democratic leader, William Mitchell, who lived across the street from the church—all going to prove that neither God nor the Democratic Party had any control over the traction interests" (Kennedy 1983:105). All the residents' attempts to reverse the destiny of Arbor Hill were in vain. One resident, Barrington Lodge, wrote to city leaders: "Before Washington Park was made, the property on Arbor Hill was as valuable as any like property in the city. . . . This was changed by the Washington Park improvement for which the people of the North End helped to pay . . . although it depreciated all their property" (Kennedy, 1983:105). The city declined his request to invest money in improving Arbor Hill. Soon more working-class families settled in, and Arbor Hill lost its position as a fashionable neighborhood.

About three-quarters of the housing in Arbor Hill was built before 1950 (70 percent), according to the 1980 census. The lower part of the neighborhood, known as Ten Broeck Triangle, consists of beautiful brownstones and brick houses. Along Clinton Avenue, houses are of similar substantial quality. But more than 90 percent of the houses in Arbor Hill are attached and consist of multiple units, and 83 percent of the residents in 1980 rented their apartments (Table 7). The streets and houses near the heart of Arbor Hill on Second Street are in the worst condition. Most of these buildings are wooden, and most of the vacant buildings in Arbor Hill are here.

Today, Arbor Hill is predominantly Black, according to the 1980 census, 73 percent of the 5,876 residents (see Table 8). Of all the Blacks living in Albany, 25 percent lived in Arbor Hill in 1980. Thirty percent of the Hill's residents lived below the poverty level, and the average years of formal education tended to be lower in Arbor Hill than in the city as a whole. Its unemployment rate was 12 percent at a time when Center Square's was only 4 percent. About 15 percent of its working residents held white-collar jobs, and about 39 percent worked for the government. However, in 1980, 50 percent had family incomes under $7,500 (low income at the time), with only 8 percent above $25,000 (high income at the time).

Table 7: Land-Use Characteristics of Arbor Hill Neighborhood

Housing	%
Occupancy	69.2
Rental units	83.3
Multiunits	70
Built before 1950	70.1

Source: U.S. Bureau of the Census, Census of Population and Housing, *1981*.

Table 8: Socioeconomic Characteristics of Arbor Hill Neighborhood

Residents	%
Black	72.9
Single	39.2
College degree	19.1
Work for government	38.7
High family income	8
Unemployed	12.1
Public assistance	32
Same house 5+ years	40.9

Source: U.S. Bureau of the Census, Census of Population and Housing, *1981*.

Although Arbor Hill has been viewed as the "worst" neighborhood in Albany since the 1950s, its residents have tried numerous times to improve the life of the community and to force the city to distribute resources more equitably, from protest strategies in the 1960s and neighborhood associations in the late 1970s and 1980s to community development in the 1990s.

The Civil Rights Movement and Arbor Hill

Blacks have lived in Albany almost since the city's founding. The West India Company sold a slave in Albany in 1650, and, although "only 23 slaves were in the County of Albany in 1698, . . . by the first federal census in 1790 that number had risen to 3,929 and was continuing to rise. Albany County was at this time New York's largest slave-holding county. By 1800, the combined free black and slave communities in the County reached 6% of the total population" (Davis 1983:8). Laws that called for the gradual abolition of slavery caused a leveling off of the city's Black population, and by midcentury, fewer than two thousand Blacks remained in the county. (Federal Census of Population, 1850). Segregation kept Blacks "generally in specific and often run-down neighborhoods and in segregated schools" (Sorin, Buckley, and Kloppot 1989:15). However, a small number of Blacks were members of the clergy, doctors for the Black community, hotel owners, hairdressers, musicians, and blacksmiths. Black residents of Arbor Hill came from professional families that had achieved a somewhat comfortable position in life.

Meanwhile, Albany's Black population had increased from 1,239 in 1920 to an estimated 2,100 in 1930, and a sizable Black neighborhood had grown up in the South End, not far from Arbor Hill (Federal Census of Population, 1920–30). With limited employment opportunities, most Blacks worked as unskilled and low-paid laborers, waiters, or washerwomen, and they had access only to substandard housing. In 1912, when the new State Education Building and the downtown park were built in the South End, some of the displaced Black families moved to Arbor Hill. After World War I, a new influx of poor and uneducated southern Blacks added to Albany's Black population. For a while, because the newcomers settled in the South End, Arbor Hill would still be a desirable neighborhood for the Black elite and upwardly mobile.

By October 1965, the city's Black population was estimated at fifteen thousand, with only about eighty families living outside Arbor Hill and the South End. These neighborhoods, by then referred to as ghettos, had problems similar to those of other poor inner-city neighborhoods. When the civil-rights movement emerged in Albany, it first "centered around liberal whites being involved with blacks for the betterment of the local black population, but as the 1960s progressed and the pace of racial change in Albany remained retarded, blacks in many instances united, separating themselves from their white counterparts in leadership roles" (Conroy 1987:4). In the sixties, one of the most influential organizations in the neighborhood was the Brothers (1966–1970), a secret society for Black men only, with meetings closed to nonmembers.

The Brothers

The Brothers had both political and social goals: to improve the harsh conditions of life for Black residents, to fight for social justice, and to create positive role models for young Black men. One of the organization's first actions was to challenge a local political machine and its practice of paying five dollars a vote. In Albany, where the machine was very powerful and rarely challenged, the attack was more a symbolic effort to build public awareness than an actual attempt to dismantle machine politics. The organization lost the court fight, but it gained visibility in the neighborhood and some support from the local press.

More successful was the Brothers' campaign to create a Welfare Union, with the help of the School of Social Welfare at the State University of New York at Albany and six local churches. As the March 3, 1967, Knickerbocker News reported under the headlines "Six Clergymen Back Brothers' Welfare Union," "The union will consist of persons on welfare rolls and will be designed to show people how to obtain the services they are entitled to, create a job clearing-house which will combat the high fees charged by private employment agencies, and establish a day-care center for the unemployed so that they can attend school or take job training."

Leon Van Dyke, a member of the Brothers, met with the commissioner of the Albany County Welfare Department to discuss the union. It was decided that the Brothers would be allowed to represent people who had to deal with the Welfare Department, and the union's watchword became "A Program for Full Employment." With the backing of area churches and local politicians, the union provided important services to local residents. As Brothers member Gordon Van Ness explained in an interview with Diane Conray on May 21, 1984, "Many individuals were being denied certain essential items by not understanding the rules and regulations. We got involved in interpretation, and with some legal assistance we were able to challenge the Welfare Department into giving that individual client whatever was due him." And according to Leon Van Dyke in a Conroy interview three years later, on November 22, 1987, the Welfare Union had made a difference. "It made the welfare bureaucrats at least know they had to bear a little bit of responsibility for their actions. Before, they had the whole show to themselves" (Conroy 1987).

Another success came as a result of the fight for free trash removal. At the time, the city charged to pick up trash, and streets in some areas of the city were in a deplorable state. With the backing of the South End Neighborhood Community Action Program, several Black residents went to Mayor Corning's office requesting city jobs as street cleaners. Their request and the public support for it confused the mayor, who was slow to react. Finally in June 1967 he gave in, and free trash pickup started. Van Ness explained the position of the Brothers in this crusade in his 1984 interview with Conroy. "We pay taxes, but in the inner city you had to pay a garbage man to pick up your garbage. In a sense, it provided employment for someone, but . . . someone was being paid for that service twice. We felt it was not proper. So we challenged the city administration on that. It was something the city didn't give in to right away. We created situations to embarrass the city into eventually providing citywide trash removal."

But the Brothers failed to penetrate Albany's political circle and gain lasting power. Blacks could not enter politics unless they went along with the machine, as Van Dyke reported in his 1987 interview with Conroy. "At that time, the Albany police and the machine were not to be messed with. They'd put you in jail for anything, and they had a reputation of beating you too . . . . They looked at it as: 'We run the show.' Mike Tepidino, all the judges, all the aldermen, all the committeemen and a number of financiers, bankers and such, were part of the machine . . . . At that time, the machine was so powerful."

Urban Renewal

The ultimate political failure of the Brothers had far-reaching consequences. For Arbor Hill, lack of political representation meant that residents could not push the city to participate and seek resources from the federal government. The party machine opposed federal antipoverty programs as "interference" in the local scene. The city had built some housing projects in the late 1940s and early 1950s, but only on a small scale. In 1955, when Albany created the Urban Redevelopment Agency to "identify blight areas" in the city and redevelop them with the aid of federal and state funds, the city still held back. Its reluctance was captured in a 1959 *Knickerbocker News* article: "This slow pace of Albany's battle against blight in general can be explained partly too by a city administration that puts a high value on its low tax rate and hesitates to rush into big risky ventures" (Rowley 1959).

Urban renewal in Albany, at least on paper, was supposed to improve life in Arbor Hill. "The plan called for the destruction of the worst buildings, but also for preserving as many of the existing buildings as possible, and planning for their improvement through a neighborhood conservation program." The Arbor Hill project envisioned a variety of new types of houses to accommodate people with different incomes. New stores and shops were to be "conveniently located" near the project. Streets were to be improved and vacant land graded for future community use. And finally, the project was to improve the tax base by making land more available for development and by replacing old buildings with new ones. "The city planned to spend a total of about $3.3 million on several projects, and to receive $16.6 million from state and federal grants. The city's portion of Arbor Hill at that time was to be $754,167" (Seyse 1987:15, 16).

According to "Albany Is Rebuilding," a 1963 report from the Albany Department of Urban Renewal, the department was responsible for helping families and businesses "who must relocate . . . to find suitable new quarters. Acquisition . . . takes time; all persons and businesses will not move at once. They will be notified well in advance so that ample time is provided to find new space. . . . Funds are available . . . for payments covering the cost of moving." The project that was designed as a major upgrading of Arbor Hill to improve its residents' quality of life instead destroyed part of the neighborhood and decreased its housing stock. The city built two private apartment complexes for low- and middle-income families, Ten Eyck Manor and Dudley Park Apartments. It also built 350 public-housing units, the Ida Yarbrough Apartments—low-rises for families and high-rises for senior citizens. But that was not enough to solve the shortage of affordable housing in Albany.

The positive outcome was the construction of Arbor Hill Elementary School, a modern structure in the eastern part of the Hill designed to resolve racial imbalance in the inner-city schools by drawing from several elementary-school districts. However, even though the school has a good academic program and receives substantial funds from the city, 90 percent of its students are Black. The new middle-class residents (some of them Black) who now live in the gentrified parts of the neighborhood do not send their children to this school. So strong is the stigma attached to it because it is predominantly Black that parents choose to pay for private school rather than risk the potentially "bad influence" of ghetto children. But one family who decided to give Arbor Hill Elementary a try said, "We are very satisfied with the school. It has everything, very dedicated teachers, good equipment, nice classrooms. In the beginning we were worried about bad kids and their impact on our son's education. But he's going to this 'bright children's' class [the school has a tracking system]. The children do not mix, only maybe a little bit at recess."

Many parts of Arbor Hill are still in decay. First Street is in the worst condition, particularly from Lark to Swan—with the exception of a few solid houses, it is a vast vacant lot. More than half the houses are gone, and those that remain are boarded up, gutted by fire, or otherwise uninhabitable. The shopping center built as part of urban redevelopment has been vacant for years. When Price Chopper, a local grocery-store chain, finally put one of its stores there, it lasted only two years.

New Black Leadership

Not until 1983 was an independent Black candidate able to challenge the local political machine. In a primary for the county legislative seat from Albany's Third District, Sandra Temple beat longtime Democratic Party leader Homer Perkins, Arbor Hill's twenty-year county legislator. In 1984 Temple replaced

Perkins as Third Ward Democratic leader. Her biggest achievements were "helping to get the Arbor Hill Community Center reopened, increasing minority representation on the board of the Whitney Young Health Center, and working with the County to create a Mobile Crisis Unit following the fatal shooting by Albany police of Clinton Avenue resident Jessie Davis" (Gold 1987:16).

The Arbor Hill Community Center, open since 1973, had been popular in the community for its classes for adults and children and its community outreach program. In January 1984, when United Way of Northeastern New York cut off funding, citing "the Center Board failure to provide adequate programming and allegedly misspending money," community residents protested to save the center. In the negotiations with United Way, Temple was the chief spokesperson, helping to reach an agreement that allowed the center to reopen in September 1985 with a new board of directors and an $88,404 check from United Way. "Now, after three tough years, it appears that the terms of the United Way's funding may soon be modified to provide a more reliable long-term source of support" (Gesensway 1988). Nearly all of the center's users are Black. According to Betty Darnette, its executive director, about 1,500 children and teenagers participate regularly in after-school and evening athletic and educational programs. The center still has a lot of administrative problems.

Another Black resident of Arbor Hill, Nebraska Brace, in 1977 won election to the Albany Common Council using as a tool the newly founded Arbor Hill Democratic Club—a political and social organization outside the Democratic Party. This organization, however, has not been successful in electing candidates other than Brace. In the 1989 elections for common council, Brace was the only reform Democrat to lose an election in Albany; the machine-backed candidate, Sarah Logan, won. Brace lost because residents believed that he could not bring positive changes in Arbor Hill.

Logan, on the other hand, although she is not part of the machine, expected that with mayoral support she could turn things around. Her approach was to implement several family-style projects. In January 1990, at a community meeting I attended titled "Rebuilding the Community/The Arbor Hill Family," she presented a program called the Mayor's Plan and emphasized the importance of cultural programs:

> So many young people helped me in the campaign, and I know that we have a
> great potential here. But we have to get our house in order. We're like a big
> family here, so let's rebuild our community. Something is wrong with our values.

We have to teach Arbor Hill children and youth social grace, good manners, to respect the family, religion, community . . . . My goal is to reach every young person in Arbor Hill. I want to engage the whole community: bankers, businesses, local public officials, and social agencies. After I got elected, I made a number of visits to all these people. And they're all interested and excited about the idea.

Logan went on conducting monthly community-leadership meetings, gathering leaders from Arbor Hill and representatives of agencies interested in Arbor Hill in her headquarters to discuss issues of concern. But the neighborhood continued to be divided: Only the leaders who supported Logan in her last election campaign participated.

The Neighborhood Association

In 1975, several residents who lived in the section of Arbor Hill known as Ten Broeck Triangle formed the Arbor Hill Concerned Citizens Association to address neighborhood problems and to advocate for neighborhood revitalization. Beginning with their area of attractive brownstones and brick houses, they saw gentrification as a way to improve their neighborhood and thought their proximity to downtown Albany and the growth of service-sector jobs would foster this process.

Most of the organizational members, White and Black, were home owners and middle-class renters. Race is not as divisive a factor in Arbor Hill as it is in other poor neighborhoods, for protecting and promoting home ownership represents a strong common interest that has mitigated its significance. One of the charter members of the organization, a longtime activist, explained to me in 1987 why neighborhoods need collective actions. "Government officials don't listen to a single voice, therefore we decided to form an organization as a place for people to come when they have problems. And we had lots of problems. We needed a playground for kids. Absentee landlords did not keep their houses up to standard. The code enforcement was bad."

Arbor Hill Concerned Citizens is not the first neighborhood association to be formed in this area. In 1971, the Arbor Hill Citizens Improvement League was founded to deal with garbage control and to develop a more cooperative spirit in the neighborhood. It launched clean-up campaigns, got the city to set up a twice-weekly schedule of trash disposal, and put flower boxes in windows and in front of houses. Its lack of success in turning the neighborhood around caused the organization to disband in 1974. Sarah Logan, a member of the league at the time, felt it failed because "a lot of apathy existed in the neighborhood. The people didn't see any use in discussing problems which had been the same for years."

But in the late 1970s, with historic preservation in full swing, the Albany Urban Renewal Agency (which later became the Albany Community Development Agency) designed a special program to make houses at Ten Broeck Triangle more desirable. The agency sponsored three auctions in 1978, 1979, and 1980, to sell twenty-seven homes foreclosed on Ten Broeck Street, with starting prices from $5 to $10,000; buyers would be rewarded with a grant of $70,000 and an $80,000 loan at 3 percent interest. Bidders needed a good credit history and sufficient income to carry out the project, with priority going to those with moderate incomes, previous residents of Arbor Hill, families, and those eager to participate in the community's life.

"Own a Piece of the Block"

When representatives of the Urban Renewal Agency approached the Arbor Hill Concerned Citizens for assistance in conducting and evaluating the bidding, a committee was formed with three members of the association and three members of the agency. Both organizations believed that the best way to stabilize the neighborhood was to encourage home ownership and discourage investment ownership (absentee owners). Although the auction was public, bidders had to write essays in which they explained their reasons for moving into the neighborhood. New residents were expected to stay in the neighborhood at least three years: "We wanted good neighbors, people who would come to live and stay here and not just make a profit," a longterm resident told me in an interview in September 1987.

In the first round, the committee had an easy job. Out of three buildings offered, two had only one bidder. But at the second auction, thirty people bid on nine buildings, and, at the third, sixty people bid on fifteen buildings. At the time of the third auction, it looked as if the purpose of the auctions—to help this depressed neighborhood develop and become more desirable—would succeed. One of the members of the committee, a neighborhood resident, in 1990 described the auctions and their effect to me:

> Mayor Corning wanted to turn Arbor Hill around. At that time we had federal funds for target-community development. The belief was that we could stabilize Arbor Hill by encouraging home ownership. Three of us from the neighborhood

association worked on the bidding process. We had to decide which bidders would represent a positive contribution to the neighborhood. Although the program was designed for low- and moderate-income people, the ones who were actually eligible were middle-income people. At the time of the auctions, they were moderate income. But over several years their incomes increased dramatically and, in effect, now we don't have any moderate-income people here.

Results were mixed. Out of twenty-seven buildings, seventeen were sold, but eight of these were never rehabilitated. They were too big or too expensive to renovate, or other personal reasons (death or divorce) made renovation impossible. Even so, living in the Ten Broeck Triangle became more desirable. The new White and Black residents were young professionals working for the state or other downtown businesses. Larry Stanley, one of these new homeowners, told me in 1987, "When I came in 1982, the area was depressed, and just a few houses were rehabilitated. I got the seed money from the Urban Renewal Agency: a $20,000 loan with 3 percent interest. The rest came from my own pocket. . . . Soon new [building] projects followed. . . . We were awakened every morning at six o'clock by construction noise. It looked as if we lived in a construction site." Most new residents shared Stanley's enthusiasm. They were proud of the history of the neighborhood, joined the Arbor Hill Concerned Citizens, and were interested in increasing opportunities for gentrifying Arbor Hill. The neighborhood association organized social events, garden parties, and house tours to induce prospective residents to visit the neighborhood. With this fresh blood, the association increased its activity.

Organizational Characteristics of the Arbor Hill Concerned Citizens

Concerned Citizens is a neighborhood association whose membership is confined to Ten Broeck but that would like to represent all of Arbor Hill. It is incorporated as a not-for-profit body, with active committees whose members work on specific issues and report to the board and the organization's membership at monthly meetings. Residents were very much concerned with the physical improvement of the neighborhood; In 1989 they demanded city services for Arbor Hill, such as stop signs, lighting on Clinton Avenue, park improvements, and parking. The organization maintains a membership list, requires dues, and publishes a regular newsletter.

The finances of the neighborhood association are based on membership dues and a spring fundraiser, a garden party called Brick by Brick. The event starts with cocktails in Norstar Bank headquarters, continues in the houses of neighborhood members, and finishes with champagne and dessert in Ten Broeck Mansion. Tickets are forty dollars. The purpose, one member told me in 1989, is that "first, we wanted to improve the image of the neighborhood and possibly attract some new residents. And we also wanted to contribute, give something back to the community. Every year we donate a portion of the money to one of the social service-oriented organizations from Arbor Hill. Also during the summer, we as an association sponsor a child or two for summer camp." The man who later became the president of Arbor Hill Concerned Citizens came to one party and decided to purchase a house himself. He described his experience to me in 1987 "Through business connections, I met the real estate agent who lives in Ten Broeck Triangle. He tried to sell me a house here, but I declined. I didn't even want to look around. Then he called me one day, and told me about the Brick by Brick party. Well, I decided to come . . . and I was delighted by the sense of community among the residents and the beauty of the houses. Then I let him show me the house that I finally bought."

Although the neighborhood association's decisions are made by the general membership, the role of the board is substantial. One important task is to enlarge the association's membership base and make the organization more efficient. One of the board members explained to me in 1989: "Our membership varies, going up and down depending on the issues. But we always had a core of dedicated residents who met regularly. They kept the organization going. Now we're discussing ways in which we can improve our organization. The suggestion is to change the membership monthly meetings to quarterly meetings. The board would still meet every month to discuss routine organizational business. That's how the Center Square Neighborhood Association is run. Then we'd have more interesting agendas for membership meetings, and more people would come."

In the last several years, leadership has come from the new residents, but the older ones are still represented on the six-member board of directors. The class and social resources of the board are suggested by their high educational and occupational attainments, which are much higher than the neighborhood's as a whole: Half of the board members have master's degrees, and the rest have bachelor's degrees. Three members have incomes higher than $40,000, one of between $30,000 and 35,000, and two of between $15,000 and 19,000. All but one are home owners. Two are married, and three have children. Four are Black, and two are White. Two members are retired professionals; four are employed. One works for the government, one owns a small business, and two are professionals. Three board members have lived all their lives, or more than forty years, in this neighborhood. The other three have lived here for from ten to two years. One of the members was a charter member of the association, three have been members for more than five years, and two have been members for less than five years. Two have been board members for more than five years, four for less. Two members belong to three other organizations besides Arbor Hill Concerned Citizens, and four belong to between four and nine others.

Racially, this is an integrated neighborhood and organization. As one board member explained to me in 1990: "I grew up in a lily-white suburban neighborhood. It was boring. Everybody was the same . . . . When I moved here I really appreciated the diversity of the people . . . . We have everybody here . . . . Our problem is not race. Black and White residents are all professionals; the majority are single . . . not that many families . . . . Demographically we are like Center Square . . . . We are different from the rest of the Arbor Hill more by class than by race."

Most of the board members have substantial ties outside the Arbor Hill community. Their professional lives and interest in the community make it possible for them to establish direct contact with many of the city's agencies and local developers. In 1989 one of them, a high-ranking state worker, described his involvement to me: "I don't own a house here, I rent an apartment. I live alone and don't need a lot of space [he is divorced with grown children]. I got involved because I have skills and knowledge that can be used to help the neighborhood. I know that this neighborhood can do better and that we can make a difference." The board members believe in the democratic process and in grass-roots democracy. They all vote, and they consider the neighborhood association a tool for the articulation of neighborhood interests and needs. One, a young single woman who recently bought a house in the neighborhood, in 1990 explained to me why she became involved: "I want the neighborhood to gentrify, and to improve its reputation. Here we are all professionals, White and Black, and the majority of the houses are renovated, but we're still treated by the city as a slum. I want the city to start paying attention to us, because we need better services . . . . This is a real neighborhood; we know each other and depend on each other . . . . I like how this neighborhood looks; it's beautiful and it's mixed . . . but we have to get rid of slum landowners, change the attitude of the city, and encourage more decent people to buy homes here." Other residents share her appreciation for the neighborhood's racial diversity, its convenient location, their beautiful houses, and the sense that they are building a community.

Some long-term residents, like this one who spoke to me in 1989, are happy that their loyalty to the neighborhood is paying off. "I've lived in this neighborhood all my life. In the fifties the decline began. Absentee landlords came here and wanted to make as much money as possible, and they turned houses into small apartments. But now it's different. These new young people are rejuvenating the neighborhood. We want to create an environment for gracious living. I like to go out and see nice-looking places, and that's what we are doing." Residents socialize with each other, on various occasions. The neighborhood association sponsors several social events to bring residents together, such as the annual Christmas-tree lighting and Christmas party. These events also provide opportunities to recruit new members. One of the board members told me how it works. "I got an invitation to the Christmas party. I went and I liked it. At the party, I heard about the neighborhood association and decided to join it. I bought a house here, and I wanted to see the property succeed as well as the neighborhood. Being business oriented, I would like more things to happen here. We still have large buildings which are not renovated. They're too big for a single family."

The neighborhood association also has something to offer its older residents and members. An elderly woman who lives alone told me in 1989: "Over the last ten years the neighborhood has changed quite a bit. More houses are fixed; the park looks better . . . . I continue to be involved because I think that I can be of some help to newcomers. And these new people are friendly and neighborly. I was sick yesterday and my neighbor came with soup . . . . We're not friends; we're neighbors."

Relationship with Other Organizations

Arbor Hill Concerned Citizens feel that it is the legitimate representative of all of Arbor Hill. The group is open to all residents and is eager to work on any issue that arises. Having a neighborhood association, some members believe, makes it possible for each citizen of Arbor Hill to get collective backing for legitimate concerns. And over the years, Concerned Citizens has been approached by people who do not live in the Triangle.

An active member of the Council of Albany Neighborhood Associations, Concerned Citizens sends representatives to sit on the Arbor Hill Improvement Corporation board and has regular contact with both the Vulcan Real Estate Corporation and St. Joseph's Housing Corporation. The association sometimes forms a coalition with the Sheridan Hollow and North Albany Neighborhood Associations to apply for common grants.

The group's relationship with Albany Democratic Party representatives is not without problems. When Nebraska Brace was alderman, he regularly participated in organizational activities. But Sarah Logan, although a resident of Ten Broeck Triangle, does not; instead conducts separate meetings to discuss neighborhood problems. She may want to distance herself from Concerned Citizens because it is sometimes called an "elite" neighborhood group. This distance has left its leaders somewhat sour toward Logan; they feel that, in the long run, the separation will undermine neighborhood efforts. In dealing with city agencies, they fear their group might be challenged as the legitimate representative of the neighborhood. It also might undermine Sarah Logan's legitimacy as an Arbor Hill representative to have another voice besides hers speak for Arbor Hill.

Current Issues

Today, major renovation of the buildings at Ten Broeck Triangle is finished. Even in this part of the neighborhood, however, residents are troubled that Arbor Hill, on the whole, is a low-income neighborhood under pressure to develop more low-income housing. The president of the association in 1990 summarized some of the neighborhood concerns by asking me: "Why does every low-income housing project have to be in Arbor Hill? The neighborhood will never improve if they continue to put these people here. What we need is not more low-income projects; we need more homeowners who will keep their property up." Members of Arbor Hill Concerned Citizens fear that the new low-income housing will increase the concentration of poverty and worsen life for everyone. Another board member explained to me in an interview in 1990: "Poor people have to live somewhere. We're not against them, but it's not good for poor people to live in a concentrated area. The children from these projects [public-housing projects on the edge of the neighborhood] are stigmatized, and they suffer. If they scatter them around it would be better for them and for us."

Residents do not necessarily oppose low-income residents living in Arbor Hill, but they are against increasing their concentration in one neighborhood. They prefer projects for mixed-income residents or low-density subsidized housing. Association members believe that these projects would help low-income residents more by making it possible to blend easily with the gentrified parts and to take the stigma from the neighborhood. Not everyone shares this opinion, as a representative of United Tenants, a citywide tenants' association, made clear to me in 1990:

I am sick and tired of hearing about the concentration of low-income people. Have you ever heard people complain about a concentration of rich people? And homeowners have a higher housing subsidy than anyone else . . . . Tenants are also interested in improving the neighborhood, but they don't feel comfortable at Concerned Citizens meetings because they don't address their issues . . . . I wonder when these neighborhood associations will realize that encouraging a stable rental situation [a low turnover of tenants] is important in creating a nice and secure neighborhood. But then they would have to encourage home owners to keep rents moderate, so that their tenants can afford to live there.

Other members of Concerned Citizens told me they privately agreed with her: "The real problem is the absentee landlords. They don't pay taxes, do not repair the buildings. Fortunes were made here. These empty buildings are empty because of neglect . . . . Tenants pay high prices for bad deals. They charged them as much rent as they could. The landlords are the ones who created the depressed conditions in the neighborhood." The problems that tenants have, as a United Tenants activist told me in a 1990 interview, are not primarily personal problems or local ones. They are national ones created by social and economic discrimination: "In this country you are allowed to discriminate according to income. People who are on public assistance cannot rent apartments easily. Landlords often do not want to deal with public services. The only apartments that poor people can rent are often in rundown neighborhoods. And because landlords know that these people don't have a choice, they ask them for any rent they wish."

The Concerned Citizens' campaign for gentrification has revealed a conflict in the Arbor Hill neighborhood, which still has predominantly low-income residents and needs more affordable housing. The association's emphasis on the residential quality of life (residential land use, services, and beautification) benefits home owners more than tenants. Indeed, the improvements in the neighborhood usually raise the price of housing and reduce the available affordable housing. Low-income residents, on the other hand, need affordable housing and have to wrestle with problems that are much harder to solve than beautification—persistent poverty, unemployment, and tenant-landowner disputes. To improve their residential quality of life, they need to improve their class position. Better and more secure incomes would provide them with personal resources that they could use to maintain themselves and their apartments, and also to share the costs of collective actions with others. Or they could work on convincing their city officials and other residents that minimum standards for human beings include safe, well-maintained neighborhoods.

But Concerned Citizens did not see demanding public programs for their low-income neighbors as one of their roles. Instead, the organization supported the city-government plan to redevelop parts of Arbor Hill through public-private partnerships. The city raised most of the funds needed for housing renovation, and it offered a historic-rehabilitation tax credit to private investors. The Vulcan Corporation, the biggest of these local real-estate corporations, became the city partner, renovated boarded-up buildings, converted them into apartments, and offered them to low-income residents at subsidized rents and to others at market-rate rents. The developer expected that the market-rate apartments would pay for the subsidized apartments.

Under the title Historic Arbor Hill, Vulcan began to redevelop parts of the neighborhood on a scale that would have been impossible for smaller investors to undertake. The corporation bought eighty-two boarded-up buildings and turned them into 233 apartments and fifteen commercial spaces. The total cost of the project was about $13 million: About $3 million came from syndicated private investments, with a tax credit for historic rehabilitation; about $6 million came from the New York State Fund for Housing, in the form of low-interest bonds; and the last $3 million came as low-interest loans from an Urban Development Action Grant. The Vulcan Corporation agreed to keep these apartments for at least ten years before selling them.

In the beginning, 40 percent of Vulcan apartments were in income-qualified programs and were offered to working, low-income people ($10,000–$21,000 a year). The size and price of an apartment depended on family size and income—tenants were expected to pay about 30 percent of their salaries toward rent. The rest would come from internal subsidies, that is, from the market-rate apartments. The remaining 60 percent of Vulcan's apartments were offered at market rates to anyone who could pay the rent.

Arbor Hill's poor reputation meant that very few people who could afford market-rate rents were willing to move there. Although the income-qualified apartments were all rented, the vacancy rate among market-rent apartments forced Vulcan to decrease the number of subsidized ones. A representative of Vulcan who talked with me in 1990 was frustrated by what she perceived was the lack of cooperation from the city:

> We have problems with code enforcement in this part of town. The city does
> not check or reinforce the code ordinances. Several buildings around ours are
> deteriorating, and that's bad publicity for our apartments. Also the Albany police
> are not cooperative. The newcomers, who don't know about the "reputation" of
> Arbor Hill, are often told when they call to inquire about the neighborhood that

"you would not want to live there," . . . and that's not true. This is a nice neighborhood. We have some bad tenants who trash apartments, but we also have good tenants. We see so many nice people here, and that makes our work worthwhile.

The charm of these apartments—the historic buildings, the beautiful views, the historic detail in the units, the hardwood floors, the high ceilings, and the convenient location—were not enough to keep middle-class tenants for long. This is a catch-22 for many neighborhood associations: Attracting middle-class residents helps improve conditions in the neighborhood, but they will not come until the neighborhood improves.

Because it had made a large financial commitment to Arbor Hill, Vulcan Corporation tried to help. It assumed a number of "improvement" activities in cooperation with Concerned Citizens to promote a positive public image, as well as influence the reputation of improved areas in which the firm was investing. As one of the owners of the Vulcan Corporation explained to me in 1990: "We want Arbor Hill to become a desirable community. The better the neighborhood looks, the more chance we have to fill our apartments . . . . And we help the neighborhood as much as we can. We financially supported renovation of the Ten Broeck Mansion [a historic Arbor Hill landmark]. We're also involved in summer camps and youth-employment programs, where we sponsor children from the Hill or offer them summer jobs. For summer and fall neighborhood clean-ups, we offer trucks and equipment." As a consequence of developer and neighborhood activity, the physical appearance of these parts of the neighborhood improved somewhat. But the historic section of the neighborhood, Ten Broeck Triangle, is still surrounded by public-housing projects, vacant lots, and abandoned buildings. Consequently, Vulcan began looking for a way out of Arbor Hill, and when the Historic Arbor Hill project was repossessed in December 1992, its total debt was $9.5 million.

The Vulcan experience supports the view that a large number of private-public partnerships operate with the understanding that the public sector has to provide the capital investment while the private partners make the profit (Clavel and Kleniewski 1990). For the private sector, the primary motivation for joining a partnership is to increase profits, and if that does not happen, they withdraw.

The Northern Boulevard Project

Some of Arbor Hill's main concerns and dilemmas around neighborhood development were reflected in the conflict over the renovation of Northern Boulevard (now Henry Johnson Boulevard). For several years, the Arbor Hill

Development Corporation had been trying to persuade city officials to allocate funds for a transportation study of this major artery that brings people from the suburbs to the city. The boulevard was not built for the volume of traffic that poured in and out every day, and the congestion burdened the surrounding neighborhood. At the same time, residents were concerned about the boulevard's appearance and the impression that it gave of Arbor Hill to the commuters, residents, and visitors who drove past its deteriorated buildings and shabby bars.

Finally, in 1988 the city decided to use some Community Development Block Grant money to pay a consulting agency to survey Northern Boulevard and its adjunct area and to propose plans for its possible renovation and improvement. The city formed the Northern Boulevard Steering Committee and invited representatives of local organizations from Arbor Hill to participate. In 1990 one of the members of this committee described to me what they did:

> The steering committee had the task of identifying critical issues that the consulting firm would address. During the bidding process we had three consulting agencies competing for the contract. Some neighborhood representatives wanted to give the contract to the Arbor Hill Improvement Corporation. We thought that as a neighborhood firm, they were well informed about the needs of the neighborhood. And also the money that they would get for the study would stay in the neighborhood. But the people from Community Agency [Albany Community Development Agency] argued that our corporation was not experienced enough for a project of that size, and therefore it was better to choose a Boston-based firm instead. And in the realization of the project, the Arbor Hill Development Corporation could be more involved. And that's what we did. Now I wonder if the city's decision would have been different if the mayor had liked the Arbor Hill Development Corporation more. For some reason, this mayor antagonizes all voluntary associations.

Another member of the committee explained to me that the disagreement between resident representatives and city officials was unavoidable: The city's plans and residents' expectations clashed.

> The city's primary interest was to foster more economic development, make Northern Boulevard more commercialized. They wanted to develop small specialized businesses and build some high-rise office buildings along the street [possibly to rent to the state]. To obtain part of the funds, they suggested putting in some low-income housing too. We [the neighborhood associations]

on the other hand wanted to keep the residential character of the neighborhood, to put some garden apartments there, to get rid of traffic, and to bring together Arbor Hill and West Hill, which are separated by the Northern Boulevard Bridge.

The project that the city finally adopted called for widening Northern Boulevard; installing turn lanes, new turn signals, and sidewalks; and constructing subsidized housing units. It was also to provide low-interest loans and grants for rehabilitating property along Northern Boulevard and for improving street facades. Over the course of the next six years, the city planned to put $10 million in improvements into this project with money from Community Development Block Grants. So far a $1.8 million, 22,000-square-foot office building has been completed, but the area has yet to become a bustling center of commerce.

Arbor Hill Concerned Citizens was not satisfied with these plans. After the project began in 1989, the drug trade moved closer to their part of the neighborhood, and by 1990 residents feared that drug problems would grow worse and spread to their blocks; these fears were exacerbated by the prospect of another low-income housing project. In a 1990 interview, the representative of the neighborhood association on the Northern Boulevard Steering Committee was bitter:

> I do not understand why the city bothered making this commission when they don't listen to us. We spent so much time working on this project, and for what? And I don't know what kind of commercial investment they're going to have there. Look at Central Avenue—half of its rental space is empty. Low-income housing, I think, is a mistake. Arbor Hill has so many vacant buildings, let people renovate them . . . . And we are also unhappy at the way the city treats the Arbor Hill Development Corporation. Just last month, they hired a Schenectady-based firm to do designs of facades for the project. When we complained, they told us that they didn't know that our corporation could do it. This agency refuses to acknowledge the existence of neighborhood resources.

The Neighborhood Watch

A major complaint that unites many Arbor Hill residents is that police protection is inadequate. The neighborhood police unit was closed in 1986, when the Police Department redeployed the fifty-two officers assigned to the Arbor Hill and South End units to two division headquarters in an effort to improve patrolling of the city. Since then, various groups have called without success for the reopening of Arbor Hill Neighborhood Police Unit. "The former Neighborhood Unit used to get the job done, but now residents are afraid due to the shooting incidents and the sale of drugs in the neighborhood. The policemen from the old police unit were your friends and your protection" (Crowe 1988).

Sponsoring a petition drive that collected 1,040 signatures, the Republican Party openly challenged the city's decision not to open a police station in Arbor Hill. "The petition urges Mayor Whalen to restore a police station in Arbor Hill that was closed two years ago [1986], after officials said it had outlived its usefulness," the *Times-Union* reported in September 1988." Whalen has stood by that decision, but this summer bowed somewhat to growing neighborhood concerns about drugs and violence by installing a police 'community outreach' post, a trailer manned by several officers, at the intersection of Northern Boulevard and Second Street" (Jochnowitz:1988). For a while, the city kept this outreach police unit in Arbor Hill. Then Mayor Whalen organized a campaign against crime and drugs. As a result an antidrug block party took place in Arbor Hill in the summer of 1988, and then the outreach police unit was taken away. One of the residents explained to me in 1989 how little had changed: "The policemen who worked in this unit didn't like being in Arbor Hill. They couldn't relate to the people. They would drive around in patrol cars, but that was it. What we need here is more foot patrols. When we recently complained to the police, they told us that they have increased the number of patrols since the unit was closed. Maybe they did, but we're not seeing them."

Residents at Ten Broeck Triangle decided to improve their own safety by organizing a Neighborhood Watch unit. Formally, Neighborhood Watch is not part of Concerned Citizens' activity, but its members are very much involved (the vice-president of the organization in 1989 was the president of Neighborhood Watch). One of the main goals of this program is to develop a better relationship with police, and to involve more people in looking out for each other. Participants help older residents crime-proof their houses and encourage all residents to call the police if they see something suspicious going on. In 1990, one participant in this program described his involvement to me:

> I often look through the window. If I see somebody who is not from the neighborhood staying here for too long, I call the police. I do the same for strange cars parked for several days in the same spot [when it is a street-cleaning day, it becomes a traffic violation and is therefore easier to get rid of them]. We

don't want anybody here who doesn't live here. Why should they hang around? They don't have any business in this neighborhood . . . . Also we watch each other's houses. My neighbor has our key, and we have his. He travels a lot. When he's away, I occasionally go and turn the lights on, so whoever might be watching the house for a burglary would think that the occupant is home.

Neighborhood Watch sponsors picnics during the summer, so members can get together socially. The president in 1990 told me they wanted

people to have a chance to meet each other, and to feel more comfortable asking a neighbor for a help. When we meet in my backyard during the summer we discuss some of the problems that we all share, but we also have some good times . . . . We have some older residents who are at home a lot. They can watch for us during the day, and tell us what is going on. Also we help them secure their houses and give them horns to use in case of emergency . . . . And the police are very responsive to our activity. They come regularly to inform us about more successful ways to protect ourselves and send us new crime statistics.

Despite the bad reputation of the neighborhood concerning crime, most of the residents feel safe living there. However, they are constantly aware that their security can be threatened by the worsening drug problem in Arbor Hill. One resident raised some of these concerns in a 1990 interview:

In this neighborhood I feel safe, I know what to look for and what to avoid. But if you go just one block up, to Swan Street, you can see them dealing drugs. It's out in the open. Nobody is concerned that police will come, because they rarely show up. I really wonder why they don't react. Everybody knows what goes on on that street . . . . Sometimes I think that the police don't react on purpose. If they start cleaning it up, they [drug dealers] might move to Center Square, or some other "nice" neighborhood. So it's better keeping them here. This is Arbor Hill. And that's why we [the neighborhood association] are sometimes bitter.

If the police's absence is a problem, so is their presence. Over the years, various neighborhood groups (but not neighborhood associations) have addressed the problem of police brutality. Some civil-rights activists have argued that the Albany police are very hard on young Hispanic or Black males. In 1984, the tragic shooting of an innocent mentally disturbed young man led to the formation of the Citizen-Police Community Board to monitor the activity of the Albany police. In 1989, the mayor suggested ways to transform the board and make it more efficient by decreasing community representation, while at the same time he appointed a new police chief who is Black, grew up in Arbor Hill, and currently lives in Colonie. Residents now expect that racially motivated incidents will decrease. For one thing, emergency telephones arrived in 1989; all neighborhoods except Arbor Hill got them in 1988, just after the city announced the appointment of a new police chief.

Community Development

Poor residents of low-income neighborhoods are aware that they need other organizations, in addition to neighborhood associations, if they are to improve their neighborhoods. Arbor Hill's problems are mostly the consequence of residents living in poverty without resources, assistance, or the means to procure them. The transfer of jobs from the city to the suburbs has made it difficult, if not impossible, for inner-city dwellers with modest means to remain in their old jobs or to be hired in new ones. The city allowed the quality of services to decline and the inner city to deteriorate as it became more and more the home of poor people. Poverty, unemployment, drugs, and lack of affordable housing in Arbor Hill have remained persistent problems that city, state, and formal agencies have ignored or dealt with haphazardly and superficially. This is why residents, together with progressive groups in the cities, support community-development strategies as solution where other programs have failed.

In Arbor Hill two organizations engage in community development: the Arbor Hill Improvement Corporation and St. Joseph's Housing Corporation. Their goals are to improve housing, to be a source of empowerment for residents, and to contribute to rebuilding a sense of community. Both organizations challenged the city's pro-growth strategies and created a workable alternative to the private for-profit sector. In that respect community development has goals that go beyond just building new housing and providing more jobs.

Members of the Arbor Hill Concerned Citizens founded the Arbor Hill Improvement Corporation in 1980 to address critical housing issues facing Arbor Hill when no resident-based development company was doing so in a comprehensive way; soon after, it became an independent organization. Since it is locally based, most members of the board of directors are neighborhood residents.

The organization has specialized in developing home-ownership opportunities for low- and moderate-income families. Under contract to the Albany Community Development Agency it also helps individual residents of Arbor Hill to submit and process applications for rehabilitation loans and grants and offers its own rehabilitation assistance to residents. It participates in New York's low-income-housing trust-fund program by purchasing and rehabilitating buildings in the neighborhood and selling them to families of modest income at affordable prices. The corporation also offers a diverse array of services to individuals interested in area property: It arranges for building inspections to determine the feasibility of rehabilitation projects, offers design and drafting services, and refers individuals to needed resources such as FHA 203k rehab loans; the Home Maintenance, Weatherization, and Restore Programs; and the Tool Library.

Although its activity is an asset to Arbor Hill, the corporation itself is in a delicate position. Most of its funding comes through agencies controlled by city hall. When in 1987 the city reassessed property, the downtown neighborhoods were most affected. The Arbor Hill Improvement Corporation offered residents help in fighting the reassessment, but the following year the corporation's new contract with the Albany Community Development Agency stated explicitly that it was not to give Albany residents any advice that was adversarial to the city's position. Because a substantial part of the corporation's money comes through this agency, it was forced to sign the contract. This problem illustrates why Arbor Hill was receptive to organizations like the Brothers. Indeed, political organizations seem essential for addressing problems at the city level.

However, most neighborhood residents could not afford to become home owners. The other organization, St. Joseph Housing Corporation, builds low-income rental housing. It offers apartments at the lowest rates in Arbor Hill and sets its prices according to the public-assistance rates. It has been able to develop housing for the poor in Albany by working on infill housing, by spreading apartments throughout the neighborhood, and by carefully screening its tenants. To make the neighborhood more livable, the corporation also sponsors social events, works on developing ties among residents, and offers incentives for children to do well in school.

St. Joseph's was founded to show that it was possible to develop housing for the poor in Arbor Hill. In 1990 one of its charter members told me how they raised the funds:

> We got $265,000 from the bank as mortgage money. The bank gave us a loan because we had good guarantees, and also because we were supposed to rent to people on public assistance. People on public assistance get money through the

Section 8 program, therefore the bank knew that we would have a constant flow
of cash. The city gave us a grant of $50,000, and another $120,000 came from the
Community Block Development Grant as a loan . . . . We bought our first seven
buildings from the county for the price of one dollar. The buildings were in such
bad shape that the county was glad to get rid of them. They were also in the
worst part of Arbor Hill. Because the buildings had historic value, we agreed to
rehabilitate them to their previous state and got a small grant from the National
Trust for Historic Preservation [$30,000] and a historic-renovation tax credit.

Today the corporation manages 120 apartments. It is still expanding and
successfully raising money from local, state, and federal agencies. However, its
activity has produced some problems. Ironically, real-estate values around its
houses are rising. The second round of houses that the corporation purchased
cost $1,000 apiece, but the third round, in 1990, cost $15,000 each. Also, for
a long time the corporation's activity faced the neighborhood associations' opposition to bringing in very low-income people to Arbor Hill. One of the
board members of St. Joseph's Corporation summarized these complaints in
an interview in 1990:

> When we started this project we had a messy relationship with the
> neighborhood associations [Sheridan Hollow and Arbor Hill]. For eighteen
> months we were fighting to obtain a zoning variance. They [neighborhood
> associations] accused us of creating substandard housing in their community,
> and that we were going to maintain low-income people in their neighborhood.
> Later, they could not understand why we were going to rent historic apartments
> to public-assistance people. I guess they thought that poor people don't deserve
> nice apartments . . . . I was a member of the Arbor Hill Neighborhood
> Association, and the president of the Arbor Hill Improvement Corporation at
> the time. They forced me to resign as president of the board, although they
> could not take me off the board . . . . Now we have a better relationship with the
> neighborhood associations. The ones who made the most problems for us are
> not in the neighborhood anymore or are not active.

Some home owners still feel that what Arbor Hill needs is more gentrification projects and projects like Vulcan's, which would bring moderate- or
medium-income people in. But the bleak prospects for gentrifying the neighborhood beyond Ten Broeck Triangle now brings more widespread acceptance of projects like St. Joseph's.

Community Development as an Alternative to Gentrification

Neighborhood mobilization in low-income neighborhoods of Albany, a service-sector city, was motivated by residents unhappy with the inadequate distribution of city resources. The lobbying and advocacy strategies of Arbor Hill Concerned Citizens have led to some positive outcomes. But because this organization's constituency—middle-class home owners—supported gentrification, it also helped fragment the neighborhood socially and, in the long run, weakened its advocacy power.

The example of the Brothers showed that low-income neighborhoods have the potential for sponsoring organizations that can argue for substantial social and political changes. The Brothers was one of the earliest neighborhood groups to oppose machine politics and fight for such change. Their lack of success resulted from racial intolerance, on the one hand, and the closed character of the political machine in the city on the other. It also shows that in order to change conditions in low-income neighborhoods, residents need political organizations to address their racial, ethnic, gender, or class concerns, but that the success of such organizations may incur a backlash or efforts to subvert them.

The activity of the Arbor Hill neighborhood corporations and other nonprofit organizations in the neighborhood shows that it is economically feasible to create low-income housing and insure that longtime residents can continue to live in the neighborhood. The relatively tight control of city hall over the corporations' activity, however, constrains what they can do. Therefore improving the delivery of services to poor neighborhoods is not enough; local empowerment is also needed.

The community-development strategy clearly can help residents of poor neighborhoods. Numerous successful revitalization efforts nationwide develop as part of more comprehensive plans that progressive political regimes promote for local development. More inclusive local policy provides opportunities to address the sources of urban poverty—lack of jobs and crime. In such political conditions neighborhood mobilization and participation can flourish.

As we can see in the Arbor Hill case, low-income neighborhoods need community-development organizations, particularly since these organizations are based on the inclusion of various interests within the community. Neighborhood residents can create and maintain stable communities not only by encouraging opportunities for home ownership, but also by increasing the pool of affordable public and rental housing. Neighborhood stability, then, can be defined as the ability of residents to continue to live in the neighborhood.

While increasing racial and ethnic diversity can lead to conflict, communities can promote goodwill and tolerance by changing the practices of community-based social-service organizations to accommodate the needs of immigrants and by sponsoring community events to bring the community together. By respecting differences, the community can also build consensus around some of the issues that all residents care about: neighborhood safety, decent jobs, and housing.

6

Schenectady, the Declining City: General Electric, Deindustrialization, and Strategies for the City's Renewal

Schenectady developed as an important center of production, research, and innovation because of huge manufacturing profits in the late nineteenth century and the growth of General Electric (GE), home based there, into a powerful corporation. However, in the 1970s, as the economy became more global, U.S. manufacturing faced greater competition from abroad. The economic role of industrial cities declined as companies like GE closed their old plants, shrank their labor forces, and started to diversify and invest in other areas of the economy and other parts of the world.

Deindustrialization in Schenectady was similar to restructuring in other industrial cities such as Gary, Indiana; Flint, Michigan; Youngstown, Ohio; and Lynn, Massachusetts. Schenectady lost jobs and revenues at the same time that changes in the national economy and government policies deprived the city of state or federal intervention to cushion the blow of these losses. A growing trade deficit, an unstable dollar-exchange rate, and rising consumer and federal-government debt squeezed budgets at all levels. The proportionally rapid increase of low-paying service, subcontracting, part-time, and temporary jobs broadened income and wealth disparities between people, neighborhoods, and cities. Schenectady's unemployed and poor population demanded public assistance at the very time that the city had less to offer. Residents also found themselves in competition with businesses as the city provided subsidies to attract new industry or to keep existing GE facilities within the community. Once a vibrant city, Schenectady went into a decline.

The Rise of the Industrial City

Situated west of Albany on the Mohawk River, "Schenectady undeniably was a daughter of Albany, yet there was very little maternal or filial love manifested by either: on the contrary, there were years of coercion, defiance and even caterwauling. Yet Schenectady until 1798 was subject to Albany" (Monroe 1914:46). The two cities still compete. Although for a while Schenectady experienced independent economic development, now Albany's economy dominates the region.

Schenectady's origins can be traced through the history of its Stockade neighborhood, one of the oldest in the country. In 1661, Arent Van Curler started a new Dutch settlement on the land that he described as "the most beautiful the eye of man ever beheld" (Bogert 1966:2). This new town was the farthest west and the most dangerous settlement of the Dutch. To protect the town, a stockade with a blockhouse at one corner was built around the settlement. From this structure the present Stockade neighborhood derives its name. The stockade itself proved useless: Only a few people and two of the settlement's original houses survived a massacre by the French and allied Native Americans who attacked from Canada in 1690 (Monroe 1914:99).

Despite its almost total destruction, the outpost was not abandoned. The settlement slowly recovered; Dutch rule was replaced by British. In 1704, the British built Queen Ann's Fort, the first of a line of forts in the Mohawk Valley (Monroe 1914:104), which served as the focus of colonial Schenectady. Boats coming from Schenectady were crucial for supplying the western British army and navy as well as the traders with Native Americans working in Ohio, Indiana, Michigan, and the fringe of the Canadian north and west (Hart 1975).

During the eighteenth century, Schenectady was one of the most important commercial centers in the Northeast. "Branches of the firm of famous merchant families, Finley and Elias, were located in London, Montreal, and Detroit, but their principal headquarters were their stores at the corner of Union and Ferry Streets in the Stockade" (Monroe 1914:125). The area was lined with wharves, warehouses, and boat-building shops, serving the traffic that plied the Mohawk. Then in 1819, a disastrous fire wiped out most of these establishments, along with a large number of nearby houses, and changed the destiny of the Stockade neighborhood. Business buildings were rebuilt, but to the south and east of the Stockade, leaving the old section almost entirely residential.

After the Revolution, the old fort was taken down and a market built (now

Arthur's Market) to accommodate both Rotterdam farmers and the farms on the great flats (where later General Electric would be built). Schenectady was becoming an industrial manufacturing center.

General Electric and Industrial Transformation

Founded in 1851, a steam-engine factory, Schenectady Locomotive Works (known as the Big Shop) by 1882, shipped 172 locomotives a year and employed more than a thousand workers. Schenectady had 13,655 inhabitants and the greatest diversity of manufacturing in its history, a development process typical of early industrial cities (Nash 1989). In the early days of U.S. industrialization, cities offered a great number of opportunities to skilled artisans and mechanics (Gutman 1976). Technological skills and possibilities for individual proprietorship or copartnership enabled them to start their own businesses.

Walter McQueen, a Big Shop master mechanic, was such a person. In 1882, he left the Big Shop over a labor dispute, bought eight acres of land along the Mohawk River, and started his own company with the backing of several prominent local business owners. When financial troubles forced him to return to the Locomotive Works, the property went into receivership with an appraised value of $45,000. Thomas Edison, who had founded Edison Electric Company in Menlo Park, New Jersey in 1878, was looking for a new location for his business, trying to evade the growing labor-union movement. For Edison McQueen's price was too high; he offered $37,500. The Schenectady Chamber of Commerce, which did not want to lose this potential large business, helped him by collecting the remaining $7,500 (Nilsson 1988: 17–23).

The Edison General Electric Company, or Schenectady Works, was founded in January 1889, bringing together all of Edison's enterprises. As the company grew, Edison's influence declined, and on April 15, 1892, when two Edison plants were merged with Thompson-Houston Company of Lynn, Massachusetts, Edison's name was dropped from the company's title (Nilsson 1988:17–23). Lynn industrialist Charlie Coffin, the owner of Thompson-Houston, became the president. A shoe manufacturer and entrepreneur, Coffin had entered the electric industry because he wanted to invest his capital in businesses where he could earn higher profits.

General Electric established plants throughout the northeastern United States and by 1900 had more than 12,000 employees, by 1919, 82,000 and an international division. By 1970, the company employed nearly 400,000 (Tichy and Sherman 1993:252–267). Its growth and success rested on several factors. The first was technological change—the transformation of water power and steam engines into electrical energy, which led to a market for industrial power. The second was a large and growing market for consumer goods, which General Electric and Westinghouse, another large electric company, fostered by developing and promoting domestic and industrial products that used electricity (Nash 1989: 53). Like all other large corporations at that time, General Electric and Westinghouse took over a number of smaller competitors. Soon, they controlled 90 percent of the industry and had oligopolistic control of their markets (Nash 1989:55).

The rise of industrial corporations like General Electric, together with the development of a transcontinental railroad network and the spread of a communication system linking major urban centers, transformed the United States from a mercantile/agrarian economy to an industrial one. The General Electric Company made Schenectady one of the nation's key locations for heavy industry. From 1886, when the city became the center of the electrical industry, its population doubled or tripled each decade until 1920 (Rich 1966:15). The rapid expansion of other companies like American Locomotive (ALCO) and Schenectady Chemicals brought the city's population to its all-time high, 95,692, in 1930 (Hart 1975).

But soon afterward General Electric alone began to dominate the city's economy. By 1930 GE was also the dominant force in Lynn, Massachusetts, which had been the leading shoe-industry center (Cumbler 1979). Such a loss of economic diversity, some believe, weakens the balance of power between the corporate sector and the community (Arensberg 1942). When the tax base and industrial activity are restricted to a limited number of firms, communities are more likely to lose their autonomy and to play a secondary role in a city's economic development (Nash 1989:52). An industrial mix and the presence of small competitive firms are essential for the economic survival of the community. No wonder industrial cities have been unable to recover when their major employer has withdrawn or severely curtailed economic activity in the area.

Social and Political Life

Schenectady grew first on the fringes of the old city, and then to the east, north, and south. Communities of Irish, Germans, Poles, Scandinavians, and Italians sprang up, forming ethnic neighborhoods. Closely built with new homes, many of them two-family houses, they were inhabited by GE employees and their families, who wanted to be close to the workplace. Besides workers,

> men of science were coming . . . from all parts of the world, artisans and mechanics were in demand, and an almost unlimited opportunity was offered for unskilled laborers. Thus the social and economic life of the city was undergoing a tremendous change. New residential areas were being developed, tenements erected, and public facilities enlarged. The city was no longer a lethargic, predominantly Dutch community, but an active, heterogeneous mixture of all nations: rich and poor, educated and ignorant, skilled and unskilled, good, bad and indifferent. (Birch 1955:136)

The street-railway system was begun in 1886 (Rich 1966:11); when the trolley lines extended beyond the city limits, widespread housing development and suburbs such as Bellevue, Mount Pleasant, and Woodlawn followed (Hart 1975:113). A residential district for company executives and their families, the General Electric Realty Plot (Hart 1984:89), appeared east of Union College, the first chartered university in New York State. Together with Stockade, this neighborhood was a desirable residential location for members of the emerging middle and upper classes.

Growth brought more immigrants, who by the 1920s made up 20 percent of the city's population—over eighteen thousand people. The most recent immigrants, especially (usually Poles and Italians), were met by a very hostile community. The *Schenectady Union Star* for June 17, 1917, advertised the construction of attractive two-family homes, but only for "white Americans of English-speaking, German or French descent. . . . No lots will be sold to colored people or undesirable foreigners." These newcomers were forced to live in the worst housing in the city. On November 18, 1903, the *Daily Union* reported that "men, women and children were huddled in small rooms, dirt and filth were everywhere present, and the stench that emanated from the place was almost unbearable. Ragged, dirty, unkept children were running hither and thither, some crying, other playing, and all totally unconscious of their surroundings." Like the immigrants of today, they were also accused of creating urban problems and exacerbating crime: "The unattached males became a source of concern for Schenectadians. Italians and Poles were not responsible for an inordinate amount of crime in the city, but their offenses, particularly those of a violent nature committed by the Italians, captured the attention of the press" (Pascucci 1984:2).

The immigrants addressed their hard living conditions by relying on ethnic solidarity and by forming a variety of benevolent societies to provide assistance for families in the event of sickness or death, or to ease the difficulties of adjusting to life in the new environment. Ethnic and kinship ties also became work relations, as employed immigrants found jobs for family and friends in the shops where they worked (Haraven 1982; Nash 1989).

An active labor movement grew up in Schenectady, so that by 1912, the city directory listed more than seventy craft unions (*Schenectady City Directory* 1912). Between 1893 and 1917, frequent strikes and lockouts strengthened workers and their organizations (Gutman 1976). The labor unions that emerged from these struggles bargained collectively to negotiate pensions, vacations with pay, medical insurance, and other benefits.

In 1911 the *Union Star* reported on November 3 and 4 that Schenectady had elected "not only a Socialist mayor, but the complete slate of Socialist officers (except one especially popular Republican sheriff who had sneaked through by a 73-vote margin), a majority (eight) of the Common Council, and eight County supervisors." The city also elected the first Socialist member of the New York State Assembly. However, the new administration was reformist rather than radical. At that time, community, labor, and corporate relationships were developed and based on expectations that companies should provide stable, well-paid jobs for union members in return for labor peace.

For these reasons, it was not unusual that George Lynn, Schenectady's Socialist mayor, would be more occupied with neighborhood conditions than with changing the social order or challenging business decisions. He built parks and playgrounds, improved public-health programs and public education, and made city government more efficient (Hart 1984:189). The political attitude of the city's administration is summarized in the mayor's message to the common council on January 8, 1912, in which he announced that the goals of his administration were, according to the next day's *Union Star*, "to improve and promote the health of the community, enlarge education to include all men and women, establish economic security, develop efficient government, and have a true economy—a thing which is not the equivalent of mere expense outing." These goals are similar to those of progressive regimes today and to their vision of urban development. The greatest difference is that current progressive city governments have realized that they have to play a much more active role in developing the city's economic plans (Clavel 1986; Clavel and Kleniewski 1990; Portz 1990).

With some of the same spirit of reform, but with a very different rhetoric, many women and some men from the more prosperous groups in the city helped establish and worked in social-service organizations like the Community Chest. Best known today as an organization on the Monopoly board, the Community Chest was first established in Cleveland in 1913 to coordinate the work and funding of charity and social-service organizations. By 1929 there were 330 Community Chests nationwide, in keeping with the precepts of the Progressive Era: to build a harmonious society by representing the best interest of the community, whose divisions and differences only needed to be reconciled. Its perspective, then, was quite different from that of the Socialist mayors and city councilors, but in practice there was little serious conflict between the two.

The Community Chests assumed that there were worthy and unworthy poor, and that all ethnic groups should strive to behave like upper-middle-class residents of U.S. cities. Since their heyday, they have often been criticized for their patronizing and even suspicious attitudes toward the poor in their communities, their lack of appreciation for other customs and standards, and their lack of imagination regarding the circumstances of poor people's lives. Nevertheless, students of the period, although they are critical of the Community Chests, commend them for some of their work. As they collected and distributed money, they "held conferences to standardize and coordinate welfare activities on a national level, developed surveys of community welfare needs, and led in the development of new fact-finding techniques, standardization of records and improved bookkeeping and accounting techniques" (Austin and Betten 1990:17). They had the predominant role in community planning until 1931, when more professional social agencies emerged and diminished their importance.

In Schenectady, the Community Chest was comprised of forty-three agencies and began operations in 1924, during the decade in which the United States adopted a policy that restricted immigration of southern Europeans. An important role for a number of agencies was to promote the assimilation of immigrant groups and their children into what they saw as the American way of life. For example, one of the agencies was the Schenectady Boys Club, which enrolled several hundred boys in low- or no-cost daily programs of recreation, athletics, hobbies, and crafts aimed at "building character, citizenship and health" (Rich 1966:16). These organizations were independent of ethnically based organizations and had an important role in assimilating immigrant children into U.S. society.

The Schenectady Junior Chamber of Commerce, also active in community affairs, primarily aimed at promoting Schenectady as a good place for business and residence. Like the Chamber of Commerce of today it strived "to build a better community and to train its members in leadership and civic consciousness through active participation in civic affairs. Since this organization was founded in 1934, the members have firmly established themselves in the life of the community through such projects as the annual Winter Carnival, Christmas programs, track meets for intermediate school children, public health and safety programs, and many other projects designed to make the city a better place in which to live and work" (Rich 1966:16).

Schenectady's economic life benefited from the increased economic activity during and after World War II. Between 1938 and 1943, the United States contributed a large share of the world's industrial production for the war effort (Perrucci et al. 1988:13), increasing U.S. total manufacturing production by two and a half times (Paterson 1973:6). The major benefactors of wartime production and government policies were large corporations like General Electric, whose growth was stimulated by federal contracts, tax-supported plant construction, and federal research and development funds.

The United States, alone of the warring countries, emerged from the war more prosperous than previously. Its industrial capacity had expanded, its land was untouched by the war, and its population had not been decimated. It had the technology, the industrial plants, the scientific expertise, and the work force needed for successful growth (Perrucci et al. 1988:15). During this period, sometimes called the "Golden Age of Capitalism" (Marglin and Schore 1990), the economy of major industrial nations grew faster and accumulated more productive capital than ever before, leading to greater gains in productivity and higher living standards than in any other period in recent history (Glyn et al. 1990).

In Schenectady and other industrial cities, it seemed that growth and prosperity would never end. Yet there were signs of change. In the 1950s and 1960s, General Electric started restructuring. It offered fewer and fewer blue-collar jobs, and more white-collar jobs. As workers retired, they were not replaced. First American Locomotive, unable to find another economic niche as locomotive production became obsolete, closed its doors in 1969. The deindustrialization of Schenectady had begun.

Deindustrialization

When the profit margin in manufacturing started to fall, manufacturing companies like GE, instead of investing in new plants and new production technology in existing cities, closed their old unionized plants in the Northeast, cut their labor forces, and opened new, nonunion, low-cost plants in the southern United States and overseas. Employment at GE in Schenectady decreased from its peak of 29,000 workers in 1970 to 11,700 in 1988 (Titterton 1988:10–16), while the overall population of the city, according to the U.S. Bureau of the Census, fell from 77,958 to 67,972. Thirty percent of U.S. plants in existence in 1969 had closed by 1976 (Bluestone and Harrison 1982), and by the end of the 1980s, manufacturing jobs were on the decline everywhere in the United States.

Capital mobility, plant closings, and unemployment have changed U.S. employment patterns (Craypo and Nissen 1993b). Declining industrial cities now offer fewer employment opportunities, and laid-off workers often have to accept a severe drop in pay, as well as in status and security (Perrucci et al. 1988:5). Loyalty to the community is seen as a liability, for to find better jobs, employees are encouraged to move. Workers often stay in their communities because they have emotional ties and financial investments—particularly homes—that make them reluctant to move when a plant closes down (Nash 1989:23). The most mobile and the first to leave are young people. Others, depending on their education, experience, and age, make every effort to stay. Some workers take early retirement. They can afford the loss in income, because their mortgages are paid off and their children are grown. Others, usually engineers with technical knowledge and experience, start their own businesses, drawing on their savings or on city funds for economic development and entrepreneurship. In Schenectady GE hires such entrepreneurs as subcontractors.

The decline in the larger manufacturing industries is often explained as an unfortunate but necessary move that capitalist development entails. Schumpeter (1950) called such changes "creative destruction," eliminating inefficient operations and allowing new economic opportunities to emerge. "As some firms go under, they release their resources to other, more cost-effective firms that offer consumers more of what they want at more attractive prices" (McKenzie 1984:85). Therefore, to overcome "technological inadequacy," U.S. firms have to modernize production and employ a more skilled labor force. These changes will lead toward more productive, more innovative firms that will be more competitive in the global market—they will benefit society in the future.

General Electric's restructuring is often held up in much of the business press as the supreme example of "creative destruction." However, GE was also one of the largest munitions manufacturers in the world, subsidized by the federal government. Today it is one of the most profitable companies in the world. As evidence, market analysts point out that in 1992, GE had higher operating profits ($7.7 billion) than all of its main competitors combined ($6.8 billion). They also note that the company outpaced its competitors and increased its profits while being the only one in the field to significantly reduce its work force. In 1992 GE's net sales were $61.9 billion with 276,000 employees; in comparison its next competitor, Hitachi, had $60.4 billion in sales with 328,000 employees.

The Transformation of General Electric

The success of GE, its supporters believe, is based on the economic strategy of Jack Welch, who took over in 1980. Welch believed that, as world competition intensified, only businesses on top of their markets (number one or two) would survive in the 1990s and beyond. Therefore, his restructuring efforts centered on improving GE performance and productivity and on cutting costs. In 1982 GE had twenty-six businesses; in 1993 it had thirteen. Those that were not competitive—by the market standards used by Welch—were closed or sold, while the core was retained.

Today GE is a diversified company with a large variety of businesses in its portfolio. According to its 1992 annual report 32 percent of revenue shares came from core manufacturing (appliances, power systems, and industrial equipment), 31 percent from capital services, 12 percent from aircraft engines, 8 percent from materials, 8 percent from technical production and services, 6 percent from broadcasting, and 3 percent from other businesses. GE is a conglomerate, a corporation that engages in a variety of economic activities unrelated to each other. It is also one of the few large diversified corporations that moves into new unrelated and often risky businesses, such as RCA (which includes the NBC television network) in 1986 or WASA, the consumer finance operation, in 1993. GE can afford to take these risks because of its large internal reserves of capital.

According to Tichy and Sherman, the company had 420,000 employees in 1980. Through layoffs and attrition, GE struck 170,000 off the rolls. Jack Welch, following the advice of his consultant, Peter Drucker, also sold businesses deemed insufficiently profitable. That decreased the labor force by an additional 160,000. Some of the 330,000 workers who were dismissed were replaced by new hires (30,000) or came with newly purchased businesses (150,000). By 1992, GE had a much smaller but more productive labor force: 268,000 employees, with sales per employee 2.5 times those in 1984.

Although GE had dismissed 330,000 employees, Jack Welch has described GE's relations with its remaining employees as unusually harmonious.

The company offers its employees financial rewards such as stock options and bonuses. In 1991, only 500 GEers received stock options; by 1992, the number had soared to nearly 8,000 (Tichy and Sherman 1993: 223). Welch has written that he is proud of having created a "boundaryless organization" by breaking down traditional horizontal barriers between organizational function, businesses, and locations; vertical barriers, such as hierarchical control and decision making; and outside walls that separated the organization from its customers, suppliers, and venture partners (234–235).

Control Your Destiny or Someone Else Will: How Jack Welch Is Making GE the World's Most Competitive Corporation, by Noel Tichy and Stratford Sherman (1993), which extols GE's management and reorganization and applauds the company's profits and the steps taken to achieve them, ignores job loss or the impact of such shifts on the work force in GE's hometown. In Schenectady alone, 3,000 manual workers, managers, and clerical staff lost their jobs in ten years, as GE reorganized and cut its work force. Such a change, especially with few other opportunities for employment available, might be expected to be devastating inside and outside the company; however, Tichy, Sherman, and Welch report no ill effects from the change in the company, based on GE's other organizational accomplishments. Welch has adopted a variation of Quality Team Management (QTM), which he has named Work-Out, in which employees meet in problem-solving forums to improve productivity. While business analysts have praised QTM as the greatest transformation in labor relations of the 1990s, labor-studies groups and union officials have been more critical—or at least more reserved. Nonetheless, a former employee of GE, who condemned Tichy and Sherman's book as an unrealistic, glowing misrepresentation of GE's practices and working conditions, reserved judgment on Work-Outs. If they could succeed in improving working conditions at the particular plant where she had worked, she would have considered them useful (Dougherty 1993).

Troubles with General Electric's Strategy

But, there is trouble in GE's empire. The problem of Kidder Peabody, the Wall Street investment bank, illustrates what can happen when a company pursues only high-profit returns. Jack Welch purchased Kidder Peabody in 1989 for $600 million and invested another $800 million to stabilize it (Pare 1994). Welch also appointed new executive leadership from GE Capital to run the investment firm. Even though the appointed chief executive was not licensed as a broker-dealer, Tichy and Sherman praised Welch's decisions and argued that the management changes increased morale at the firm and led to its unprecedented profitability (1993:115).

The new management, consistent with GE policy, wanted to make Kidder the leading investment firm. To do so, they made a risky decision to enlarge the company's portfolio: "With Kidder's equity at the time a slivery $283 million, the enlarged portfolio posed a significant danger because losses on the securities would mean a big hit to the company's equity. Theoretically, a mere 3.2% decline in the value of its portfolio could have wiped out Kidder's entire net worth. But with deep-pocketed GE in the wings it was a risk that Kidder was willing to take" (Pare 1994:40). Not everything worked according to the management's plan. When the new managers arrived, a large number of the "old" key people left because they were unhappy with GE's decision to fill the key positions with GE executives. As distrust grew, rumors spread that GE would sell the company once it was stabilized. Faced with these problems and eager to turn higher profits as soon as possible, the management of Kidder Peabody ignored standard financial practices, a risk that did not pay off. What Tichy and Sherman in 1993 described as "unprecedented profitability" was fictive. The fraud was exposed in 1994, when Joseph Jett, Kidder's chief government-bond trader, was accused of fabricating $350,000 million in profits.

Jett was not the only one to blame, claims a journalist for *Fortune Magazine* (Pare 1994:41). Citing the Lynch report, the GE internal investigation, he stated, "Time and again questions [about Jett's unusual trading profits] were answered incorrectly, ignored, or evaded. One important reason for those oversights, the report states, was Jett's importance to Kidder's bottom line. 'As his profitability increased,' it says, 'skepticism about Jett's activities was often dismissed or unspoken.' " This scandal, although it tarnished GE's reputation, was not seen as a great financial loss. The *Fortune* article explained that "against the corporate backdrop—annual earnings of $4 billion, $2.03 per share—the $210 million charge that the company took in the first quarter to account for the phony profits works out to a barely visible 12 cents a share. Welch describes the charge as 'nothing, a peanut.' "

But this peanut is not GE's only financial misstep or scandal in recent history. Between 1985 and 1993 the company had to pay more than $100 million in fines for criminal and civil penalties, mainly for cheating and overcharging the Defense Department and governments of other countries on sales of military equipment (Pare 1994:46). GE's profits and practices thus are not always in the public interest, and GE does not necessarily serve its own best interest. Although GE now views these scandals as a problem, the restructuring that destroyed the livelihoods of thousands of workers and the stability of their families and communities is not so perceived.

The phrase "corporate hegemony" describes the power that large firms have. National and global corporations control local conditions because they have the ability to grant or deny jobs and revenues to communities. In this way they determine labor relations, manufacturing operations, and the outcomes of community economic-development activities (Craypo and Nissen 1993a: 224).

Schenectady, Lynn, and other deindustrializing cities did not lose jobs because they were unwilling to change, learn, or improve, but because it was cheaper for GE and other companies to move their plants elsewhere. Similarly, fewer jobs, the threat of plant closings, and the emergence of a pool of low-paid, part-time, and temporary workers forced employees to make concessions on wages and benefits (Perrucci et al. 1988:23). I find it hard to believe that the union-management cooperation now advocated can reverse the loss of jobs. Instead, "to regain the ability to protect their members' economic and job interests" and "to ensure adequate services and social amenities to their residents," unions and communities need new forms of institutional power (Craypo and Nissen 1993a:225).

Other research on plant closings and economic restructuring also challenges the "general decline of American economic dominance" idea. Deindustrialization, these writers insist, was caused by a conscious investment decision and disregard for existing labor and communities (Bluestone and Harrison 1982; Perrucci et al. 1988; Nash 1989). U.S. Steel, which changed its name to USX Corporation after diversifying into oil and gas production (half of its business), is one such example. The company was able to spend billions of dollars to acquire oil and gas companies because it extracted concessions from workers and abandoned the industries where they worked (Perrucci et al. 1988:1).

General Electric, General Motors, and USX could afford to restructure in the way they did because companies in the United States were not forced to compensate communities and workers for the damage and loss they inflict. Cities and unions do not know enough about what is happening in the centralized administrative bodies of the companies that control their destinies. Because companies do not have to disclose information about their operations, plant closings and job reductions have often come as a surprise.

For workers who continue to hold jobs, restructuring the U.S. economy created a new system of industrial relations based on a human-resources model, as the GE strategy exemplifies. It emphasizes flexible work rules and job classifications and introduces worker participation in direct-production processes. However, GE did not change the power relationship between its managers and employees. It is clear to everyone in GE that Jack Welch and other top managers—while they might ask employees for work-related input—continue to make all the important decisions. Workers and communities will continue to be vulnerable to corporate power.

Meanwhile, corporations justify the loss of good manufacturing jobs, the decline in living standards and working conditions, and the loss of community prosperity, stability, and quality of life by pointing to increasing profit margins for shareholders. The advice that John Biggs, chair and chief executive officer of TIAA-CREF, a teachers' pension fund, gave its members about investments in foreign stocks explains it all: "The argument against buying foreign stocks is that foreign countries frequently put employee and community interests ahead of shareholders' interests" (Biggs 1994:6). When profit margins are the bottom line, human costs do not matter. Within this framework, the destruction of communities through deindustrialization makes sense.

City Revitalization

As GE cut jobs during the 1970s, Schenectady city officials played what has been called the "bystander" role (Portz 1990). For a decade they watched in dismay and hoped in vain that layoffs would be temporary. By 1983 they realized that the GE pullout would not be reversed.

Corporate Strategies

The city and Schenectady County formed the Economic Development Corporation to lure new businesses, jobs, and young people back to the city. Its major goal is to diversify the economy of the area by encouraging public and private employment, developing new service jobs, and promoting growth in manufacturing jobs. The director of the corporation told me in 1989 that "the city decided to throw politics out the window and to turn all of its attention to revitalization efforts. The corporation is now sponsoring small and medium-sized companies. We also sponsor an employment training center." Corporate strategies in general meet with such enthusiasm and approval that people do not even see them as political decisions. To achieve jobs for the community and a healthy local economy, local governments provide economic incentives, such as financial-assistance packages to a business firm or to a retraining center for workers.

Portz (1990) calls this policy an "offset" response. Local officials might help the unemployed by offering job-search assistance, income support, and retraining. But they are more likely to use city resources to create a good business climate, to cut wages as a way to keep manufacturing production, or to discourage unionization. Consequently city governments provide businesses with a capital infusion, tax reduction, tax abatements, and free land or vacant buildings (Clavel and Kleniewski 1990). Because cities must compete among themselves for their economic survival, by now virtually every city has a glossy brochure describing the benefits of doing business in its community.

Local governments, Portz suggests (1990: 9), use offset policies as a compromise that will maximize worker and community welfare while preserving a firm's right to control its economic resources. Yet when GE pulled out of Schenectady because the market for turbines had shifted to Asian countries, there was very little that the city could do to bring GE jobs back. Schenectady needed to find a new economic niche. One choice, according to city officials, was to invest in service-sector jobs. In 1988 a local publication, *Metroland*, reported that "one of the biggest projects in the city is the construction of an $80 million, three-building office complex and parking garage in the downtown area. It is scheduled to be completed in the spring of 1990, bringing with it some 600–800 jobs. Officially, the latest unemployment figures of 2.7 percent, are the lowest ever in the county and 4% in the city" (Titterton 1988:10). The office complex ran into financial difficulties as soon as it opened for business. In 1994 the State of New York bought one of the office buildings, Broadway Center, for $12.1 million. The city of Schenectady got $150,000 for its $700,000 investment, or about twenty-one cents on the dollar. The state Urban Development Corporation, which got $500,000 for its $5 million investment, or about ten cents on the dollar, will be able to get title to the building for one dollar after twenty-five years. Also two state agencies, the Department of Taxation and Finance and the Division of the Lottery, became new tenants.

GE continues to reduce employment at its Schenectady plant, cutting employees in 1994 from 8,000 to about 6,000. Company officials promised not to cut more jobs in 1995, but beyond that, they refused to reveal their plans for Schenectady's plant. In March 1995, GE announced another round of layoffs: 980 people lost their jobs.

Many local residents still do not think Schenectady has been revitalized. Most new businesses there are small enterprises that offer few permanent jobs with benefits. Vacant storefronts and nearly empty streets, especially in the evening in Schenectady's downtown, are not signs of prosperity.

Government-Labor-Community Coalitions

An alternative to corporate strategies has been tried in some cities where populist or progressive governments take an active role in designing economic policy, working more closely with labor and community groups than with business firms. These government-labor-community coalitions have explored a variety of avenues to influence business decisions. One strategy is to pass a plant-closing law, which requires advance notification of a plant closing from the business firm. Usually a city then organizes a public hearing to determine whether the closing is necessary and demands that the company provide severance pay for workers, job-transfer privileges, funds for worker retraining, and lump-sum payments to the community. Such legislation, believe the authors of *Plant Closings: International Context and Social Costs,* places employment and the human and social costs of unemployment at the center of economic decision making and also slows capital flight, because it makes disinvestment less attractive. Some firms learn that modernizing an old facility is less expensive than building a new one in another location (Perrucci et al. 1988:153).

Another policy that addresses company flight seeks financial compensation for tax abatements provided by the city to keep companies in the community. In the 1980s property-tax abatement became an important economic-development tool. In northwest Indiana, for example, nearly all investment projects undertaken by existing and new companies, regardless of company need or benefit to the community, got tax abatements. "In 1988 Hammond [Indiana] gave tax abatements totaling more than $15 million (given out over the life of the abatements) to 16 companies. On the 'statement of benefits' application, the recipient companies had promised to create 804 new jobs but had actually created only 74. Furthermore, there had been no public participation in the tax-abatement process before the abatements were granted and no oversight or accountability once the abatements were given" (Nissen 1993:216). To demand accountability from companies granted tax abatements, a community-labor coalition was organized. The Calumet Project for Industrial Jobs, a grass roots labor group, helped draft what became a city ordinance that established public hearings for all tax-abatement requests, required companies to write annual reports to the city about their compliance with job-creation promises, and introduced hearings or fines for companies that failed to keep their promises.

The main goal of a tax-abatement ordinance is to make public the process under which companies get subsidies. Private firms have been able to avoid public disclosure because existing laws protect their privacy. Yet when individuals apply for financial help or a loan, their privacy is suspended: They must reveal all their private financial and other relevant information to the source of funding. Why should corporations, which use public funds and are legally defined as if they were individuals, not follow the same procedures? Why should a privileged status allow them to hide their operations?

In Chicago, a local government, labor, and community coalition forced Playskool, Inc., a subsidiary of the Milton Bradley Company, to honor its loan obligations. In 1980, Milton Bradley received a million dollars in industrial revenue bonds (IRBs)—low-interest, tax-exempt loans designed to help firms make capital outlays for plants and equipment. In return, the company promised to create four hundred jobs in its Chicago plant. Instead, the company decreased the number of employees and in 1984 announced that it would close its plant. The city reacted by filing suit against Playskool. In an out-of-court settlement with the city, in early 1985 Playskool agreed to return the IRBs and keep the plant open for another year, as well as "to establish relocation and training programs and funds for the displaced workers" (Fasenfest 1993:127, 129).

These policies demonstrate that communities can do something about their economic problems. Progressive or populist regimes change the rules of the game. They "add new players, create new roles, and demand new results from the economic development process. Economic life can no longer be shaped solely by corporate actors" (Portz 1990:11). Such players, roles, and results differ markedly from Schenectady's, where relying on the business sector thus far has failed to create a new economic role or fiscal stability for the city.

Neighborhood Mobilization around Crime

Widespread loss of employment has devastated Schenectady and other industrial cities. Large lay-offs affect not only the people employed in a single sector but, in a ripple effect, other sectors of the local economy. The quality of local services (garbage collection, police protection, education, and neighborhood physical maintenance) suffers as the city loses revenues. In Schenectady some schools were closed; social programs were reduced or terminated. Today, the same amenities that made the city an important industrial center—

its geographical location; traffic connections with major centers like New York, Buffalo, and Montreal; and abundant cheap labor—are making the illegal-drug trade a growth sector in Schenectady's economy.

Residents of Schenectady are disturbed by the signs of physical and social deterioration of their city and neighborhoods, especially visible in poor sections like Hamilton Hill, whose residents do not have the personal resources to compensate for the loss of city services (see Map 4). The signs of poverty show up in the physical and social disorder of neighborhoods, "evident in the widespread appearance of junk and trash in vacant lots; it is evident, too, in decaying homes, boarded-up buildings, the vandalism of public and private property, graffiti, and stripped and abandoned cars in streets and alleys. It is signaled by bands of teenagers congregating on street corners, by the presence of prostitutes and panhandlers, by public drinking, the verbal harassment of women, and open gambling and drug use." Such conditions signal a breakdown of the local social order; if not addressed, they can lead to further destabilization and decline of a neighborhood. They drive people out and discourage others from moving in. In such a neighborhood, house prices and investment in the neighborhood drop as crime rates and the residents' fear of crime increase (Skogan 1990:2).

What can be done to reverse the trend of neighborhood decline? The best policies address its causes—mainly unemployment, poverty, and inadequate social services. But instead of dealing with causes, declining cities like Schenectady are encouraged by the federal government to look for private-sector solutions to city problems or are expected to do more with less money. In the hope of reversing neighborhood decline, residents and city officials also concentrate on eliminating signs of social and physical disorder from the neighborhood. They organize neighborhood clean-ups, collect money to fix sidewalks, or launch campaigns to boost the positive image of their neighborhood. However, the increase in crime (whether real or perceived) alarms people most.

Residents want more police presence and protection. While saturating a community with police can result in a significant decrease in crime, this is a very expensive—thus, rarely used—policy. The criminal-justice system (including the police) can in most instances only react to crime, not prevent it, goes one theory; police should teach the public that crime prevention is primarily its responsibility and should help neighborhoods help themselves (Lavrakas 1985:87).

In some cities and neighborhoods, this is already happening as partnerships develop between the police and residents. Residents organize neighbor-

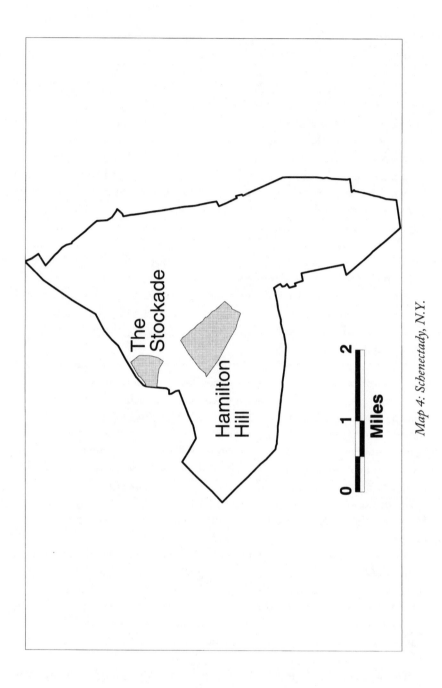

Map 4: Schenectady, N.Y.

hood or block watches or hire private security companies and private guards to patrol their neighborhoods. But the neighborhoods that use private services also want a tax break for their efforts. Under current law, business-improvement districts are already getting tax breaks, so residents are exploring the possibilities of creating community-improvement districts. The drawback is that such districts drain more resources from already poor cities.

Community organizations, some suggest, might be our best hope for reshaping the destiny of threatened urban neighborhoods (Skogan 1990). This is what happened in Schenectady.

Neighborhood Watch

One of the most popular neighborhood programs in recent years has been the Neighborhood Watch, in which local residents take a direct role in preventing crime. People are motivated to participate in such activities because they gain control over what is happening in their neighborhoods (Curtis 1985: 215), as residents of the Stockade in Schenectady confirm from their own experience. Residents that participated in Neighborhood Watch felt empowered, and some even felt more safe. This "civilianization" of police work (Skolnick and Bayley 1986:217) in some cities goes even further: Community residents have responsibility for some tasks traditionally handled by patrol officers.

Residents' involvement in neighborhood safety was a common early practice in U.S. cities. Only when police protection became a formal city service did that involvement decline. Schenectady formed its first Committee on Safety in the late eighteenth century, with a watch house and foot patrols of two men "to go round through all the streets in the Towne every hour." The watch house for the required sentry was the old Dutch church in the Stockade neighborhood. Committee records show that one of the most important concerns of residents at that time regarded "slaves on the loose." A resolution stated "that the Town Watch be very diligent in apprehending all Negroes that may be found to run on the street after ten o'clock, [and] that if they take any of them up[,] to confine them in the watch house" (Hart 1975:62).

The Stockade's Neighborhood Watch in some ways resembles its predecessor. When residents in this mostly White neighborhood watch for potential criminals, Black passersby make likely suspects. Crime, according to Boston's mayor, Thomas Menino, is very much a race issue. He was quoted in the *Boston Globe* for September 19, 1994: "People talk about crime, but that's just a smoke screen. They say crime, but they mean race. It's the most important issue we face as a city."He could have been talking about Schenectady.

Recent research has found that Neighborhood Watch has been most successful in homogenous and middle-class communities and has failed in racially and economically heterogeneous neighborhoods because it cannot mobilize a broad and representative cross section of the community. Also these neighborhoods have a hard time reaching consensus about the nature of crime in the community and the tactics that might be most effective (Bursik and Grasmick 1993:117). This is exactly what happened in Hamilton Hill, where the Neighborhood Watch had to be disbanded.

Neighborhood-Based Crime-Prevention Programs

In their effort to find solutions for loiterers, illegal-drug sales, and prostitution, Hamilton Hill residents, social agencies, and community and religious organizations came together in 1985 to start Project SAFE (Sexual Exploitation of Youth). The program's objective was to help prostitutes by offering them counseling, medical care, shelter, and peer support. It succeeded in making street prostitution much less visible than ever before, although prostitution did not disappear from the Hill. One of the project's organizers told me in 1989 that "the word has really spread. The pimps know Schenectady has cracked down, and the girls know they have a place to go."

Another organization, Clean Sweep United, also addressed the issue of crime. Organized by a group of women who used grass-roots tactics and protest to make Hamilton Hill safer, the organization had about one hundred members, most of them White women living on the Hill and frustrated by the lenient criminal-justice system in Schenectady. In 1988, when the organization was formed, there had been twelve violent shootings on the Hill. Drugs were dealt openly in the neighborhood, but not many arrests followed; the police complained that the plea-bargaining system made their arrests fruitless. Members of Clean Sweep United felt that the city was trying to conceal or minimize the drug problem (Rabrenovic 1995).

As a consequence of Clean Sweep's activity, about a hundred more arrests were made. Schenectady police arrested so many people that the jails overflowed, and they had to rent trailers. The organization's members were especially pleased that the two biggest drug dealers were sentenced to fifteen years to life in jail. However, after the organization reached its main goal (more strict sentencing, and no plea bargaining), it kept a low profile. Because not all drug-related problems were solved, and selling drugs on the Hill continued, some members decided to continue their efforts by joining the Hamilton Hill Neighborhood Association. There, they believed, they could continue to work on important neighborhood problems, especially ones caused by drugs.

Community Policing

Hamilton Hill's neighborhood association addressed the crime issue by joining the city's task force on the relationship between the police and community residents. For residents of the Hill, whom the police see as potential criminals rather than as victims, police harassment is a major issue. Because most police do not live in the neighborhoods they patrol, they rarely develop personal attachment for the community (Curtis 1985:215). The situation is especially difficult for poor neighborhoods. Hamilton Hill's reputation has stigmatized all its residents. As one Black resident told me, "If you are Black you are suspected of being a drug dealer, and if you are White you must be here to buy drugs. Everybody is under suspicion. . . . The cops don't patronize our restaurants. They don't come to sit with us, to know us better. They come when you don't need them, and when you need them they're nowhere in sight."

To build a more constructive relationship between the police and residents, the city started community policing. This is one of Schenectady's newest policies designed to help poor neighborhoods and includes using a foot patrol, team policing, or putting a local office in the neighborhood. Community policing shifts the police role from a reactive to a preventive policy (Skogan 1990:91), and it improves communication between residents and the police. It makes it easier for residents to pass information to the police, and also to demand action from them (Bursik and Grasmick 1993).

In 1994, Schenectady invested about $100,000 to increase police patrols and started the major drug sweep "Operation Crackdown," which led to ninety-nine arrests, ninety convictions, and sentences of from three to nine years. Police representatives were happy to announce that the number of violent crimes in the city had decreased and were hopeful that the arrests and stiff sentencing would slow the migration of drug dealers from New York City (Kava 1994:A6). The success of this police action is similar to Clean Sweep United's mobilization in 1988. However, cracking down on crime can help reverse the trend of neighborhood decline only if it is complemented by policies that address its roots in unemployment, poverty, and too few social services. Even the police admit the limitations of crime sweeps. "The more and more we crack down, the more and more educated they [criminals] become" (Kava 1994:A6).

Schenectady's Future

Schenectady's history illustrates that nineteenth-century industrialization shares some features with twentieth-century restructuring: In both eras, cities competed among themselves to attract companies looking for cheap labor and subsidies. In the past, Schenectady benefited from such trends, only to lose in recent years. There is a risk in being a one-industry town. Because cities have little power over the global economic forces that lead to increased capital mobility, they are at the mercy of their major employers.

The restructuring of Schenectady deprived the city not only of revenues and population, but of its purpose as well. It became a city without a mission, its future uncertain. To turn the city around, residents and city officials, advised to become more entrepreneurial and to find a new economic niche, tried to foster a "good business climate" and encourage service-sector employment. So far these efforts have not paid off. In the meantime, local services suffer and the city becomes an even less desirable place to live.

As an alternative to corporate strategies, local labor-community coalitions can sometimes win and can even play an important role in creating public policy on labor and economic issues in their communities (Fasenfest 1993; Nissen 1993). Knowing there is something that people can do is in itself empowering. It gives people hope for the future and encourages them to participate in local struggles. Ultimately, it can also contrast the company's interest in maximizing shareholder values with community and labor interest in creating what Franklin Roosevelt called the Economic Bill of Rights, a policy that would "guarantee a job to everyone who wanted one at a fair wage, adequate housing and education, accessible medical care, and equal opportunities for all citizens" (Perrucci et al. 1988:155).

Neighborhood mobilization in Hamilton Hill, Schenectady's poorest neighborhood, has demonstrated that this city has resources and strengths. Although residents face enormous difficulties, they are not giving up. It is in their power, not that of General Electric or some other big firm, to come up with the model for the future development of this city.

7

The Stockade: Defending the Gentrified Neighborhood in a Declining Industrial City

The Stockade (also known simply as "Stockade,") is a neighborhood cherished for its historic past that continues to be a desirable place to live despite the changes in Schenectady's economy. Its strength lies in its population: a stable core of residents with the resources and dedication to preserve this oasis in the city. Like the residents of other poor cities, residents of the Stockade face problems: how to maintain the residential amenities of their neighborhood, and how to protect themselves from the overall decline of the city—especially from the attendant increase in crime.

The Stockade Neighborhood

The Stockade, a Historic District neighborhood, is bounded by the Mohawk River on the north, Liberty Street on the south, North College Street on the east, and Binne Kill on the west (see Map 5). The neighborhood, according to the 1980 census, had 1,519 residents and 1,168 housing units, with an occupancy rate of 84 percent. Most of the buildings in the neighborhood were built before 1950, are attached, and have only one unit per structure (see Table 9). For an inner-city neighborhood, the Stockade has a relatively low percentage of rental units (27 percent).

The residents of Stockade are almost all White (2 percent are Black). Half of them have lived in the same houses since 1975 (see Table 10). More than

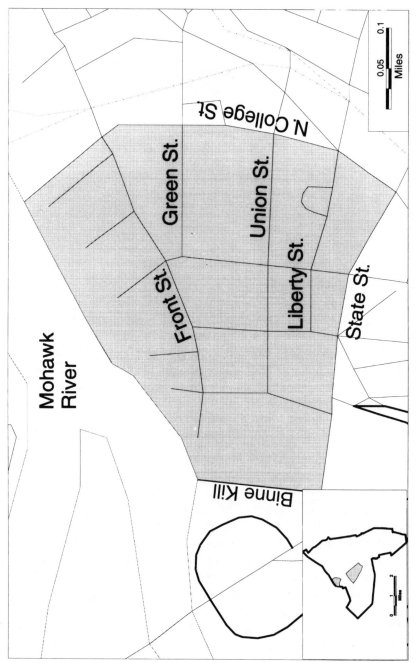

Map 5: The Stockade Neighborhood

Table 9: Land-Use Characteristics of the Stockade Neighborhood

Housing	%
Occupancy	83.9
Rental units	27
Multiunits	4
Built before 1950	98

Source: *U.S. Bureau of the Census,* Census of Population and Housing, *1981.*

Table 10: Socioeconomic Characteristics of the Stockade Neighborhood

Residents	%
Black	2
Single	61
College degree	52.6
Work for government	25.3
High family income	19.2
Unemployed	5.6
Public assistance	19.5
Same house 5+ years	50.2

Source: *U.S. Bureau of the Census,* Census of Population and Housing, *1981.*

60 percent live in single-family households, yet only 8 percent have children. More than half have college degrees, and 42 percent work in managerial, professional, or technical jobs. The income of the residents, however, is not the highest in the city. In 1980, 20 percent had family incomes higher than $25,000 (high income at the time), and 30 percent had incomes lower than $7,500 (low income at the time); nearly 20 percent were on public assistance.

Visitors are often brought to Stockade to be shown that Schenectady, known as a "company town," has a rich past and much to offer new businesses and their executives. In the late 1980s, Stockade became more affluent, and rents have gone up. In the real-estate section of the March 18, 1989, *Schenectady Gazette,* a one-bedroom apartment went for $450, at the time considered high for Schenectady. Even some residents from surrounding suburbs moved in, charmed by the neighborhood amenities. Now it looks more like other gentrified neighborhoods. For a city that hopes to see its decline reversed, Stockade has great symbolic value.

The old Stockade was destroyed in the Massacre of 1690 and then partly damaged in fires that ravaged the western part of the community in 1819 and 1861. But some of its historic buildings have survived (Bogert 1966) and are now considered the trademark of the neighborhood. Portions of two pre-Massacre houses, for example, form parts of more recent structures. At least seventeen houses date from the first quarter of the 1700s. In some, the age is readily apparent, while in others subtle structural evidence is obscured by successive renovations. Several churches are further reminders of Stockade's colonial past. The First Reformed Dutch Church was organized in 1680. The present building is the fifth one, erected in 1869. Saint George's Episcopal Church was built just outside the fort gate in 1759 to serve the British garrison. The First Presbyterian Church was organized in 1769, but the present building is the second one, built in 1809. Many of Schenectady's oldest families, descendants of merchants, lawyers, and doctors, still live in the Stockade. Alicia Shanklin, one of the oldest residents, in 1989 shared with me some memories of the time when Schenectady was still an important industrial city: "I was born in this neighborhood in the house built by my grandfather. My father was a doctor and worked all his life here in Stockade. We liked this neighborhood. The life was rich then. A lot of stores and all sorts of things were around. Everybody knew everybody. We were like a village."

In the first quarter of this century, some parts of the neighborhood started to decline. A "gray area" of rundown homes was developing to the east on Ferry, Green, and Front Streets. In the early forties, Front Street was "gray" enough to be seriously considered for a low-rent housing project (Bogert 1966). Land speculation by a few wealthy residents saved the neighborhood. They realized the potential of the area and decided to buy property there. When the stock-market collapse in 1929 made bank financing impossible, they obtained private money, bought several deteriorated buildings, and converted them into apartments. The renovation of these buildings stabilized the neighborhood and helped reverse its decline (Bogert 1966).

During World War II, when new families came to Schenectady to work for General Electric, some larger houses in Stockade were turned into apartment buildings to alleviate the housing shortage. At the time, the neighborhood was economically mixed and had a transient population. The further development of high-tech industry in Schenectady, such as the Knolls Atomic Power Laboratory and General Electric's new Research and Development

Center, increased the demand for good apartments in stable neighborhoods. Many young engineers from General Electric, in the city for training, lived in Stockade apartment buildings. However, many apartments were substandard, and tenants often moved out as soon as they could afford to.

In the 1950s some residents who were permanently employed in the city yet still in need of housing learned about a government program that gave them an opportunity to pay off a mortgage and for $5,000 or less own a historic building. "Finding the money to rehabilitate these almost substandard dwellings was no longer a problem. The banks now knew that the area was becoming stable, and were more than willing to take new mortgages and to make loans for alterations, repairs and restoration. Without this financial support, no reclamation or rehabilitation would have been possible" (Bogert 1966:9). The financial support available for these neighborhood improvements was in sharp contrast with the banks' reluctance to invest in low-income neighborhoods. This is how neighborhoods like Stockade (and Center Square in Albany), whose new residents and home owners were mostly White professionals, were able to prosper.

The new residents were excited by the quality and value of the houses they bought. To preserve their investment in the neighborhood, they formed a neighborhood association and became its most vocal members, sharing a belief that their neighborhood was a unique treasure that must be carefully protected. As one of the founding members of the association told me in 1989: "There is a special flavor in this neighborhood—a neighborhood of diverse residents who take pride in their community, responsibility for their neighborhood, and pleasure in its ambiance." But the "diversity" in this neighborhood differs radically from that in Albany's neighborhoods. In that respect industrial cities are different from cities where public employment has risen; the state government's presence in Albany contributed to the increase of the Black middle class. There is very little ethnic and racial diversity in Stockade. Like many other urban neighborhoods, its diversity is based on occupation and income, residents' age, and family life-styles (see Table 10).

Creating a Historical Neighborhood

The Stockade Neighborhood Association was founded in 1957 with the intention of tightening the neighborhood's housing code, and it dedicated itself to preservation, protection, and beautification. The association was composed mostly of property owners who envisioned creating a historic neighborhood and were frustrated by the lack of understanding for neighborhood historic value among their fellow residents and in the city administration. They realized that only together could they achieve their goal. A member of the association who was also a member at that time explained to me in 1989 that: "it was very difficult for individuals to fight the misuse of the buildings and the destruction which was going on. After an incident when a woman was nearly knocked down by an angry neighbor's car because she complained about the inappropriate 'improvement' of his house, we decided to organize the group. Well, you can knock down one person but not the whole association. Besides, as an organization we can put collective efforts behind our demands. It looks less personal. In that way, we can protect ourselves and still achieve success."

But the biggest issue the organization faced was the demolition of older buildings. You cannot have a historical neighborhood without historic houses. One of the association's first fights was with St. George's Episcopal Church, which wanted to demolish a historic house to put a parking lot in its place. The neighborhood association failed to prevent the demolition, and the church knocked down the building. This dispute arose because the neighborhood had different uses for residents who lived in the neighborhood and cherished its historical past and church officials who had to meet the needs of parishioners. The president of the neighborhood association attacked the church in the local newspaper for its lack of sensitivity, and for its arrogance as a wealthy institution whose members came from outside Stockade and did not care about the needs of the neighborhood.

The association also learned a lesson: It needed to find a permanent solution for historic preservation. Members turned their efforts toward having the neighborhood zoned a historic area, lobbying successfully for support from the city administration for an ordinance. For a year, a committee of city-council and association members studied the problem, then drafted an ordinance enacted into law by the city council on May 14, 1962, the first historic-zoning ordinance in New York State (Bogert 1966). The ordinance was only a partial success, because it protected only buildings built before 1825, at that time considered the ones with true historic value.

Fighting Neighborhood Change

In the years since the ordinance was enacted, the association has had plenty to do. It battled the Mohawk Club over a new parking lot, the Army Corps of Engineers over a copper dam on the Mohawk River, and a local developer who wanted to build a motel.

In 1965 the Mohawk Club, a private club of local business owners, bankers, church leaders, and city and county officials, filed for permission to replace the building at 13–15 Union Street with a parking lot. Club officials argued at the Historic District Commission's public hearing that they would build a "model" parking lot in the Historic District. The neighborhood association representatives argued that the building had historic value and should be preserved, but since it had been built after 1825, it was not protected by the historic-zoning ordinance.

The neighborhood association succeeded in postponing demolition for a year, but eventually the Mohawk Club was granted a permit to build its parking lot. Some members of the association believed that the club won because its members were a "cohesive group of influential leaders of Schenectady." This conflict had its origin in the same issue as the conflict with St. George's Episcopal Church: Stockade had other users besides residents of the neighborhood.

The neighborhood association did not have to wait long for new challenges. In 1968, the U.S. Army Corps of Engineers came up with a proposal to build a levee to protect the Schenectady banks of the Mohawk River from floods, an earthen structure twelve feet high and eight feet wide at the top. The cost of the construction was estimated at $2,444,000, of which Schenectady would pay $30,000 and New York State $90,000; annual maintenance costs were estimated at $112,000, of which Schenectady would pay $17,500. The proposal was supported by the Schenectady Chamber of Commerce, which wanted to use the project to develop a marina on the Binne Kill and its islands as recreational sites by the Schenectady Yacht Club and by the New York State Society of Professional Engineers.

But the levee was opposed by the Stockade Neighborhood Association, which appointed a special committee to discuss the proposal. As reported in the December 1968 issue of the association's newsletter, the committee agreed that flood control was needed in the area but concluded that the proposed levee would be detrimental to the Stockade area and would not stop flooding, because it failed to alleviate floods in other areas of the basin. The organization urged the Schenectady City Council to request further study of the problem, aimed at a more universal and more acceptable solution (*Stockade Spy* 8:2).

At a public hearing on November 4, 1968, the association's viewpoint won support, and the Army Corps of Engineers was urged by the city to reopen the program for further study. A lack of funds prevented a new study's being either proposed or made, and the association won by default. But the neighborhood still needs a levee. In the conflict between neighborhood needs and aesthetics, the neighborhood won a battle but lost the war. Floods are still common in the neighborhood and cost residents money and inconvenience.

In the process of consolidating the neighborhood as a historic residential district, the neighborhood association sometimes had to fight even its own members. In 1969, the Historic District Commission received an application for the construction of a motel behind the property on 50 Washington Avenue from the Handalaer Corporation, owned by two local residents. One of them was chair of the Historic Commission and a previous president of the Stockade Neighborhood Association.

Alarmed, the neighborhood association's members opposed the project and warned the commission, according to the October 1969 *Stockade Spy,* that it would "destroy one of the few historic residential areas in the country. The addition of a motel would not only be an eyesore, but it would reduce current home values, bring more traffic into an already crowded road area, and possibly spur the entry of other motels and hotels which could completely destroy the historic image of the area." The overflow crowd of neighborhood members at the association meeting not only voted unanimously against construction but also decided to initiate a process to change the city ordinance to prevent the threat of possible future construction of motels and hotels in the area.

The Historic District Commission decided to refuse the building permit for the motel proposal but turned down the association's proposal for the change in the ordinance, advising the association to turn to the city council. The neighborhood association took this issue seriously, circulating two sets of petitions through the neighborhood: one by home owners, and another by residents. Combined, they held nearly five hundred signatures. On August 1, 1969, the association submitted its request for changing the historic-zoning ordinance to the City Clerk's Office. The request was sent first to the City Planning Commission for study. In September 1969, the commission recommended that the city council adopt the change. In October 1969, the council completed a new city ordinance incorporating the changes requested by the neighborhood association. By that time the city had realized that Stockade was a city treasure, and that by protecting it, the city could only benefit.

The Beautification of the Stockade

Although Stockade was recognized as a historic neighborhood, it still needed work to become more attractive. From its beginnings, the neighborhood association had stressed the importance of physical improvements. In the early sixties, property owners purchased and planted more than a thousand dollars' worth of trees to replace those lost to Dutch-elm blight and widening of streets. The Stockade Neighborhood Association used funds raised through membership dues to help them and also subsidized the cost of cutting into the concrete sidewalk so the trees could be planted (Bogert 1966). In the summer of 1961, during the celebration of Schenectady's Tercentenary, the association asked owners of historic houses to purchase and fly replicas of the flags that had flown over Schenectady at the time of the construction of their homes to demonstrate to the city and neighborhood residents how old and important Stockade is. In other efforts to improve the neighborhood's appearance, the association campaigned for the elimination of overhead power and telephone lines and the clean-up of the Mohawk River frontage.

The organization continued to have problems with nonresidential uses of the neighborhood. When the Boy Scouts of America bought one of the old Stockade buildings for its programs, the association worried about the impact of the noise and traffic on surrounding residences. When association members asked the Boy Scouts to put either offices or less-disturbing activities in the building, the scouts refused: They owned the building, and they believed they had the right to do whatever they pleased with private property. The neighborhood association organized a protest campaign, mailing letters to members, friends, acquaintances, and neighbors asking them to boycott the Boy Scouts' membership and pledge drives. This tactic succeeded; soon the Boy Scouts agreed to the association's suggestions.

In the 1950s and 1960s, the association also had difficulty with city officials, especially those from the Building and Code Enforcement Departments, who would neither respond to protests nor object when contractors began construction in the neighborhood without a building permit. Association members often called and complained, with little success. Over time they learned to identify early signs of the new projects and make official complaints in advance. "We would call the Building Department and tell them about the particular project, only to hear that it was too late to stop them," one association member told me in our interview in 1989. "It was also hard to find the person who was responsible to take any action against the violator. Well, we learned from our failures. We all watched carefully for any suspicious activity in the neighborhood and reported it immediately. The officials could no longer claim that they did not know about a project, and they had to do something about it." These efforts led to consolidation of neighborhood-association power and transformed the group into an influential organization.

Organizational Characteristics of the Stockade Neighborhood Association

Throughout a succession of leaders and members who have all shared an appreciation for the neighborhood, the Stockade Neighborhood Association's best resource has been its long organizational history. Until 1963, only property owners could serve as officers. Soon, however, the organization realized that this rule was unfair and changed it. Organization members—property owners and renters alike—are united around a common belief that they live in a unique place. This sense of community summarized by a past association president, quoted in the association newsletter, the *Stockade Spy*, for October 1969: "Stockade is alive. It is a neighborhood. It is a living museum. It is a catalog of architectural styles. It is a political ward in a city. It is a small town. It is a sophisticated urban space. It is my home and it is lovely." Residents draw on this kind of sentiment to encourage each other to stay in the neighborhood and to continue to defend its vitality, despite the decline and deterioration of their city.

The association was incorporated in 1973. As a legal entity, it can maintain and retain gifts of property. It has active committees, publishes the *Stockade Spy* monthly, and addresses a broad range of issues. Like the Center Square Neighborhood Association in Albany, it has drawn a clear boundary around its neighborhood. The organizational goal is narrow: to protect and improve property within those designated boundaries. This narrow focus is one factor that typically facilitates neighborhood participation: In small, natural neighborhoods, "regular, face-to-face discussion of the issues is possible by all who would take the time to be involved" (Berry, Portney, and Thomson 1993:49).

The association has developed several resourceful organizational tools, among them the *Stockade Spy*, started in 1961 to keep members informed of activities, to be a neighborhood information center, and to keep residents up-to-date on personal happenings. It reinforces the image of the neighborhood as a village where residents want to know the doings of their neighbors.

Another very effective tool is the organization's ten-member board of directors, whose participants over time have all used their personal resources and networks to help the association's causes. In 1990 I interviewed eight members of the board (the other two were business leaders who declined to be interviewed), who turned out to resemble the members of the board of Center Square Neighborhood Association. Five had college degrees, and three had master's degrees or Ph.D.s. Five were married; six had children. Six were home owners. All were White professionals, including three in educational institutions and three running small businesses. They had relatively high incomes: five higher than $40,000, two between $35,000 and $39,000, and one between $20,000 and $25,000. All eight had lived longer than five years in the neighborhood: four members between five and ten years, and the rest longer. Four board members had joined the organization less than five years ago, and four had been members of the board for less than five years.

As we might expect, all eight board members joined the neighborhood association because they liked the neighborhood and wanted to protect it. One of the newest told me she joined even though she preferred the suburbs. "When I got married, my husband and I were offered this family house, if we would renovate it. I was raised in the suburbs, and I don't really appreciate city life. I do not like noise, lack of parking, too much traffic, lousy services . . . but this neighborhood is so special that it will always have some people who want to live here and insure that it remains intact. . . . I joined the neighborhood association because I was interested in neighborhood preservation, and I didn't want to be the last person to know what was going on in the neighborhood." The majority have been inspired by the current association president's determination and energy, and some of them were recruited by her, among them an English teacher at Union College, who described her as "an active go-getter. She gathers people around herself. . . . She heard that I was interested in writing and she called me and asked me if I wanted to be editor of the *Stockade Spy*. That's how I got involved. . . . I just like the idea of community. As a single person, I really need it. You can't live only on your work interest. People also need community."

The president of the neighborhood association since 1988, a developer who owns a number of houses in Stockade and in Albany (Center Square), moved to Stockade in 1978 and became active in the community when she started working on a renovation project. As she put it, "I got involved because I like knowing everybody and getting things done. Also, I have a flexible schedule which allows me to work on association matters. I'm good at that. . . . Our organization is run by the board. The board is an informal group. Everybody chips in. Half of the members I recruited were not even members of the association before. I was looking for people with information and connections that could help the association in its work." The president's success illustrates that real-estate developers and residents can have a common interest. As a business leader she has brought her talents to the organization, including an understanding of the need for network ties and information and how a neighborhood association can benefit from the resources of its members and residents. This is why she and others on the board have encouraged the recruitment of people with money and influence to move to the neighborhood. But as one resident, a renter, pointed out to me, that can be a problem too. "I don't like that this neighborhood is becoming more elitist. For some residents, the world begins and ends in Stockade. A lot of energy is used for such small local interests. . . . The neighborhood is still heterogeneous [home owners and renters], but it's becoming more difficult for tenants to stay here. I would like to invest more in my apartment, but I don't know what will happen with this building in the future."

To maintain its visibility in the neighborhood and to provide a place for residents to meet each other, the association has sponsored an annual Memorial Day picnic in Rotunda Park on the banks of the Mohawk River and an annual Christmas-tree lighting and Christmas party. The president believes that these events help recruit members. She has also used her power as a land owner to encourage tenants to join the neighborhood association. "I still wish we'd get more people involved," she told me. "We have some older sections of this neighborhood where residents don't participate in our activities. . . . Now more tenants come to the meetings. I'm asking all my tenants to get involved, because all the residents of the Stockade are, by definition, members of the association. Some pay dues; some do not." The association expects members to pay dues but is not strict about collecting them. Instead, it sponsors fund-raisers like the annual Villagers' Outdoor Art Show, where local artists exhibit their work and residents from the suburbs come to stroll, buy, and have a pleasant outing in the city. But the main fund-raiser held yearly on the last Saturday in September, is the Stockade Walkabout, a house tour that allows residents to show off their renovated houses and make money for the organization.

The association has benefited from its cooperation with other organizations as well, mostly those devoted to historical preservation. The Stockade Heritage Foundation, for instance, was established in November 1979 as a neighborhood-preservation corporation to preserve, rehabilitate, and improve the physical aspects of real properties in Schenectady County listed in the National Register of Historic Places. Since most of the county's historic buildings are in the Stockade, the neighborhood association is the foundation's natural ally. The association also counts on the help of two other organizations: the Schenectady County Historical Society and Friends of the Stockade. The historical society, founded in the last century, has flourished with the formation of the neighborhood association, with which it has extensive connections. In the 1960s, the society instituted a program of placing data markers on buildings whose construction could be authenticated as before 1825 (Bogert 1966). Today older members of the neighborhood association are its active participants, and the association holds its regular meetings in the historical society's building, keeps its records there, and shares with the society the money from annual tours. The Friends of Stockade, which consists of former residents, was formed in 1963 for those residents to keep in touch with events in Stockade. Over the years, the organization has been willing to finance various neighborhood projects.

In some of their more recent battles, residents and the neighborhood rely on all these resources to compensate for Schenectady's shrinking support.

Defending the Historical Neighborhood

The decline of Schenectady affected the residential composition of Stockade. Some residents left for the suburbs, or for jobs in other communities. Because most new residents are upper-middle-class single professionals and couples without children, the number of children has decreased, and some schools have closed. Some of the smaller buildings that had been converted into apartments have been turned back into single-family units. But, Stockade is not becoming an exclusively single-family residential neighborhood. Well-established apartment buildings and the sluggish housing market in the city have made this neighborhood more tolerant of multifamily dwellings.

The neighborhood association has had a good relationship with local developers, who have been sensitive to the historic nature of the neighborhood and have tried to design apartment buildings in that spirit. In turn, they and land owners have used the neighborhood association as an ally in attracting upwardly mobile renters.

The gentrification of the neighborhood is also visible in new shops and businesses oriented toward the needs of the new upscale residents. But the neighborhood has only one large grocery store, Arthur's Market, a family-run concern in business since 1945. In 1989 the current owner explained the store's success to me: "When my father started this business, there were fifteen grocery stores [in Stockade]. Now they're all gone. We survived because we changed. We put up some money to make us look more attractive. We offer personal service, cooked meals, we cash checks, sell stamps, or even rent videotapes. Now we issue charge accounts for our customers. Business is very good."

Elderly people like to live in Stockade because of its easy access to downtown Schenectady, Proctor's Theater, city parks, the library, and the grocery. Even though they complain that many of the neighborhood's businesses have moved to malls or have been forced to close their doors, they are happy with Arthur's Market, whose owner often meets their special needs. Some of these older residents are active in the Schenectady County Historical Society and help with the annual or special tours that the society organizes.

However, Stockade has not been able to escape Schenectady's current economic and political troubles. Residents have complained about bad services and the city's slowness in dealing with problems. The neighborhood association carefully observes whether the historic-zoning ordinance is enforced and occasionally has problems with some property owners. One of the new residents and board members explained to me in 1990 why he is troubled: "Some people cannot fix their houses because they simply do not have the money. But others just don't care. My neighbor, for example, is letting his house deteriorate. He does not want to sell it (we offered to buy it) nor fix it. He doesn't live here, but he says that the house has emotional value for him (he promised his mother that he would never sell it). And now we are stuck. We have even thought of moving." Residents, sensitive to visible signs of deterioration, are concerned about broken sidewalks. In the city of Schenectady, property owners are responsible for maintaining the sidewalks in front of their homes. The president of the neighborhood association told me why the group responded to this problem: "Lots of sidewalks have to be replaced because they represent a safety hazard. Especially during the summer and fall when large numbers of people come to Stockade, the sidewalks are a liability for their owners. To encourage residents to fix them up, we started giving grants up to $300 for whoever upgrades his sidewalk."

Two recent issues show how hard it is to protect a neighborhood when a city is falling apart. The first was a conflict between residents who wished to maintain the use of the Riverside School building as a school and a large real-estate firm that wanted to transform it into luxury condominiums. The other was the increase in crime in the neighborhood.

Fight for the School

Riverside School's troubles started in 1973, when due to the decline in Schenectady's population, the board of education decided to close some schools and merge others. At that time, Stockade escaped the cuts and the school stayed in the neighborhood. In 1978, when another school consolidation occurred, Stockade succeeded again in keeping the school but only by accepting consolidation with the open school from Hamilton Hill. In 1980, in the third wave of school closings, the Stockade finally lost the school. Residents acknowledged the realities of Schenectady's fiscal problems: The school district did not have enough money. However, they were concerned about the future use of the school building. When Brown School, a private school, showed an interest in buying it, the neighborhood association lobbied the school board to accept the offer.

A real-estate agency, Blake Realty, also wanted to buy the building to convert it into thirty to thirty-five condominiums to be sold at $75,000 to $100,000 each. The conflict developed between residents who wished to preserve the use value of the building as a provider of services for neighborhood residents, and the developer, who wanted to raise the exchange value of the building by turning it into condominiums.

However, not everyone in the neighborhood would benefit from keeping the building as a private school, only residents who could afford to pay tuition. The school would attract more traffic and give rise to more noise, especially during drop-off and pick-up times. Like the neighborhood garage in Center Square, it would provide services for some people and annoy others, but the neighborhood association favored Brown School as a use for the site, probably because it was a prestigious educational institution and the neighborhood is affluent enough that many of its residents could afford to send their children there.

The association decided to plan its strategy for influencing the decision behind closed doors. Before bids for the new use of the building were submitted, some members of the board of education assured the neighborhood association and the Brown School that, since the school would win the bid, the school's bid did not have to be the higher. In the end, the Board did indeed have to accept the higher bid, $126,600 from Blake Realty.

The loss of the building was a blow to neighborhood residents. A member of the neighborhood association's board, the father of a student in the Riverside School, described his disappointment to me in 1990:

> I was involved in the school issue from the beginning. My son was there as a kindergartner. The school had 120 children from kindergarten to sixth grade. The school was important for the neighborhood, not just as a school, but for social events too. We all went there each election day to vote. . . . But we also understood that the city needed a better tax base. . . . Therefore when we heard about the Brown School's intentions, we were thrilled. But the school board tricked us. . . . Now my son is going to a private [parochial] school. Other Schenectady public schools are not good. And we don't want him to be bused around.

Residents who had expected city and school-board officials to be their allies also felt cheated. Together with the Brown School, they tried vainly to change the board of education's decision, but by 1985 the condominiums were a reality. The only satisfaction for the residents has been that Blake Realty has not done well selling or renting them. But bitterness against the city remains, for some neighborhood association members. One of them concluded from this defeat that "in this city you have to find out who the members of the game are. Politics are very important. The city administration does not know what is good for the city. They have this unique neighborhood here, and instead of preserving it and paying more attention to it, they play games. We constantly have to alert these elected officials to pay attention to our needs. . . . Luckily we have a strong leader. Susan [the president] knows how to get things done and who to call." Residents of Schenectady's Hamilton Hill would second this opinion. The deterioration in city services and the lack of clear vision for the city's future have them worried as well.

Some people who participated in the struggle for the school did not have children but believed it was for the common good of the neighborhood. One of them told me, "In each battle you learn something new. Now we know not to take people at their word. We are now much more conscious. This neighborhood still has people working together for the common good. What we need to do, though, is to get more people involved. To be more concerned about the unique historical significance of this place." The historical significance of the neighborhood could not protect it from crime, a major issue that gentrified neighborhoods like Stockade share with low-income neighborhoods like Hamilton Hill. What has kept them from joining forces is the parochialism of the residents in gentrified neighborhoods, who have been primarily concerned with their own neighborhood problems and have felt that they could respond better if they acted alone.

Neighborhood Watch

The drug trade and prostitution in Stockade have increased as a result partly of the general deterioration of Schenectady and partly of the spillover from Hamilton Hill. The neighborhood was shocked to learn that some drug dealers actually lived in Stockade. Some residents' feeling of security ended with a police bust of some of their "decent" neighbors, even though the police action had been initiated and facilitated by the Stockade Neighborhood Association.

The organization has always been aware of safety problems. In November 1971, for example, the *Stockade Spy* carried a message frofm the president urging members to watch out for crime because "if the Stockade Association is going to take positive action, such as requesting additional police protection, it must be documented that, indeed, things are happening which justify extra help. It is important that all violations be reported." This concern is not unusual. The large number of crime-prevention programs in urban neighborhoods are initiated primarily by organizations already active there (Bursik and Grasmik 1993) and are effective because they are tailored to a particular neighborhood (Greenberg 1985).

To increase security in the Stockade, the neighborhood association sponsored a Neighborhood Watch. Its objectives according to the organization's president in 1989, were "to organize residents to look out for each other's safety, and to help Schenectady's law-enforcement officers protect people and the houses of Stockade against crime. It would show Stockade residents how to cooperate with each other, and with the police, in a common cause—a safe home and neighborhood." Although this strategy has had limited success, it is widely used in relatively affluent, homogeneous urban neighborhoods (DuBow and Emmons 1981). In a combination of residents' private efforts and police cooperation, residents use their interpersonal ties and social control to detect signs of crime, acting as the "eyes and ears" of the local police (Rosenbaum 1987:106).

Typical of collective actions, not every neighborhood resident participates in neighborhood or block watches—usually about 10 to 20 percent (Greenberg 1985). More likely to participate are middle- to upper-middle-income residents, as well as those who are married and have children. Home owners and residents who have lived in the neighborhood longer also participate more.

The early Neighborhood Watch in 1982 attracted around fifty Stockade residents. Each was assigned a membership number, to be used to report suspicious or criminal behavior in Stockade. But the program had more symbolic than real value. In 1988, however, the association knew that the neighborhood had a real problem, and that the police were not providing protection. An older resident who had participated in the Neighborhood Watch at that time described to me in 1989 how they forced the police to take more action. First, the police told the residents,

> they needed evidence. Well, we decided to provide the evidence. Some older residents were home a lot. Therefore we asked them to sit and watch what went on outside on the street. The police told us what to look for. And if they saw something suspicious, like young people who had expensive cars but didn't seem to work, and had a lot of people visiting them, I would take their license number and later give it to the police. . . . When they saw our evidence, they did not have a choice; they had to do something. They sent specialists for undercover surveillance. We provided apartments which they used. . . . Now all the crack houses are gone.

Elderly residents like the ones in the Neighborhood Watch in Stockade often help in neighborhood surveillance. They have time and are at home during the day. Resident surveillance and involvement in law enforcement, a common practice in nineteenth-century America (Bursik and Grasmick 1993), is also used in other countries. China and the former Soviet Union, for example, relied on the help of elderly residents to keep an eye on the neighborhood and report suspicious events to the police, a form of local social control believed to keep crime rates low.

The problem with citizen surveillance is that it limits the individual rights of residents and discriminates against some groups, usually minorities or anyone who who differs from the standard profile of neighborhood residents. The underlying logic of these tightly controlled communities is that if you don't live in our neighborhood, you don't belong there, a principle that turns the neighborhood into a private space, an enclave separate from the city's public space.

Some other actions of the Stockade Neighborhood Association show how that exclusivity happens. To secure cooperation with Neighborhood Watch, the president of the association sent letters to all absentee landowners: "I asked them for cooperation—to check out new tenants and to be sure that they were not engaged in illegal activities. I also sent them application forms for membership and offered them a subscription to the neighborhood association newsletter. I informed them about the variety of ways that the organization could help them in renovating and maintaining their historic buildings and stressed the importance of such programs for improvement of their property value." The association continued to publicize the Neighborhood Watch and to warn people about the neighborhood's vulnerability. The fear of crime makes people suspicious of their neighbors. Some residents now see the presence of young people as a problem, as did this 1990 interviewee: "The root of this drug problem is the fact that we have always been tolerant of different behavior. We didn't ask questions. We had such a variety of people. A lot of students from Union College live here, but now we are much more careful. Before, I thought that this guy, who was later busted for drugs, was just popular and had a lot of friends. Now I know better. I watch what is going on."

However, it is not easy to limit access to the Stockade, nor are all problems drug related. The neighborhood, near the river, is popular during the summer. Once again the residents' desire to keep the neighborhood residential conflicts with the interests of others who come from outside. One of the residents I spoke with in 1990 commented, visibly upset: "During the summer, lots of people from outside the neighborhood come here to have parties down on the river. They are noisy, fights often break out, or they just create more parking problems. The police here do not react quickly enough. What good are the police if they don't respond?" Similarly, when the neighborhood association has lobbied the city or encouraged residents to invest in maintaining neighborhood amenities, it has acted under the assumption that only neighborhood residents will use them—but this is not the case. One of the board members I interviewed in 1990 explained what happens: "We have this public swimming pool in the park near our home. But our children can't go there, because it's taken over by the kids from Hamilton Hill. They first destroyed their own pool, and now they have to come here. During the summer the police come three to four times a day to intervene. I don't know why they take them here [the children come by bus]. They should fix their pool." As the board member implied, the growing disparities between the haves and have-nots in Schenectady and the scarcity of resources in the city are pitting one neighborhood's residents against another's. Instead of addressing the issue on the city level, Stockade parents, concerned only for the safety and well-being of their children, are quick to see Hamilton Hill children as troublemakers: "These kids [from Hamilton Hill] create problems for our children. Once my son was riding his bicycle with his friend. When he came home, he left the bike in the garage. Later that day, when he wanted to take the bike again, it was gone. He remembered that some big Black kids were telling him how nice his bike looked. Well, for days I went to Hamilton Hill, just to drive around and see if I could find the bike. I don't know what I would have done if I'd seen it, but I didn't."

Many well-heeled residents have been able to take care of their safety needs without worrying about crime or feeling that residents have to monitor the behavior of passersby. One of the new residents said, "This is the city; you take normal precautions. We have a burglar-alarm system, I don't walk alone after dark in some parts of the neighborhood, and my neighbors and I watch out for each other. My bikes were stolen from the shed in my backyard, and once somebody attempted to break in, but the alarm went off. But I feel safe." This reasoning lies behind the feeling of many of Stockade's residents that they need not participate in solving Schenectady's problems, an attitude reflected in the neighborhood association's decision not to join Schenectady United Neighborhoods, the local neighborhood-association network. The president says frankly that Schenectady United Neighborhoods "address specific issues which are time consuming. We already have a good relationship with all the actors in this city. It's not in our best interests to share our resources with them."

In a city on the brink of collapse, it is surprising to find residents unworried about their future, but, as a board member and long-term neighborhood resident explained to me in 1990, neighborhood characteristics influence residential experience. "Today, Stockade does not really have any big problems. Our residents, especially homeowners, are in stable economic situations, and that brings financial stability to the whole neighborhood. It is relatively safe, and the city sees us as a source of pride. . . . This is a neighborhood that the Chamber of Commerce publicizes to outside visitors as 'the place which must be seen.' . . . Therefore the city is responsive to the neighborhood's needs." How can residents justify the privileged position of their neighborhood in a city as poor as Schenectady? Some believe that they are successful because they worked hard to protect the neighborhood, and that other neighborhoods can do the same. Others argue that they contribute to the city by preserving and maintaining the neighborhood as a treasure for Schenectady. As one member of the neighborhood association put it: "Some people have a prejudice about this neighborhood. It is not true that we are elitist. We care about the rest of Schenectady. Every year we organize house tours, and we open our homes for them. We want others to enjoy and take pride in the historic aspect of this place. Stockade is not just ours; it belongs to the whole city. . . . It is our Williamsburg. And we have to preserve it." For twenty dollars, even Hamilton Hill residents can enjoy the treasures of Schenectady. But they do not feel that these treasures belong to them too. Preoccupied by failing schools, closed factories, crumbling infrastructure, crime, and poverty, they lack the time or energy to take pride in the Stockade.

The Neighborhood as a Private Community

The history of the Stockade neighborhood and its neighborhood association shows that even declining industrial cities have neighborhoods that are desirable and pleasant to live in. Not everyone in declining cities is poor and jobless. The loyalty that residents feel toward their community and their willingness to work toward neighborhood improvements are resources that makes it possible to defend them.

However, Stockade residents face a dilemma: to promote their neighborhood as a democratic, inclusionary, and diverse neighborhood, or to tightly control access, promote homogeneity among residents, and become a more elitist and exclusionary neighborhood. The neighborhood association's orientation to keeping problems out leads it toward this second option, which alienates some residents: The association does not promote collective interests, but the interests of a relatively small number of people.

In declining industrial cities, the lack of resources encourages private solutions to city problems, which leads to "privatization" of neighborhoods. Like the "private city," which has been defined as a community of private money makers (Warner 1968), what we see in Stockade is the emergence of the private neighborhood, a community of home owners who want to restrict the use of their neighborhood to residents. The question then becomes, To whom does a neighborhood belong? To residents who live and invest in it or to the whole city? As long as a neighborhood receives public services, the city can claim ownership. But what happens when a neighborhood hires private security guards and garbage collectors? Or buys a street and closes access to the neighborhood to nonresidents?

The private neighborhood develops a private government that in the name of neighborhood safety and services suspends residents' privacy and sometimes even some civil laws. Neighborhood organizations can have a great influence on the development of a neighborhood, but often their activity goes unchecked, a high price to pay for saving a neighborhood.

Not all residents of Stockade feel comfortable with their neighborhood's privileged status, nor do they want to live in a private neighborhood. What makes city life exciting, after all, is its openness and diversity. These residents, who also realize that neighborhood problems will persist as long as Schenectady lacks a vision for the future, are the ones who can be mobilized for improving the whole city, not just Stockade. Residents of declining industrial cities have a common interest: living in a place that is human and democratic.

8

Hamilton Hill: A Low-Income Neighborhood
Struggling for Survival

In neighborhoods that face the double disadvantage of being poor in a poor city, there are limits to how far lobbying and protest strategies can go in improving residential life. In such neighborhoods it is difficult for neighborhood associations to mobilize needed resources, define common interests, and overcome neighborhood fragmentation, even if they do everything right. The political, economic, and social fragmentation common in U.S. cities is particularly detrimental in poor neighborhoods, because it pits one weak group of residents against another. It also reduces the possibility of using protest—the only resource the poor have, some researchers believe—to draw attention to their harsh living conditions.

Poor residents are transient, and their poverty not only contributes to the sense of neighborhood instability in low-income neighborhoods but undermines their attachment to a neighborhood and their solidarity with their neighbors. Community groups in such neighborhoods have a harder time defining common interests and organizing residents around them. Hamilton Hill, the poorest neighborhood in Schenectady, is a good example of how economic restructuring fragments a community and inhibits collective action. Poor residents of Hamilton Hill lack adequate incomes, social services, police protection, and decent housing, conditions related to the restructuring of the U.S. economy as a whole and General Electric's drastic reduction of jobs in Schenectady in particular. The city's tax base has shrunk, and the number of jobs, real-estate values, and the quality of local services have declined, forcing many residents to move. At the same time, competition for jobs and resources has increased the conflict between ethnic groups in the residential communities that survive and has left little room for them to organize to address neighborhood problems.

All of a neighborhood's residents are affected by the physical deterioration of their neighborhood, by a rise in crime, and by a decline in local services. But they may have different views on who and what causes neighborhood problems and on how to solve them. The strategies long-term residents and home owners in Hamilton Hill supported were designed to keep the "wrong people" out and to bring the "right people" in. However, most Hamilton Hill residents *are* the "wrong people"—poor people.

The Decline of Hamilton Hill Neighborhood

In the nineteenth century, Hamilton Hill, with its easy access to Schenectady's factories, emerged as a typical ethnic working-class neighborhood. The Hill was known as the Bower Woods or Bower Hill, from the Dutch name for the higher lands lying between Albany Street, Veda Avenue, and Paige Street. forested with tall, stately pitch-pine trees that extended eastward to Albany. Today's name was derived from Hamilton Street, named after Henry Hamilton, one of the owners of the Bower lands along the summit of the hill that were deeded to the city in 1842 (Hart 1975).

Hamilton Hill developed rapidly as a residential neighborhood in an industrial city, bounded on the east by South Brandywine Avenue and on the west by Veeder Avenue, where the county jail stands now. State and Wyllie Streets defined its northern and southern boundaries respectively (see Map 6). Hamilton Hill was always fragmented along religious and ethnic lines, with each ethnic group congregating at its own church, a source of economic and social support. "The French who had lived on Stanley Street attended Sacred Heart; the Irish, clustering on Emmett, Craig and Steuben Streets, went to St. Columbus; the Albany Street Germans went to St. Joseph's; and the Italians along Schenectady and Strong Streets attended Our Lady of Mount Carmel" (Kurp 1986:A17).

The residents gained a sense of community by sharing their daily round. The main Hamilton Hill shopping district was Albany Street, a busy retail area with a variety of specialty stores, some of which remain today, even though Hamilton Hill is known as a crime-ridden neighborhood and shopping malls have put many small inner-city retailers out of business. For busi-

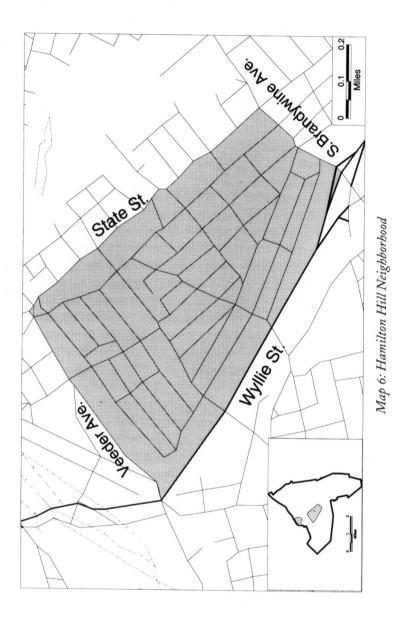

Map 6: Hamilton Hill Neighborhood

nesses like the Albany Pork Shop, founded in 1900 by a German family;
Ralph's Cleaners, established by Irish settlers in 1910; and Schenectady
Hardware, begun in 1920, the Hill offers amenities worth staying for: low rent
or low taxes and infrastructure (a smokehouse for the Albany Pork Shop, for
example). Most of the remaining stores are specialty shops that have not suffered from the neighborhood's bad image. They are a source of pride for residents and a sign of neighborhood vitality, in contrast to the drug trade and
prostitution also thriving on Albany Street, building on its new reputation as
a center of crime.

Economic Restructuring

The decline of Hamilton Hill began in the 1950s when GE started reducing
its investment in Schenectady. Closing the plants set in motion a residential
exodus from Hamilton Hill, and gradually residents displaced from more expensive cities moved in. Many of the new residents—Puerto Ricans, Do-
minicans, and later Vietnamese, Cambodians, and Afghans—differ from the
members of previous ethnic groups who moved to the Hill: They were not attracted by job opportunities, but by low rents—they could not afford to live
anywhere else. For the same reasons more African-Americans also moved to
this neighborhood.

Some evidence suggests that the concentration of poor minorities in certain neighborhoods is a consequence not of economic factors but of racial residential segregation (Massey and Denton 1988; see also Wilson 1987). In
Schenectady, a mostly White working-class city, even the small number of
minority residents faced residential segregation. Hamilton Hill gradually
became a ghetto, as minorities moved to Schenectady and settled there. In
January 1989, the director of the Better Neighborhoods, Inc., a community-
development agency, explained to me that "70 percent of the people who are
buying a house at Hamilton Hill through the help of our corporation are
Black. . . . The minority residents, voluntarily or involuntarily, are accepting
their limited position in the housing market and are more willing to live in
this neighborhood despite its shortcomings."

The median sales price for a house was $18,000 (compared with $31,500
for Schenectady), according to 1980 census date, and 70 percent of the housing is owned by absentee land owners. The houses are mostly wood construction, and 23 percent had more than three units. Nearly all buildings (99 percent) were built before 1950. Although some of the housing in Hamilton Hill
could be characterized as unsafe, the neighborhood in 1990 did not have ma-

jor abandoned areas; some houses had deteriorated or were abandoned, but never to the extent that the whole neighborhood was a slum (see Table 11).

For the most part, Hamilton Hill residents in 1980 were White (73 percent). About 40 percent of its residents have lived in the same house longer than five years, and 59 percent of those employed work in Schenectady. Only 13 percent had college degrees, and 50 percent of the adults have never completed high school, (compared to 33 percent in Schenectady as a whole). A high concentration of households living below the poverty level (30.8 percent in 1983) or on public assistance (26.3 percent), made this neighborhood even poorer. The median household income was just over half that of Schenectady as a whole ($7,996 compared to $13,108); 48 percent of the households had incomes below $7,500 in 1980, and only 6 percent had incomes above $25,000 (see Table 12).

Table 11: Land-Use Characteristics of Hamilton Hill Neighborhood

Housing	%
Occupancy	82.3
Rental units	66
Multi-units	23.2
Built before 1950	99.4

Source: U.S. Bureau of the Census, Census of Population and Housing, 1981.

Table 12: Socioeconomic Characteristics of Hamilton Hill Neighborhood

Residents	%
Black	26.1
Single	30.1
College degree	13.4
Work for government	22.7
High family income	6.2
Unemployed	15.6
Public assistance	33.4
Same house 5+ years	39.5

Source: U.S. Bureau of the Census, Census of Population and Housing, 1981.

The concentration of low-income residents combined with declining property values, drug-related crimes, prostitution, and steadily worsening local services were not due only to economic restructuring. Public policies promoting suburbanization, funding urban renewal, and reducing federal funding for social services all contributed to Hamilton Hill's crisis. When the city administration failed to use federal funding available in the 1960s to improve services or renovate houses, the neighborhood became overcrowded and unsafe.

According to Jim Murphy, a community activist from Hamilton Hill, one of the city's first actions to address neighborhood problems came in 1968, when Schenectady used urban-renewal money to "renovate" the neighborhood by demolishing "unsafe" old buildings on the Hill and by providing money for some residents to move away. However, since urban renewal did not provide any new housing, the Hill's housing shortage worsened.

Schenectady was not abone in its disappointing use of urban-renewal funds. At the time, local political and economic elites across the United States "were interested in slum clearance, but not in low-cost housing for residents displaced by clearance." When some cities, Schenectady among them, tried to respond to the housing shortage by planning more public housing, they failed to gain the support of the neighborhoods chosen as sites. It is likely that public-housing projects were unpopular because they were large in scale, and because they would concentrate racial minorities in a neighborhood, since public housing was racially segregated. Nationwide, "less than one-fourth of the housing units were replaced, and many of these were too expensive for those who were displaced" (Judd and Swanstrom 1994:138, 146).

Schenectady officials' plan to ease housing problems throughout the city in 1968 by building a public-housing project at Hamilton Hill met with strong opposition from residents of the Hill and surrounding neighborhoods, who Murphy says believed that "it did not make sense to tear down the buildings to decrease the overcrowded conditions, and then again concentrate poor people in the same area. During the debate over the appropriate location for public housing, the city council changed from a Democratic to a Republican majority. This new council was not interested in public housing, and the issue was dropped." With so little affordable housing available, people on public assistance must wait three to five years for public housing. In 1988, the Municipal Housing Authority had 304 families waiting for Section 8 certificates, and 414 families waiting for places to live.

Hamilton Hill did not fare better with other federal programs. The Neighborhood Development Program, designed to combine human services, general aid, housing efforts, and health improvements in the neighborhoods, was terminated in the late 1970s without achieving its objectives—encouraging public participation, building moderate- and low-income housing, preventing slum blight, and alleviating emergency situations. But a steady flow of resources, such as food stamps, welfare benefits, and support for social services, kept the Hamilton Hill neighborhood afloat until economic and federal-policy changes in the late 1980s combined to transform it from a working-class neighborhood to a ghetto. The new policy emphasis tried to shift onto private institutions a burden they could not take up, as the Reverend Mr. Grinsby, a priest from the Schenectady Inner-City Ministry, a religious organization with a social-service mission, recognizes: "The median cost of a house in the city of Schenectady is now [in 1988] $74,674; federal policy has neglected housing for the past eight years and left a wide gap in affordable housing. The private sector, even with the best of intentions, cannot provide housing for low-or moderate-income families without subsidy. The economics simply don't work." The picture was the same in communities nationwide. And instead of bringing relief, the corporate policies that followed in the 1980s made the urban plight worse. "Economic and political forces no longer combat the poverty—they generate poverty" (Goldsmith and Blakely 1992:1).

Corporate Strategies

The city's response to its economic decline, urban poverty, and inner-city decay was to adopt corporate strategies to revitalize the local economy. It expected that the creation of a good business climate, tax exemptions, and subsidies to private businesses would increase job opportunities for local residents and create a healthy tax base. But Schenectady was competing with other cities who offered the same benefits to businesses. These corporate strategies diverted the money from local services and, instead of helping neighborhoods like Hamilton Hill, harmed them.

In the mid-1980s the city applied twice for the State of New York Economic Development Zone Program, whose purpose was to assist distressed areas through a variety of financial incentives and economic development benefits designed to attract new businesses, or to enable existing businesses to expand and create more jobs. State incentives in this program were focused on unemployed and needy people to insure that they benefited from the new jobs. Schenectady's application was rejected both times. Joe Allen from the Hamilton Hill Neighborhood Association blames city officials who used statistics about Hamilton Hill to apply for the money but failed to demonstrate that the neighborhood would benefit from the investment. However, he did not believe that the neighborhood would have benefited from these Economic Development Zone, or enterprise-zone, projects. Much research supports his assessment, indicating that enterprise zones were never intended to generate additional business volume for the nation, but rather to redistribute businesses from one location to another (Judd and Swanstrom 1994:302), a policy so limited that it could not assist the cities but only shift economic losses about.

The activities of the Albany Street Merchants Association illustrate how little a community may benefit from business-oriented federal assistance that does not take the needs of community residents into account. When in the 1970s federal money was available to help local businesses, five Albany Street merchants formed the Albany Street Merchants Association, so that they could apply collectively for a grant to build a parking lot for out-of-neighborhood customers. The president of the association, the owner of a local store, believes that Hamilton Hill is a good neighborhood for business, that "people spend money here." His family owns the meat-specialty store and the small processing plant nearby. Tax incentives are not what keep his business here. "It would be very difficult for us to find another location or neighborhood which would allow us to have a smokehouse there," he explains. "If the city was successful in getting economic-zone money, we could even expand more. Our customers come here from all over the Capital District." He admits that only one of his fifteen employees is from the neighborhood. Even if he could expand, he would not be likely to hire new employees from the Hill.

Enterprise zones and similar "revitalize-the-ghetto schemes" have rarely been successful (Lemann 1994). People from the neighborhood need training, and services like day care, before they can take advantage of newly created jobs. In a 1989 interview, one of the residents who is active in efforts to find solutions to neighborhood problems agreed: "It is tempting to assume that any kind of development will help the poor as much as it does other citizens. Not so. Because they typically lack job skills, the poor cannot take advantage equally of all kinds of employment. What people from Hamilton Hill need is more local efforts to encourage manufacturing jobs." But others see the prospect for employment, especially the likelihood of manufacturing jobs, as bleak. Some city officials, social researchers, and local residents share the view expressed in an interview with a local magazine by the local police officer who patrols the neighborhood: "Hamilton Hill's never going to change, jobs or no jobs. Because unless these people get into some really serious educational programs, these people are only going to take care of the menial jobs. They're going to be the dishwashers and the street sweepers. I'm just telling you that they could bring in 5,000 jobs tomorrow, and it wouldn't affect Hamilton Hill one iota" (Dunn 1986:28). To help residents of poor neighborhoods, we must first address the problems of family disintegration, the rise in the number of impoverished mother-only households, and the lack of adequate education skills and a work ethic (Kasarda 1993). All these policies require resources that Schenectady has not had. Instead the city used scarce public funds to help create new business ventures, mostly small enterprises that offer limited employment and do not provide benefits like health care; such businesses often fail after a year.

Hamilton Hill is not only economically but educationally depressed, although there has been some effort to improve the public schooling of at least some of its children. In 1988, Schenectady established its first magnet school, Yates Arts and Education Magnet School. Besides basic elementary studies, it provides an extensive arts program intended to draw students from all over the city. The goal was to reduce racial isolation within a district and to give students better educational choices. In 1989 the minority participation in this school was about 30 percent.

The parents of some of Hamilton Hill's children who attend the school have been pleased. As one of them told me: "My granddaughter is going to the Yates Magnet School. They have such nice activities, and she is doing fine. The bus comes every morning to pick her up. Also three times a week she goes to the Washington Irving School for extra math tutoring. They have computers there, and she is learning to use them." But other Hill parents argued that it was not enough to offer a good education only to children lucky enough to attend a magnet school. Most children in the neighborhood went to Hamilton Hill School, with the most racially isolated student population in the city (53 percent are minorities). The problems of the educational system were not new. In Schenectady, as in other one-industry cities, most young adults had expected to work in the city's main industry, in this case General Electric. Only now, with no jobs to go to, has the inadequacy of the educational system become apparent.

Sister Georgette Dix, who has worked with Hill young people, was aware of another problem facing them: the absence of any other activities. "For young adults in Schenectady, White or Black, there is nothing. You don't go to the Boys' Club and shoot basketball anymore . . . but in this city nobody cares. We used to be such a nice neighborhood. Sometimes you think they are doing this on purpose. This is prime land here. When it gets so cheap, some developer will buy it, and rich folks will move in." Meanwhile, the drug trade and prostitution were two occupational opportunities available for Hamilton Hill youth.

Social Services

Despite all its problems the neighborhood has enjoyed an active community life that explains how people survive despite their poverty. The art center, Carver Community Center, the health center, Boys' and Girls' Clubs, and the library, begun during better times when more resources were available for community-based projects, offered after-school programs, health education and prevention, creative art activities, or just a safe environment for the children of the neighborhood. The Hamilton Hill Drop-In Art Center has been a "mecca of black culture between New York City and Montreal," according to director Margaret Cunningham. Opened in 1968 to provide activities in arts and crafts for Hamilton Hill youngsters, the center has always been short of funds but in 1990 helped about 160 adults and children to study painting, theater, Black culture and history, puppeteering, and dance. The programs were set up to develop self-esteem in its members, for, as one local resident commented to a reporter, "then they don't need drugs and don't have to hop into bed" (Kurp 1986:A16).

Hamilton Hill, like other poor neighborhoods, needs voluntary and social-service organizations to help residents deal with neighborhood problems and to provide support and a sense of community. But residents of the Hill's social organizations were ineffectual because of a lack of resources, poor coordination among social agencies, and a limited, crisis-management orientation. Besides, most public agencies, such as the health center, did not provide services that corresponded to the needs of poor people. In an interview with a local magazine, a policeman from Hamilton Hill said, "Amazing thing is, you can't get hold of anybody after 9 o'clock at night or on the weekends. What good is it? What good is a social program that has normal business hours? Well, unfortunately, people that live up on Hamilton Hill don't have normal business hours" (Dunn 1986:29). Social service agencies for residents of Hamilton Hill were better equipped to provide long-term support than to respond adequately to crises and emergencies.

Nonetheless, many poor families like those in Hamilton Hill depend on such organizations for emotional, informational, and instrumental assistance. For example, teen-age mothers who have access to low-cost child-care services, family financial assistance, and vocational training can achieve economic independence (Mayfield 1991). Similarly, welfare payments help women leave abusive relationships and poorly paid jobs (Naples 1991). In some communities, residents have organized around the delivery and quality of social services, positively affecting other collective action. In the 1960s women built powerful welfare-rights and tenants movements that challenged their limited access to economic resources and political power (Pope 1990). Although it had limited success, this strategy enabled women to gain political power to influence welfare policies, and to participate in articulating solutions to housing problems.

That residents' efforts to become more active in gaining direct control over the delivery of services, or over programs and development projects that will directly serve their neighborhoods, can be effective and important has been the subject of some study (Davidson 1979; Susser 1982; Burnett 1983; Mayer 1984). For a large number of residents at the Hill, fighting for the improvement of services became a paramount task. However, social-service agencies often wield a double-edged sword. They can be both the avenues to power and the means by which the power structure influences and controls local communities (Uriarte and Merced 1985:30). Social-service organizations tend to have limited programs; they "attempt to clean up the social damage after it has already been done rather than address its structural sources" (Mollenkopf 1983:293).

Residents of Hamilton Hill recognize the problems and limitations of their neighborhood. Some hope that one day they will be able to move out, while others have resigned themselves to the conditions of their life and think that nothing they can do will change them.

The Hamilton Hill Neighborhood Association

When in 1974 some concerned residents founded the Hamilton Hill Neighborhood Association, their intentions were to address issues not dealt with by the city. Though the organization had sixty members, only about thirty—mostly home owners—came regularly to meetings. They represented the most active members of the association, the ones "concerned all the time."

Over the years, the neighborhood association has been primarily interested in improving the physical condition of the neighborhood. One of the early members of the association told me that "the neighborhood association dealt with the problems of absentee landlords and burnt-out buildings, which endangered safety and were eyesores. The neighborhood association was successful in getting rid of these buildings. Also it was engaged in some smaller projects; it had the city pave some streets and put in some trees." The members worried that if they did not deal with abandoned, burned buildings fast, the more buildings would be burned, making whole sections of the neighborhood unlivable.

Although the Hamilton Hill Neighborhood Association sees itself as a civic, nonpartisan organization, it cannot ignore the social issues of poverty, limited resources, and class and race divisions that are consequences of the economic and political characteristics of Schenectady. In some ways, old and new issues develop from the same problem. Poverty, racial discrimination, welfare, and unemployment have been discussed on numerous occasions; these are the issues that require the cooperation of other social and political organizations on the Hill.

Organizational Characteristics of the Hamilton Hill Neighborhood Association

The Hamilton Hill Neighborhood Association is a loosely knit, informal group of local residents. Although it has a charter and is incorporated, it has neither a board of directors nor a block-captain system. One of its former presidents explained to me, "We used to have a block-captain system, but then we decided against it. Some parts of the neighborhood had active block captains. They would mobilize residents to come to the meetings when allocation of some grants was discussed. Then the well-organized parts of the neighborhood would lobby for the grants to go there. We thought that this was not a fair deal. Grants should go where they are needed." Most members own a home or small businesses in the neighborhood and are interested in improving the quality of life there. They believe in the power of the democratic process, and the organization regularly sends representatives to meetings that address development of the city and of Hamilton Hill. Some of the members, although active in the organization, do not see themselves as committed to the neighborhood. As one of them explained her involvement to me:

> The city does not always care what we think about the issues, but we make them listen to us. I used to live in this neighborhood as a child. My grandfather came here from Italy. He and my father used to work for GE. Later we moved. When six years ago I needed an apartment, I realized that the only one I could afford was in Hamilton Hill. I was not thrilled, but I also knew that this was not such a bad neighborhood either. . . . When my economic situation improves, I will probably move. . . . I don't like the city; I like the country. . . . I got involved in

the neighborhood association because I am stubborn, I am not a quitter. Nobody's going to force me out if I can help it.

Some members work for the government, and others are business owners with extensive contacts throughout the city. One of the neighborhood association's ex-presidents is a councilman for the city.

> I lived in the Hill all my life. It was always ethnically diverse. That's why these new immigrants settled here. Other neighborhoods would never take them. . . . When I became a council member, I was their youngest member. I campaigned throughout the whole city and had support from other wards, not just from Hamilton Hill. People knew my affiliation with the neighborhood association. As a Polish American, I got Polish votes, and the fact that my wife is Italian helped me in getting Italian votes. Also, it's strange that I'm a Republican, and Hamilton Hill residents are basically Democrats. But for Hamilton Hill, party politics were never important. What matters are issues. . . . Yes, I like the Hill. My family lives here too . . . but I don't know how much longer we're going to be here. My wife doesn't like it. She works in Albany, and she's ashamed to tell them that we live in Hamilton Hill. All this bad publicity in the newspaper or on television makes this neighborhood look like a slum.

Association activity is very much structured by the characteristics of the neighborhood: The activity rises and falls with issues. The membership is racially and ethnically heterogeneous, but economically more homogeneous. Most members were home owners who shared a common interest in preserving their investment in the neighborhood, which allowed them to overcome racial and ethnic differences. Not everyone active in the association is sympathetic to their poor neighbors. One member who is economically better off than the rest of the neighborhood is frustrated by the persistence of poverty in the Hill:

> This state is all wrong. The city gives too much to welfare, and not enough to encourage people to work. That's why we have all these people coming here. They know that here they can get money. My friend, a schoolteacher, asked her kids what they wanted to be when they grew up. Three children said that they wanted to be on welfare. They believed that being on welfare is a job! . . . Schenectady was first destroyed by unions; they were too greedy. Imagine, they wanted fourteen dollars an hour for sweeping floors! That's why GE went to Mexico and now pays two dollars for that. What we need is a better city government. . . . Well, I like it here; my neighbors are nice. As a single mother,

with my own business, I'm out a lot. My downstairs neighbor keeps an eye on
my son. Although I own some property here [two partially rented houses], I
prefer to rent. Rent is cheap, and the apartment is nice. And I don't have to
think about fixing up the house. The drawback of living in this neighborhood is
that my son can't keep his bicycle here. It would be stolen in a second. He keeps
it at his grandmother's house.

Close proximity and similar problems do not necessarily create community or
help residents to better understand each other. If they did, the association
might have fewer problems with membership.

To increase neighborhood participation, some have suggested organizational changes, as one member told me: "Some people would like to come to
the meetings, but they are afraid. We have our meeting every third Thursday
of the month. Our meetings are in the evening, but if we alternate between
Saturday afternoons and Thursday nights, maybe more people can come.
Also, we talked about car pools. People who are afraid can get a ride and be
escorted home. That will increase security." The neighborhood association
also planned to sponsor a block party to boost community spirit, promote the
Hamilton Hill neighborhood, and get more members. For now, the organization publicizes its activities by distributing fliers that say, "Dear Neighbors
and Friends: Never have so few made so many important decisions that have
a potential impact on so many!—Come out—be heard—get involved."

The problems of Hamilton Hill have also been addressed by other organizations that the neighborhood association has maintained contacts with over the
years. Their members and leaders often worked for some of them, like Carver
Center and the Inner-City Ministry. For example, the association has an ongoing relationship with the Albany Street Merchants Association. They often
come together when they have common interests. The Schenectady Inner-City
Ministry is another frequent ally. According to a flier available from the group,
this organization was founded in 1967 by local churches "to relate the resources
of the churches to the human needs of the city. . . . [The Inner-City Ministry]
provides joint services to meet unmet needs; and provides leadership for constructive change on urgent community problems." Among the projects it sponsors are an emergency food program (food pantry), a housing task force (to provide security-deposit money, address homelessness, and discuss affordability of
housing), the Learning Tree Cooperative Nursery (for preschoolers), Project
SAFE, and nutrition outreach and educational programs (a food-stamp program and Women's, Infant's, and Children's School Meals). For Hamilton Hill
residents, these programs are of crucial importance.

The neighborhood association was also an active member of Schenectady United Neighborhoods, a cross-city organization founded in 1979 to pressure the city to remove snow and ice from the streets as well as to increase other services. But city officials soon saw this organization as a troublemaker, accusing its members of turning against the government instead of working with it. The city controlled the resources that the local organization needed to continue its efforts. Lack of funds and the constant feud with the city led to its eventual demise.

Another citywide organization suffered a similar fate, the People's Advisory Service (funded through the community-development budget), formed to provide tenant-landowner reconciliation services and promote fair-housing practices in the city. But it also helped other neighborhood groups oppose the city administration and city council on policies that they did not support. The city retaliated by prohibiting the use of a photocopy machine in city hall for duplicating fliers and other materials not approved by city officials. The members complained in vain that the copy machine was bought under the grant from the community-development agency and did not belong to the city, and soon the People's Advisory Service also became inactive.

The disappearance of these cross-city organizations left the Hamilton Hill Neighborhood Association alone to deal with other voluntary groups and public officials. In 1990 Schenectady United Neighborhoods was reestablished, but without much zest. Its members all come from depressed and declining neighborhoods, and the more wealthy neighborhoods are not represented.

Image-Bolstering Promotion

The association's early goals were to improve the image of the neighborhood and to encourage middle-class people and businesses to move in. Self-help activities have a long tradition in neighborhood involvement. They often develop around common interests for improving the safety and security of a neighborhood through block watches and patrols, neighborhood clean-ups, and management of open space (planting and careing for trees, turning vacant lots into gardens, or maintaining the neighborhood park). Sometimes residents turn their interests toward bolstering neighborhood spirit and improving the image of the neighborhood through block parties, neighborhood fairs, or promoting a community's history and cultural heritage (Gittell 1980).

Hamilton Hill Neighborhood Association chose that route, also stressing neighborhood amenities: an excellent central location and proximity to major traffic routes and to Schenectady's downtown. The affordable real estate was publicized by fliers with a picture of Hamilton Hill and the motto: "Hamilton Hill, the Next Great Neighborhood in Schenectady." The neighborhood also sponsored "We Love Hamilton Hill Day" in 1979. Some people even suggested in 1980 changing the name of the neighborhood to escape the stigma attached to it.

Finally, in 1981, several organizations, such as Better Neighborhoods, Inc., the Hamilton Hill Neighborhood Association, People's Advisory Services, the Albany Street Merchants Association, and Schenectady Inner-City Ministry, met to plan and promote rehabilitation programs for Hamilton Hill. To encourage local developers and landowners to repair their deteriorated rental properties, the city council adopted a $125,000 Rental Rehabilitation Program in June 1982. This program gave each land owners a grant to cover some of the costs of renovating and constructing new housing. Other plans called for free paint projects, development of tool libraries, and neighborhood clean-ups. The neighborhood association even sponsored an annual bike-around for children and young adults. These developments encouraged the residents, who felt that change was on the way.

However, by 1983 the effect of the promotional campaign had dissipated. The bike-around was taken over from Hamilton Hill by the city to promote downtown redevelopment, and most participants were out-of-town professionals. Another 15 percent of local businesses left Hamilton Hill. Not many middle-class people wished to live there, which forced the neighborhood association to address neighborhood problems more directly. It had also become clear that to make any headway, the association needed to work more closely with other local organizations.

Neighborhood Mobilization around Crime Issues

In November 1986, an interview with a frustrated policeman from Hamilton Hill, published in one of the Capital District's newspapers, upset both the residents of the neighborhood and city politicians. The picture that the policeman drew was depressing: In a city divided by a partisan government, residents were fighting for survival. Born and raised in Hamilton Hill, he described it as a place ruined by crime and poverty, and as one of the most depressed areas in the city. According to him, little was being done to help residents cope with the problems. The police were trying to keep peace and order, but the situation was beyond them. The conclusion of the article was especially bitter: "You know, the problem is that, at this level, [the residents are] way past help. It's got to start on a much higher level than me. Because by the time they get to me, they're past hope. We're the ones that get dumped with them. We've got to deal with these people every night, and go around with them every night. And end up boppin' them over the head. I don't blame these people. I blame the people that are sitting there over in Albany [the state government]" (Dunn 1986:27).

Community reaction was strong. Residents who felt that the problems affecting Hamilton Hill had been ignored did not like their neighborhood characterized as the home of people who have nothing. But they also demanded that the city government start offering some solutions to Hamilton Hill's problems and lack of adequate services. A few weeks later, the *Knickerbocker News* published a special front-page article about the Hill based on interviews with prominent residents, who painted a brighter picture of the neighborhood. People who could afford to move out and chose not to described the Hill as their home, and the community as worth fighting for: "Here, at least you get to say hello to people. You've got to lock your doors, but that's just urban living." But they did not deny that crime is a serious issue on the Hill. Many residents constantly worry about robbery. Prostitution and drugs are major problems. Some said that a man could not walk on the street without being approached by a prostitute. "Here, street prostitution has always been heavier than anywhere else in the Capital District. A prostitute could earn $1,200 to $1,800 a week" (Kurp 1986:1A).

Fighting Crime in the Neighborhood

To improve community-police relationships and crime prevention, in the mid-1980s the city opened a Community Police Center in the neighborhood, where police aides (not police officers) provided assistance to neighborhood residents. Their major task, however, was to prevent crime, and they were funded by the County Youth Bureau (State Division for Youth) and by the city. The center became a visible part of the community. The police aides patrolled four area schools, talked to residents about home security, registered bicycles, and conducted seminars on preventing burglary, rapes, and assaults. They also ran property-identification and drug-abuse awareness programs. This effort was further beefed up in 1994, when Schenectady got a $975,000 grant from the U.S. Department of Justice to hire thirteen community-police officers. The thirteen-officer unit has three bicycle-patrol officers and works out of the Hamilton Hill Police Community Center rather than the downtown headquarters.

Another attempt to deal with crime was the Neighborhood Watch. The state's Office of Crime Prevention sponsored this program by distributing relevant literature and radios to members, urging them to call the police and report what they saw without getting involved themselves. In 1983, Hamilton Hill had the largest Neighborhood Watch unit in the city, but soon some of its members were under attack for using racist and obscene language over the radios. In 1989 one of the Black residents described the Neighborhood Watch to me as "a bunch of redneck guys. They were all White and thought that the radios gave them some power in the neighborhood. They were not sensitive to minority residents. Another difficulty for this program was the size of the neighborhood. In some areas people know each other and watch out for each other. In other parts, it's best not to get involved. Some people know about their neighbors' criminal activity, but they reason if they stay out of it they are safe." Residential polarization over the Neighborhood Watch forced the president of the neighborhood association to intervene and change the leadership of this crime-prevention group. Finally the organization broke up. In 1995, some attempts were being made to revitalize the program. However, based on previous experience, some residents interested in the program stress that it is more useful to limit Neighborhood Watch to certain parts of the neighborhood where residents know and trust each other, instead of trying to cover the whole neighborhood.

Frustrated by the failure of such efforts to fight crime, a group of women from the Hill organized another citywide organization, Clean Sweep United. They used grass roots tactics and protest to address its primary focus—making Hamilton Hill safer by exposing drug-related problems. Some theorists argue that protest tactics are the only resource the poor have (Piven and Cloward 1979). Perhaps because protest strategies allow women a creative use of their resources linked to their traditional gender role as mothers, women-based organizations often adopt them. West and Blumberg (1990) describe how women have mounted protests that gained attention and sympathy by using social stereotypes to challenge their opponents, using symbols of their roles as wives and mothers, like pots and pans, to publicize their demands and ridicule their opponents. With an imaginative use of familiar symbols and theatrical devices, women have often been able to increase public visibility for their demands and to force some effective intervention. One of the Clean Sweep United protesters told me in 1989:

> We tried to talk with the mayor first, but when she did not respond, a bunch of
> us decided to do something. We went to the mayor's house and sat on her stoop.

"If we can't have lunch on our stoops, we're going to have it on yours," we told her. Next we went to the Schenectady County district attorney's neighborhood and told his neighbors that we were going to continue to come back and disturb them until "their neighbor" stopped letting drug dealers loose [through the plea-bargaining system]. Well, the district attorney said that we didn't bother him, but his wife and neighbors were concerned. Nobody likes strangers wandering in their neighborhood.

Although these tactics worked, the organization's actions were not applauded by everyone. Some public officials and residents accused the organization of being radical and—because of women in leadership positions—"hysterical." Fighting for police protection, while hardly a radical goal, was unusual in this instance because women were active, held leadership roles, and were more aggressive in their pursuit of drug dealers. They accomplished the major goal of the organization: to make the city and its residents aware of the drug problem. The members believed something had to be done and felt that they were taking risks in order to save their neighborhood and their families. A single mother who was one of the organization's more vocal members described her involvement to me: "Participating in this organization was dangerous. We would go and beam a light on the house where drugs were being dealt to prevent customers from coming in. Or we would take license numbers and give them to the police. Sure, I was scared, but I was more scared by the prospect of my son being shot playing in the backyard. That's why I decided to do something. Better to be shot doing something than doing nothing at all."

Criticism came as well from civil rights activists who disagreed with Clean Sweep's actions and found its focus too narrow. One of the activists who had worked in Hamilton Hill for years said: "Drugs are manifestations of other problems, such as poverty, powerlessness, and unemployment. More sweeping law enforcement, more prisons, and stiff sentencing, although important, could not solve the problem. Instead, Schenectady needs more economic opportunity, especially for minorities, and more drug-rehabilitation programs." This opinion is shared by some researchers who have studied local actions and found that protests over services tend to be transitory and fragmented (Saunders 1981). Organizing around specific local issues may prevent participants from seeing connections between their individual problems, the problems of their neighborhoods, and social conditions (Gottlieb 1992)—and consequently from linking their struggle to more enduring political movements. The real challenge to single-issue organizations is how to broaden their agendas as well as their membership base. Otherwise they disappear from the local political scene. The limitation of Clean Sweep United was that it challenged only some aspects of Hamilton Hill's status as a disadvantaged neighborhood—lack of police protection and law reinforcement—the kind of protest actions sometimes labeled ameliorative social movements (Chafetz and Dworkin 1986).

Some leaders of Clean Sweep United were aware that they lacked the support of minority women from the neighborhood and made an effort to achieve a more racially balanced membership. One member involved in outreach actions explained to me that they "didn't want to be seen as an all-White group. In the beginning we had only one member who was Black. When you deal with drugs, it also becomes a race issue. On the Hill, everybody was sensitive to the drug problem, White and Black alike. Therefore, we started encouraging more Blacks and Hispanics to join us." But that was not an easy task, and the organization continued to have primarily white members. The lack of cross-racial and cross-ethnic coalitions shows that, for poor residents, race and ethnicity are powerful divisive forces. Even in the face of life-threatening common problems—their poverty and the dangers of living in a neighborhood with a crime rate—they remained divided, and Hamilton Hill itself became contested terrain. Who had the right to live there? Who was responsible for damaging the neighborhood? By concentrating solely on the consequences of poverty (drugs and crime) and not on its causes (unemployment and racial discrimination), White women ignored issues that were important for minority women and their families.

Clean Sweep United kept a low profile after achieving stricter sentencing and no plea bargaining. However, sales of drugs on the Hill continued, and some members joined the neighborhood association, where they believed that they could continue to work on important neighborhood problems, especially ones due to drugs.

The consequences of these local struggles for the women that participated in Clean Sweep United went beyond making their neighborhood safer to positively affecting their sense of attachment to their neighborhood, their sense of community, and the development of their political consciousness. Through their collective efforts these women met other people from their neighborhood and began to feel they belonged to a community, which they, in fact, were creating. As others have pointed out, political participation offers women the opportunity to cement friendships and to act rather than feel stifled by their frustration (Bookman and Morgen 1988). The women who continued to be active in the neighborhood association began to think in more political terms, to see how their problems were related to the political and economic conditions of their communities, and they became more committed to changing these conditions. They also began pressuring the neighborhood association to broaden its agenda and to adopt tactics similar to Clean Sweep's.

From Protest to Legal Strategy

Neighborhood residents view houses used for drug distribution, and vacant houses used by the homeless, drug addicts, gangs, and children, as threats to the safety of the surrounding neighborhood. The vacant houses are often haunts for local gangs, whose disputes spread through the streets. Occasional fires and vandalism affect everyone. In addition, some parents are concerned that their children will be hurt playing in or outside these houses.

Some of the new members of the neighborhood association, with experience in Clean Sweep United, devised a legal strategy to fight this housing problem. The woman who developed the idea described how it came about:

> The tenants of the house next to mine were selling drugs. When their "high" customers came to complain or to buy drugs, they did not always know which house was the "drug house." They banged on my doors instead, wandered in my backyard. They already broke the fence. I called the landlord and the police a number of times without success. Then I heard from Gail about the "bawdy law." The law apparently gives the right to the neighbor of the house where the vice is taking place to act as landlord and evict the tenant. But nobody ever heard of such a law. I went first to the city and then to county court, but they didn't know much about it. Finally, here [at work in a state office], I went to the legal library and found the law. It was designated in the nineteenth century against prostitution houses. But it also states that it can be applied to other vices. Then I went to court and made a case against the landlord.

The law states that the neighbor who complains about the vice has to present evidence that, in fact, vice is taking place (two arrests per year are enough). Then the court will notify the property owner, who has thirty days to evict the tenant and can be fined (in 1990 $5,000) for noncompliance, at which point the neighbor is given the right to evict the tenant. In this particular case, the owner evicted the tenant himself, and the case did not go to court. Since then the neighborhood association has been trying is trying to persuade the city to take an active role in implementing such a law. The city would make money, and neighbors will gain more peace in their neighborhood.

The Hamilton Hill Task Force

The neighborhood association also played an active role following an incident involving the arrest and harsh treatment of a Black man by two white police officers. A special task force was set up to deal with the general problem of police insensitivity and harassment. The problem was multidimensional: Some youngsters from Hamilton Hill were involved in drug dealing, others only sporadically went to school or were unemployed. Soon, as the result of task force efforts, school districts were given some extra money to employ specialists in dealing with dropouts to identify children at risk, to pick them up from the streets if necessary, or to help them find jobs.

The task force addressed the relationship between the police and the community. The police had often overreacted, turning small incidents into major problems. Together with the Schenectady Community for Social Justice, a group organized because of the incident involving the black man, the task force prepared several proposals, which the two groups presented to the mayor and the police. They included providing sensitivity and community-relations training for the police, making arrest procedures public, and hiring more minorities. Inner-City Ministry's the Reverend Mr. Grinsby commented on the plight of one minority group, which typified the neighborhood's minority-employment problem: "Everybody knows that we have a new Spanish-speaking population. The Spanish Apostolate estimates an immigration of ten to fifteen families per month. Although our community is becoming much more diverse, we as a community did not respond adequately. . . . Our track record on minority issues is not good. For example, the city has approximately a ten percent minority population, yet our Police Department has only 2 minority members out of 150; our Fire Department has none."

Regarding other problems facing Hamilton Hill, the task force concluded that buildings in the neighborhood were continuing to deteriorate and that abandoned buildings were the central offices for drug dealers and burglars. In 1988, the neighborhood association surveyed the neighborhood, listing all vacant and abandoned properties, and submitted the list to city officials. Members demanded that building inspectors inspect them, and they forced owners to repair them or board them up. One of the local owners felt the cure was worse than the disease:

> I don't know what we accomplished with this list. Before we had forty vacant buildings, and now we have eighty! I have one of these houses. I volunteered to put it on the list myself. [He expected the city to provide resources for repair.] I

want to renovate it, but the city already sent me a note that I have thirty days to bring my property up to standards. I couldn't do it in thirty days. Therefore I'm going to apply to the rehab program. Let the city pay for my rehabilitation. You know this program? It's a program which reimburses you for part of the cost of rehabilitation. Only you have to keep it as a rental property for awhile.

Hamilton Hill's housing problems are characteristic of poor neighborhoods. Property owners enjoy higher profits from rentals because of the lack of tight code enforcement. The mail carrier for Hamilton Hill, who is also active in the social and political life of the neighborhood, presented the tenant's point of view, emphasizing the roles played by absentee owners and the housing crisis:

> Some landlords complain that welfare tenants trash their apartments. That is true, but not in every case. You have good tenants and bad tenants, but you also have good landlords and bad landlords. The bad landlords use these examples of bad tenants to justify their neglected apartments. We have people here who are lawyers and doctors and who live in the suburbs but own property in Hamilton Hill. They don't care about the tenants, they care only about how much money they can get. But let's expand this problem a little further. Demand for housing is growing here. We now have more homeless people. I'm amazed by the number of people who are now living together. You see all these names on the mailboxes, one after another. . . . But let's expand the problem even further. The unwed mothers, for example, can get public assistance only if they live in separate households. Therefore, they move out of their parents' houses and increase the demand for housing too.

Life for poor people, according to the Reverend Mr. Grinsby, is no easier here than anywhere else: "Families end up paying, in my experience, 50 percent and more of their income for shelter costs. Obviously this creates enormous strain in a household. The slightest crisis could lead to eviction. In addition, the 'doubling up' of families in housing units is more common, though hard to estimate." It is widely believed that the city keeps the poor concentrated in this neighborhood, and that it uses them as a bargaining chip: As long as the poor are there, the city can receive some state and federal grants and subsidies.

Affordable Housing and Neighborhood Revitalization

One of the task-force recommendations was that the city seek funds to build more low-and moderate-income housing. The neighborhood association supported the proposal but insisted that better code enforcement was also needed if the project was to succeed. Joe Allen, the president of the association, argued that the whole area should be brought up to the city's code for safe and sanitary buildings. New houses surrounded by deteriorating houses would deteriorate. Members of the association and task force also believed that encouraging home ownership would lead to a more stable neighborhood.

Better Neighborhoods, Inc., a community-development agency, then applied for a Community Development Block Grant and in 1989 was awarded funds for subsidizing the cost of houses. As a result, a new housing project designed for Hamilton Hill called for twenty-four to thirty new duplexes for moderate-and low-income families. One apartment in each house is owner occupied, and the other is a rental unit, which should help owners pay the mortgage. The local neighborhood corporation was in charge of accepting and processing applications for the houses. Applicants had to have incomes between $19,000 and $36,000 (depending on the size of the family), have been employed for at least two years, and possess a good credit history. In 1990, twelve houses had been finished and sold, at a cost of $85,000 each. Local and state subsidies reduced the cost to $55,000, still affordable only for moderate-income families.

However, the project is seen as a sign of better times coming to the Hill. One of the active members of the neighborhood association, a long-time resident, told me she feels positive about the changes: "People are starting to fix up their houses. If everything is run down, there's no purpose in doing it; soon the house would look the same as before. But now with these new houses, the neighborhood is going to be better. Who knows, when these new office towers are finished, maybe some of their employees will decide to come and buy a house here. It's a nice neighborhood. Good location, and people are friendly. We have a park nearby. The city promised to put some bathrooms there, too. Yes, the neighborhood will definitely be better."

To address the neighborhood association's concerns over code enforcement, the city has introduced a rental-certificate program for Hamilton Hill and its surrounding streets. Schenectady building inspectors look for health and safety hazards in buildings with two or more rental apartments whenever new tenants move in and issue a certificate verifying the apartment's safety if it complies with the codes. But the program's success is threatened by the lack of inspectors to do the job. Also, neighborhood residents and the association are not pleased that the program is limited to the Hill and doesn't extend to the city as a whole.

Because Schenectady is a poor city, it needs help from the state and federal government. And in December 1994 it got some. Together with two other cities in the region Schenectady was awarded a $3 million grant from the U.S. Department of Housing and Urban Development Enterprise Community Program and a $3 million matching grant from the State of New York. The grant requires neighborhood and community participation and allows the use of money for commercial and business development, for neighborhood improvements, and for family and youth programs. It is up to neighborhood organizations to insure that they are not excluded from participating in, and benefiting from, the project.

What Next? Rebuilding Poor Neighborhoods

Large job losses turned Hamilton Hill from a poor but stable working-class neighborhood into a transient and fragmented community whose residents' major concern became how to stop further deterioration, a difficult task in a declining industrial city whose resources for supporting neighborhood improvement are limited. Impoverished neighborhoods are forced to compete among themselves for resources they all need but only a few will get, and this poor distribution of resources keeps most residents in the lowest social stratum. Lacking money and political power, Hamilton Hill has had little chance to gain resources to improve conditions by lobbying the city government.

Realizing that, the members of the Hamilton Hill Neighborhood Association became much more involved in building coalitions and alliances with other groups and organizations in and outside their neighborhood. Although the accomplishments of that neighborhood mobilization are modest, they are still important. The existence of active organizations has kept some residents from moving out and has energized others, who see they can do something about the conditions of their community. It also it made harder for the city to ignore neighborhood problems.

Neighborhood and community organizations are a resource for Hamilton Hill, showing that, as others have documented, people who live in poor communities are able to initiate and actively participate in urban struggles (Susser 1988; Heskin 1991; Stoecker 1994). However, to sustain gains that local organizations make, residents have to work toward improving the social and economic conditions of their communities. The problems of crime cannot be solved only by stricter sentencing and more policing; they also require for their solution developing programs like Project SAFE in Schenectady (see Chapter 6), strengthening families, and developing neighborhood social-support systems.

The example of Clean Sweep United shows some of the strengths that poor neighborhoods can muster in the face of enormous difficulties. This organization was led by women who often bear heavier burdens than poor men do—their wages are still uniformly lower, and they are often solely responsible for the economic and emotional well-being of their children. Although trapped in their neighborhood by poverty, they took action to stop violence against themselves and their children, to insure enough resources to feed, clothe, and house their children, and to gain the right to be heard in the political arena. Several active women at Hamilton Hill were able to use their personal relationships to mobilize other women in the neighborhood. A protest strategy allowed them to gain public recognition and to force public officials to address their concerns: to protect their neighborhood, and consequently their children and families. However, this organization also exemplifies the weaknesses of poor neighborhoods. Clean Sweep United, began as an organization of White women, was not able to overcome racial barriers, and remained an organization of White women. This is one of the most difficult challenges that urban movements in poor neighborhoods face. To overcome the social fragmentation of their neighborhood, White women of Hamilton Hill will have to develop new strategies to involve minority women in their activities.

That may happen as they become more aware of the true causes of their neighborhood problems. The struggle with the city officials helped some women to develop their political consciousness, to see beyond their own immediate concerns for the safety of their families to build alliances with minority women. Their membership in the neighborhood association offered them the opportunity to work for the well-being of the whole neighborhood. They brought with them the skills and experience that made them valuable and important members of these new organizations.

However, there is a limit to how much women and men can obtain for their communities using these techniques. To sustain gains they have made, they must work toward improving the social and economic conditions of their communities. Rebuilding the neighborhood has to be connected with larger redevelopment policies, such as meaningful, skill-based jobs; the improvement of urban infrastructure; better housing, education, and health care. In Ecuador, for example, as women organized around consumer and service demands, they saw the need to gain jobs and housing for themselves (Lind 1992). Similarly, for some women in Mexico, their way of life has been changing "from individual survival strategies to collective ones that place pressure on political parties and government bureaucrats" (Stephen 1992:90).

In socially fragmented neighborhoods, residents not only have to address multiple issues simultaneously, but they must cross ethnic, racial, class, and gender lines in the process. However, the success of their collective action does not depend solely on their ability to organize and overcome fragmentation but also on political opportunities made available by local and national governments. Since the early 1980s, the federal government has severely cut many social programs that were helping poor residents and neighborhoods. What we need now are policies that unite rather than divide urban neighborhoods, cities, and suburbs, or pit one ethnic group against the other.

The new federal-state grant gives Hamilton Hill residents an opportunity to use their organization and participate in decision making. We know from past experience that the existence of resources does not insure that poor neighborhoods will benefit from them. Often government polices divide rather than unite residents. Moreover, the requirements for neighborhood participation in this case do not guarantee that poor neighborhoods will be allowed to participate fully. Not only Hamilton Hill but the whole city has to find a new mission for Schenectady: not just economic development, but also the development of a livable community for its residents.

9

Neighborhoods, Strategies, and the City Context

Many residents of cities and neighborhoods across the United States are struggling to keep their communities livable by improving the delivery of municipal services, and by increasing citizen participation in local decision making. Innovative city and neighborhood programs show that residents, social agencies, organizations, and businesses have not given up on cities and can work together to address urban decline. In Hartford, Connecticut, Aetna, a large insurance agency, works with the local schools and provides resources for minority students to attend college. Volunteer doctors and nurses have addressed the lack of medical care in Racine, Wisconsin, by establishing free neighborhood health clinics for uninsured working poor residents. In Boston, Massachusetts, a nonprofit community-development corporation uses neighborhood resources and grants from corporations and foundations to build affordable rental housing and to provide opportunities for home ownership.

These responses, consciously or not, challenge the idea that social needs such as housing, education, and health care are the responsibility of individuals only or should be met only through the marketplace. They are public needs that must be addressed with public services. So though all the actors in collective urban actions may not share the same political views and may even be strongly opposed to each other, their common desire to improve conditions in a city represents a political opening for building coalitions to restore the public sector to the city.

When a city's residents organize to preserve or improve social conditions, they are motivated by a desire for a more livable community. The city is not only a place to make money and maximize profits, but also a place where people live and enjoy their daily round; it can be a source of support and security. The question remains, What can people in different kinds of neighborhoods and cities do to create a livable urban community?

I have examined neighborhoods and their collective actions in a service-sector city and in a declining industrial city, urban environments at opposite ends of the scale. While such cities often have similar histories and may lie near each other, they have emerged from urban restructuring with very different outcomes because of the interplay of economic and political factors. In both cities I looked at, Albany and Schenectady, neighborhood mobilization concentrates on the quality of residential life, using lobbying and advocacy to make local government more responsive. For some neighborhoods in Albany and other service-sector cities this approach has helped residents influence land use in their neighborhoods or obtain more resources for neighborhood-based services. But what can neighborhoods do in Schenectady and simular declining industrial cities when the local government has too few resources?

Neighborhood Mobilization and the City Context

The characteristics of cities—the city context—influence resources available to neighborhood organizations. Because the resources of service-sector cities and declining industrial cities are stretched thin in different areas, they face different problems, which in turn influence neighborhoods to mobilize differently. In service-sector cities, the focus is on taking an active role in decision-making about local development. In declining industrial cities, the focus is on maintaining and improving city services.

The fiscal crisis of state and federal government and the more globally oriented postindustrial economy are forcing city or local administrations to become more entrepreneurial and forge alliances not only with businesses but also with other actors in the city. In the 1980s and 1990s citizen and neighborhood groups, foundations, and nonprofit organizations have become much more active participants in new comprehensive plans to integrate local economic and social development. Their involvement supports Long's claim (1973) that local development is a political as well as an economic process, and that more citizen participation in city decision making will encourage more efficient and equitable development. But as my analysis of neighborhood organizing in Albany and Schenectady shows, this cooperation does not come easy, nor is it always voluntary.

Neighborhood Mobilization in Service-Sector Cities

Service-sector cities have more diversified economies than industrial cities have. The major expansion in office building and employment in administrative services for both government and private industry makes their central business districts active places. The local economy provides many well-paid professional jobs, a sound fiscal policy, and a probusiness climate. Not just large cities like New York City, San Francisco, or Atlanta benefited from service-sector growth, but also medium-size cities like Albany, New York, and Cincinnati, Ohio.

Economic restructuring has made service-sector cities the successful model of urban development. The economic transformation is carried out by pro-growth political regimes and accomplished with corporate strategies. Economic and political actors, who see the city primarily as a place to make money and maximize profits, create pro-growth coalitions that are the driving force of economic change. But, because economic development benefits businesses at the expense of residents, it also provokes and stimulates neighborhood mobilization as a reaction to "value-free" development and to aggregate growth portrayed as a public good (Logan and Molotch 1987).

Residents of service-sector cities form place-based organizations for two reasons: to influence land-use policy in the city and to distribute the benefits of economic development more equitably. They are opposed to intensifying land use in their neighborhoods and communities and to the economic logic that sees residential communities as commodities—places to be sold and bought (Čapek and Gilderbloom 1992). Residents use collective action primarily to influence the city's administration or political regime and real-estate developers. They use neighborhood associations as lobbying-style organizations to address their residential concerns: reliable urban services, tougher zoning regulations, and a greater say in local decision making. As taxpayers they demand accountability from local elected officials and believe that a healthy local economy provides enough resources to create and maintain livable communities in the city.

In service-sector cities, neighborhood associations are the most prevalent way of organizing. That they represent the interests of home owners in a neighborhood—or the home-owning class—makes them the main organizations for gentrified neighborhoods. The driving force behind neighborhood mobilization in service-sector cities is residents, the people who invest their money, energy, and time into revitalizing urban neighborhoods, who cherish the amenities of urban life, and who are dedicated to preserving cities as cultural and social centers. They are well educated, work in well-paid service-sector jobs, know the political system, and have connections with influential officials.

The neighborhood association is seen as a successful model of local mobilization because it can take advantage of these resources. Such associations also benefit from their organizational resources in the form of formalized structures, well-connected board members, and persistent leaders—essential for successful influence on local decision making. However, by emphasizing place-based interests, the neighborhood association attracts more middle-class home owners than poor tenants. Important issues such as education, poverty, and affordable housing do not get addressed, for they are viewed as less important to the well-being of the neighborhood than land-use issues. Association members are also aware that more spending on social services will increase their taxes and make it harder to sell their houses or to attract new residents.

Neighborhood associations in service-sector cities play a different role in low-income neighborhoods, where they form in response to the economic consequences of corporate strategies that have created a two-tiered system of neighborhoods and of jobs. On one side are well-paid, skilled jobs that contribute to an increase in personal income and wealth, and on the other are low-paid, low-skilled jobs that hold no prospects for upward mobility or a better life. People in poorly paid jobs live in neighborhoods without adequate services and do not have the personal resources to improve their areas or move to ones better served by the city.

Housing in low-income neighborhoods is deteriorating, and many residents have lost their jobs or are employed part-time. To survive, many of them engage in illicit activities, which contribute to their neighborhood's notoriety as a dangerous, shabby part of town. Mobilization in such neighborhoods centers on demands that the local political regime be more even handed with city resources. Residents organize to make their neighborhoods safer and more stable and to help avail the poor of opportunities for employment and job training. In these neighborhoods, the major goal of neighborhood associations is to stop further deterioration by encouraging gentrification. But because there are fewer home owners, and gentrification is not a realistic option, their strategies do not pay off. More successful are broad-based coalitions of local community groups, neighborhood development organizations, and housing corporations using a combination of advocacy and community-development strategies to persuade the city administration to support them and provide resources. Together, these public and private agencies back entrepreneurial economic strategies such as indigenous growth, new business start-ups, and job creation (Eisinger 1988; Clarke, Gaile, and Saiz 1994). The purpose of these policies is to create assets within communities, "assets that are visible as commercial space, industrial properties, and affordable residences, and assets owned by individuals such as job skills, education, and an increased sense of self-worth" (Rubin 1994:419). The more inclusive local policies provide opportunities to address the sources of urban poverty, lack of jobs, and crime. Under such political conditions neighborhood mobilization and participation flourish.

Neighborhood Mobilization in Declining Industrial Cities

Economic restructuring stripped declining U.S. industrial cities of their traditional economic base without replacing it with other sources of income. With their specialized economies, the loss of industrial jobs had a severly damaging impact on them. Factories closed down, people lost jobs, and city revenues declined. Stable working-class families became poor families. Lack of money and hope for the future led to abandonment and deterioration of housing and neighborhoods. Cities like Schenectady, New York; Lawrence, Massachusetts; Dayton, Ohio; and Detroit, Michigan, have more problems than service-sector cities but fewer resources to deal with them.

In declining industrial cities, neighborhood mobilization centers more on city services than on influencing land-use policies. To succeed, neighborhood and community organizations need the support of the whole community. However, class and racial divisions fragment the city and make neighborhood mobilization less successful.

Gentrified neighborhoods in these cities do not want to influence local development, as in service-sector cities, nor are they looking for progressive regimes to address neighborhood problems. Their goal is to insure the delivery of services to a small number of residents of a few relatively prosperous areas. Their organizations have a good relationship with their pro-growth local political regimes, unlike neighborhood associations in service-sector cities. Poor neighborhoods, however, are left to struggle alone to reverse the trend of neighborhood decline.

Gentrified neighborhoods in declining-industrial cities also use their own resources to buffer themselves from the rest of the city by erecting walls and fences around their neighborhood or by buying public streets and forbidding access other city residents, as one St. Louis, Missouri neighborhood did; by proposing secession from the city, as Staten Island, New York City, did; or by erecting iron gates, as did the Five Oaks neighborhood in Dayton, Ohio. The Community Association Institute has estimated that nearly 4 million Americans live in closed-off gated communities, and that about 28 million live in communities governed by private community associations. And the popularity of these communities is expected to grow; the *New York Times* reports that the Walt Disney Company plans to develop a complete private city for 20,000 residents (Egan 1995:22)

This strategy is sometimes known as the "defensible space" concept, developed in the 1970s by Oscar Newman, an urban planner who worked on its implementation in St. Louis, where, he says, residents "have been able to create and maintain for themselves what their city was no longer able to provide: low crime rates, stable property values, and a sense of community" (Newman 1981:124). He believes that traffic-engineering techniques, stricter code enforcement, and home-improvement incentives can stabilize urban neighborhoods. The problem with Newman's model is that it fragments a city even further and allows better-organized residents to gain more city resources for their neighborhoods. It does not address the real problems of declining industrial cities, namely the lack of vision or resources for local development.

Low-income neighborhoods in declining cities get very little support from their local political regimes. These cities themselves are poor, and even politicians who sympathize with poor people's demands can do little. Poor neighborhoods are in competition with a city's other declining neighborhoods, which are in much better condition. Often the most spurned of the city's neighborhoods, they have very limited possibilities for improvement.

The residents of any poor neighborhood vary in ethnicity, race, class, and time in residence. Some who used to have jobs in the city's industrial base but are now unemployed or underemployed feel trapped in their neighborhood. Their tenure is involuntary, and they are not likely to see the neighborhood as a community worth preserving. But some long-term residents who could leave have elected to stay despite the decline. They work or are retired and have an economic and emotional investment in a neighborhood that they like and want to protect. They remember better times and are driven by the wish to recreate the once livable community they have lost. And they demonstrate that even the poorest neighborhoods have people who stay because they want to, not because they have to. They also have resources such as education, income and knowledge about the political system, and a willingness to use such resources to change conditions. They are the people who form neighborhood associations and fight for neighborhood improvements.

Neighborhood associations in poor areas want to persuade the city administration to address the deterioration. They would like to attract new middle-class residents, but they know that they can't. The crucial question for poor neighborhoods, as for gentrified neighborhoods, is how to deal with crime. The racial mixture and heterogeneity of neighborhood residents, however, make strategies like Neighborhood Watch less effective than in prosperous neighborhoods. Attempts to create a safe environment constantly confront the lack of alternative employment for residents engaged in illegal activity and police insensitivity and brutality to all residents regardless of their engagement in local crime. For poor neighborhoods the police are often part of the problem, not part of the solution. Simply increasing the police presence is not enough. Neighborhood groups know that they have to come up with additional strategies.

More than service-sector cities, declining industrial cities need neighborhood mobilization to achieve a livable community. Their problems are more urgent, and they are less likely to have local political regimes with a vision and plan for redevelopment. Community-development strategies that are improving conditions in some low-income neighborhoods of service-sector cities are not a realistic option for low-income neighborhoods of declining industrial cities with fewer resources for such development.

However, declining industrial cities have other resources. Social and religious organizations in these cities play a more important role in improving living conditions than they do in service-sector cities. Their primary goals are to provide services for residents, and to find ways to raise additional resources for improving the neighborhood. Together with neighborhood organizations, they pressure their city officials to apply for outside resources that will help improve services for poor neighborhoods.

Deterioration of the city, and especially crime, are not going away. They worry not only residents of low-income neighborhoods, but also residents of middle-class neighborhoods who cannot afford "defensible space" strategies. Residents of both types of neighborhood want to reside in livable communities, but they lack a vision of how a whole city can become a livable community and how to mobilize for a safer, better-maintained city. For cities to take their situation seriously they need a sense of crisis, "a belief that, if changes are not made, conditions in the city will deteriorate even further" (Gittell 1992:183). In declining industrial cities, the sense of crisis is coming from poor neighborhoods. To save their neighborhoods, they have to save their cities.

Rebuilding the Declining Industrial City as a Livable Community

How can a declining industrial city become a livable community? A place that is safe and has a stable population and social institutions can have hope for the future. In the early decades of the twentieth century, some researchers argue (Coleman and Hoffer 1987), Americans lived in functional communities where residents and local social institutions, such as schools, shared the same or similar social values, norms, and sanctions—the middle-class values of "hard work, diligence, respect for the teachers, and good behavior in school." This commonality represented the "social capital" of the community and helped parents to socialize and to control their children more effectively. In such communities, students from disadvantaged families also were able to achieve further education and social mobility. The local social capital weakened the effect of students' personal background on their educational opportunities. The decline of such functional communities "leaves parents, whether middle class or lower class, without a strong set of social resources, able only to draw upon whatever individual resources they have." But parents still need community to help them rear children. Economic necessity forces both parents to work and to juggle family and work demands. They have to do well at work, but also keep their children safe and healthy and help them resist the temptation to join street gangs, use drugs, or succumb to other negative aspects of peer pressure. They are counting on day care, schools, and structured child and youth programs to assist them. Instead of functional communities, parents today choose "value" communities, that is, private or public schools whose educational philosophies attract both them and their children. In these educational communities a high degree of value consistency develops among all parties involved, which has a positive effect on children's education (Coleman and Hoffer 1987:8).

The restructuring of the U.S. economy, the influx of new immigrants, and the advent of a more conservative political climate are powerful forces that have set the stage for relationships of cooperation, conflict, adjustment, or isolation among the residents of our cities (Lamphere 1992:11). Researchers from a Ford Foundation project on the relations of newcomers and established residents in six U.S. communities found that fragmentation there was caused not solely by cultural differences among ethnic groups, but also by the structure of the institutions with which people deal. Corporations, school systems, city governments, and organizations that provide housing and social services maintain old separations and divisions between people and often create and foster new ones (Lamphere 1992).

One way to overcome neighborhood fragmentation is for residents to acknowledge their common interest. Most residents of poor neighborhoods, even some of those engaged in criminal activities, want to live in a safe home, find a job that pays decent wages, and send their children to a good school. They rely on their salaries, welfare payments, and help from kin and neighbors to provide for themselves and their children. What undermines their efforts is the instability of their economic situation and the characteristics of their neighborhoods. Their children are more likely to be exposed to random violence or tempted to join street gangs because gangs are active in their neighborhoods. They also have fewer structured school- or community-based activities to keep children busy and safe. Poor parents, like middle-class parents, need help. But they do not have the money to buy services for their children like camps or day care, nor can they afford "value" communities. They have to rely on each other and take advantage of the resources that they can muster.

The interests of individuals and community are interdependent. Communities "are not merely environments to which an actor adjusts as he or she would to a new climate, but they also influence to a great extent the person's most inner desires, preferences and moral commitments." Community and individuals work together toward a common purpose or goal and share the same primary moral standing, which subjects individuals "to the shared understandings, the collective consensus of the community." Such a "responsive community," is also "a non-coercive community that appeals to the 'nobler' part of the self, and one that in turn the self finds compelling" (Etzioni 1991: 125, 148, 147).

Community helps individuals cope with their problems and makes it possible to find collective solutions for them. However, common interests, values, and norms that bind people together and make their communities "functional" or "responsive" do not develop in a vacuum but as part of social interactions promoted by social institutions. When people organize or join community and neighborhood organizations, they are primarily driven by a desire for a livable community. But collective efforts to create a livable community do not depend solely on residents' ability to organize and overcome fragmentation of their neighborhoods, but also on social, political, and economic opportunities made available by social institutions.

The stability, order, and safety of a neighborhood are achieved by affordable housing, responsive educational institutions, reliable medical care, and access to police protection. "Without homes and jobs within the community, the young people see no future and take little effort to gain the skills needed

*But coercion is essential
to its success.*

for later survival" (Rubin 1994:420). Homes and jobs create common interests that bind people together. In a diverse society like the United States, it is up to social institutions to promote such common interests. Inclusion and respect for differences make individual success possible. The livable community that results goes beyond creating "functional" community or achieving "responsive" community.

Social institutions such as schools can mediate relationships among people in a community, even when its ethnic composition is changing. Experience suggests that when children do well in school, it is because the school and family promote and support academic achievement and success, the school has a stable student population and a low teacher turnover and welcomes and facilitates parents' involvement as aides and as members of Home and School Associations, and, finally, teachers who live outside the neighborhood maintain ties within it. By way of contrast, children have been shown to have problems in both schools and communities where ethnic and racial divisions and poverty have created fragmentation, indicated by high teacher and student turnover, when competition for jobs, housing, and school resources has turned one group of residents against the other. Consequently, poverty, instability, and the lack of common goals and understanding among teachers and parents affect the children's interactions and academic success. "The teachers and administration blame the parents, the parents blame the outsider professional and the school district, and a strong boundary separates the English-speaking and Spanish-speaking adults and children" (Goode, Schneider, and Blanc 1992:197).

Marxist and other theories suggest the problems of poor neighborhoods— social inequalities and poverty—persist because they are the normal consequences of a capitalist economic system. Competition among cities for economic resources pits one city against the other, creating few winners and many losers. Within the cities, the capitalists or pro-growth regimes are primarily interested in maximizing profit. Their interests conflict with the interests of city residents, who see the city as a community and want to preserve its residential amenities. Overcoming such conditions of capitalism, these theories suggest, demands fundamental social and economic change that cannot be achieved by protest and lobbying but only by social revolution.

The real dilemma of the poor neighborhood, especially in the poor cities, is what to do when the revolution never comes. How can a neighborhood confront larger economic and political forces? There is no easy answer to this question. But one thing is clear: To rebuild poor neighborhoods like Hamilton Hill in Schenectady, residents must become involved in rebuilding the social infrastructure of the neighborhood to turn it into a livable community.

At least three options for such rebuilding exist. The first solution starts at the neighborhood level and builds on neighborhood strengths. A neighborhood alone cannot solve problems such as poverty, unemployment, and crime. But many neighborhoods are making life better by using collective action to rebuild residents' support networks and to make local human-services more responsive to local needs. When they succeed, it is because residents, small businesses, civic and religious organizations, and human-service organizations have learned to trust and work with each other. They build on and expand the social capital of the neighborhood.

The second solution addresses the economic development of the city. To rebuild livable communities, people need stable jobs that pay decent wages. Neighborhood and community organizations believe that strategies that stress investment in people and neighborhoods can lead toward that goal. Because human capital is the key element in contemporary economies (Reich 1991), a city's investment in people can contribute to economic development as well.

The third solution is based on policies initiated outside the cities. The city is seen as part of a regional and national economic development. The life of urban residents will improve by implementing comprehensive health-care policies, increasing state and federal investment in education, and facilitating transfer payments to families (Goldsmith and Blakely 1992). Within such a context, declining cities can be transformed into residential communities. As livable communities, they contribute to the development of human capital that helps the economic development of the region and the nation.

Strength out of Poverty

A neighborhood's problems—poverty, social isolation, the accumulated effects of social ills—can be addressed by using and developing the neighborhood's organizational, physical, and social resources. In the process of assessing the disorganization and break-up of individual poor families, we have ignored both the potential for and sometimes a successful use of existing social capital in poor neighborhoods. The real issue for residents of the inner city is not that a community is lost—because it is not—but that it is constantly under threat from more powerful economic and political forces.

For local solutions to work, communities need to rely on and rebuild community- and value-based institutions such as neighborhood organizations, churches, and social clubs. They are source of leadership, they build and maintain a sense of community, and they connect residents with other similar organizations outside the neighborhood. Collective action brings people together. Through mobilization and confrontation, participants gain a sense of togetherness that helps to establish unity and cohesion in the organizations and in the neighborhood. Through such actions, long-lasting ties of mutual support are forged, and they help residents survive poverty.

Most low-income neighborhoods have multiethnic populations. People from different cultural backgrounds have different ways of solving problems. As working couples, first-generation immigrant families, single mothers, laid-off workers and their families, or individuals down on their luck, they work, hustle, and use a variety of public- and-private support programs to survive, despite the sometimes inhuman conditions in which they live. Some of these residents hope that their individual conditions will improve and that they will be able to move to another neighborhood. Others, however, develop an emotional attachment to the neighborhood and see their future tied to its future. Together with other residents, they already participate in or can be mobilized to join activities of community and religious organizations in their neighborhoods and can learn how to take advantage of the existing resources.

Neighborhood resources come from local residents, organizations, and social institutions. The economic resources of residents come from salaries, pensions, social security, and public-assistance income. Although these are not sufficient to cover all the needs that poor people have, they are a source of income and are used to pay for housing and food. Some resources, like Aid for Families with Dependent Children (AFDC), are not necessarily recognized as such. Instead of being seen as income that makes it possible for families to survive, recipients are stigmatized as unproductive members of society. The public perception of child-based policies contrasts with other social policies. Social security, for example, is seen as respectable income, while AFDC is not. This pervasive attitude implies that rearing a child is an individual responsibility and an unworthy social task. Neighborhood-based organizations challenge such attitudes by embracing women and their children, and by sponsoring community-based activities that help them in socializing and supervising children.

Residents can use collective action to address inadequate local services. Not only do poor families have low monthly incomes, but they also are overcharged for local services, such as housing and groceries. Just because people pay market-rate rents, for example, does not mean that they live in decent housing. It is hard to address this problem individually. Together, residents can fight for tenants' rights or can form alliances with outside agencies, such as community-development corporations, nonprofit housing corporations, or tenant cooperatives to increase the supply of affordable and decent housing in the neighborhood.

Similarly, poor people cannot force supermarket chains to open or maintain stores in poor neighborhoods, but they can organize shopping trips to suburban shopping centers. Nationwide, older residents are already doing this. Because they are not able to drive, they asked supermarkets to charter buses to help them shop. There is no reason why residents of poor neighborhoods could not do the same, making shopping more convenient and cheaper. In some neighborhoods residents have responded to shopping problems by sponsoring grocery cooperatives run by residents themselves, a source of income for people who work in the stores, and a source of profits for the community. Also, the failure of retail and service businesses to deliver goods and services to the local urban market creates opportunities for minority businesses such as Americas' Food Basket to develop their niche and rebuild the economic vitality of urban neighborhoods (Porter 1995:60).

Social, health, and education institutions are other resources in a neighborhood, as well as part of its social infrastructure. However, they are more likely to be seen as sources of problems than of help. The lack of financial resources and the increase in need for services make the work of these organizations difficult. The poor quality of services residents receive is blamed on lack of money and staff, but the failure of schools to educate children is not only due to a lack of money. It is also based on the absence of trust among teachers and parents. Teachers often believe that children are dull and unmotivated, that their parents do not care about their children's educations, and that there is little that school and teachers can do.

Similar attitudes are found among other human-service workers. Social workers, police officers, doctors, and nurses often believe that their poor clients are passive victims of misfortune or are responsible for their own hardships. By pitying or blaming them, these professionals cheapen the services their clients do receive. Clients are rarely seen as participants in a collective effort to find solutions to their problems, putting poor people, who deal the most with human-service organizations, at a disadvantage. They lack information about the services and resources available. Often they do not have the skills for bureaucratic interpersonal communication and consequently fail to articulate their needs and worries in a way comprehensible to human-service workers. Because clients are expected to conform to organizational rules and regulations in order to receive their benefits, human-service organizations have few incentives to change their practices or to take clients' needs into consideration. Poor people often have no choice about the quality of services they receive; human-service workers "usually have nothing to lose by failing to satisfy clients" (Lipsky 1980:55).

Residents of poor neighborhoods can also address these types of problems through collective action. In some neighborhoods, residents become members of organizational boards and task forces and participate in organizational evaluations, taking an active role in overseeing how money is spent for services that their neighborhoods receive. But more is possible. Neighborhood residents could become human-service workers. Community-based employment includes training residents to become teacher aides, run family day-care centers, work in after-school and sports programs, or provide home-care services for senior citizens.

Such professional training could work to make human-service organizations more responsive to clients' needs. Every such organization has some employees who are deeply interested in improving its services. Concepts such as community policing, community health care, and community schools as ways to improve delivery of services are gaining recognition among practitioners, policymakers, and clients. Community policing in Newark and Houston significantly reduced disorder and police repression, improving the quality of life (see Skolnick and Bayley 1986). Human-service workers who know a community and its residents well and are involved in community life are able to better assess and deliver services (Gutiérrez 1992). In some communities human-service workers interested in change are already working with local residents to eliminate the "blame the victim" syndrome, to focus on real needs, and to cut through professional boundaries and treatment ideologies.

Community-based programs also stress coordination and cooperation among a variety of services, with prevention and development as major goals. Programs such as family planning, childhood vaccination, parenting and nutrition classes, and sports activities are not expensive. They use existing facilities and rely on the human resources in the community. For example, a retired nurse can be recruited to run a nutrition program. Immigrants will learn English faster if they have an opportunity to interact with their English-speaking neighbors, or to participate as volunteers in schools and other programs.

The empowerment of clients and their families leads to an improvement of the quality of life in their neighborhoods. The prevailing belief is that only paid work gives people self-worth. But communities and local human-service organizations could not survive without work that local residents put in maintaining their families and communities. By recognizing family and community-based activities as work, we also provide people with feelings of dignity and self-worth. For public policy this is important, because we start from a position of strength, not weakness.

Human-service workers also benefit from the empowerment of their clients and communities. Their working conditions improve, and they receive more professional recognition and respect from their clients. More involved and empowered clients can make human-service organizations more successful. Also, a more empowered community has more chances to gain the attention of city officials and fight for more resources for local organizations. More importantly, based on the success of their programs, poor neighborhoods can also apply for outside private and public funding. This is vital, because poor neighborhoods cannot be self-sustaining.

This neighborhood-based mobilization must be distinguished from the highly touted but ineffectual self-help strategies. The improvements of life in the neighborhood are not seen as separate from the rest of the society. Empowered residents may take a leading role in articulating neighborhood-development priorities, for instance: Which types of economic activities, social policies, and public services are best for them, their neighborhoods, and their cities? By respecting the diverse cultural foundations of the neighborhoods, local organizations build on strengths.

Local Economic Development and Livable Community

What type of local development can help declining industrial cities such as Dayton, Ohio, Lawrence, Massachusetts, or Schenectady, New York? Major corporations have abandoned these cities as they follow the precepts of global economic restructuring, and federal and state governments have similarly cut back on programs—never bountiful—that helped poor residents and cities. These communities obviously need more economic activity to employ and sustain their residents.

There are two ways to go about a city's revitalization. The first is to start with economic development, and the second, to start with the development of services. In the debate about where a declining city should put its resources, economic development is often presented as the primary concern because it is expected to create jobs and increase city revenues. Residents' needs for services and safe and livable communities are seen as secondary. But it is possible to see a connection between these two sets of goals.

Cities that can prosper are the ones that can respond to challenges of global economy. High-value production—economies of scale—seen in previous economic development are being replaced by increasingly flexible, high value-added production—economies of scope and quality. Companies that succeed are often smaller and employ skilled, technical, and professional employees. They also need research, development, and marketing firms nearby. Wealth and the potential for gain are no longer best measured by fixed assets (plants and equipment), but by accumulated knowledge and experience—human capital (Reich 1991). In today's economy, what makes a city a good place for business is the quality of its labor force.

Therefore, to rebuild their economies, cities must invest in their residents. Cities need livable communities, because core human-capital institutions—families, schools, job-training organizations—are locally based (Fosler 1991; Clarke and Gaile 1994). No economic development can proceed in a city without safe and livable communities.

An analysis of new manufacturing enterprises in Sun Belt cities supports these claims: Firms that invest in the United States need a skilled, flexible, and innovative labor force. Their workers are looking for safe, pleasant neighborhoods in which to live and raise families. Companies choose cites that have livable communities because they help them solve the problem of recruiting a skilled labor force. "The quality of the local education system, recreational and cultural possibilities, and the availability and cost of housing, weigh more heavily in combination than relative wage rates" (Lamphere et al. 1993:39).

Many who have studied these issues believe that it is possible for cities to respond to problems of deindustrialization in a proactive way (Clavel and Kleniewski 1990; Gittell 1992; Clarke, Gaile, and Saiz 1994). Instead of recruiting businesses, local governments can engage in entrepreneurial activities; locate their own competitive advantage; build on strengths and develop partnerships with business firms to stimulate innovative business ventures, develop new products, exploit untapped markets, and encourage investment in scientific research and human development.

Evidence suggests that poor cities are more likely to choose entrepreneurial strategies than are well-off cities (Clarke and Gaile 1994). The accumulation of urban problems is forcing city administrations to come up with innovative ways to organize their cities' economies and to address urban social needs (Gittell 1992; Goetz 1993). Their entrepreneurial activity challenges the view of public officials as being guided by short-term political incentives (Clarke, Gaile, and Saiz 1994:5–6). And their interest and willingness to invest in meeting poor residents' social needs—housing, education and health care—shows that it is possible to tie economic development to social development.

One of the criticisms of local development is that even if it were successful, so many in-migrants would be attracted that nothing would change in the long run. The price of land would increase, and housing would become more expensive. To prevent these outcomes, development should be based on the characteristics of current residents and provide job training and education that make them competitive in the job market. To avoid land speculation, cities can give incentives to developers to build affordable housing and cooperatives and can provide loans to small businesses and entrepreneurs to purchase the land for their business operations.

Life in the city will improve where progressive or entrepreneurial regimes define prosperity in both economic and social terms. Even the poorest city has some resources. It receives money from the state and federal government, has a local economy that produces some revenue, and has home owners who pay local taxes. Local regimes may invest in improving the school system, health care, and police protection, and in rebuilding the physical infrastructure of the neighborhood. However, this is contrary to current practices in poor cities like Schenectady and Flint where the local regime squanders scarce city resources trying to foster economic development through constructing office complexes, garages, and convention centers. In doing so, they further erode the living conditions of the city and drive existing businesses away.

In the absence of an entrepreneurial or progressive local regime, it is up to neighborhood- and community-based organizations to save cities. They do that by demanding that cities use existing or seek additional external resources to provide and improve services for poor people and poor neighborhoods. But poor people cannot succeed alone; they need the support of middle-class residents. It will take a coalition of poor and middle-class neighborhoods to successfully pressure city government or to elect a new one to address these demands. The poor and the middle class have different kinds of resources, and by pooling them local residents improve the chance for success.

How can a poor neighborhood like Hamilton Hill in Schenectady elicit the cooperation of middle-class neighborhood residents who are able to maintain some of their services by living in secluded neighborhoods? It is up to low-income communities to show middle-class neighborhoods that by supporting services that help the poor people, they can improve conditions of their cities and make them more economically viable. For example, increase in crime is a direct consequence of the economic and social neglect of poor communities. Residents of poor cities have a common interest in keeping children in school, that is, in improving the educational system. Social institutions are also more likely to help poor people if their tenure in the neighborhood is more stable. A safe, stable city is a goal that many in the community can support. Seeking out those common issues and interests can help build diverse, active, and committed coalitions.

To develop cooperation and understanding among residents of declining cities we need "an approach grounded in both an awareness of class and material concerns and a politics of inclusion that seeks as a priority unity among culturally diverse constituencies" (Delgado 1993:103–104). In his analysis of the work of People United for a Better Oakland (PUEBLO), an organization in Oakland, California, Delgado describes how the residents of poor neighborhoods in that city were able to establish alliances around common needs. PUEBLO's goals were to force local human-service organizations and the city government to better respond to the needs of Oakland's diverse residents. The group addressed issues in education, health care, and environmental protection. It launched campaigns, like the Campaign for Accessible Health Care, to increase the number of multilingual employees in county facilities and make free immunizations available to county residents. The organization also tapped outside resources. The combination of "formal skills training, exposure to other social movement activists, and structured internal discussions developed a leadership core in PUEBLO able to envision and develop a multiracial organization with a broad-based representation" (121). The organization also developed access to national networks, through which it obtained results of research on health-care and environmental issues and used these in the struggle for better services.

The use of extralocal ties parallels the strategy used by gentrified neighborhoods. Residents draw on their own resources but also reach outside the neighborhood for additional support. To be successful, they need the support of political leaders, the advice of experts, and positive media attention. When poor communities call on the resources of people and institutions with technical knowledge and experience about community and social struggles in many different places, they are able to conduct more effective campaigns in their communities. Several national and international community-organizing and -development networks already exist in the United States, with the primary task of sustaining neighborhood mobilization in poor neighborhoods.

National Urban Policies

It is practical and useful to rebuild cities. But is it realistic to expect that the residents of declining cities can or will do it alone? The suburbs became livable communities and desirable places to live because the government provided resources for their construction and infrastructure. Similarly, in the 1970s and 1980s the government again stepped in to help gentrify urban neighborhoods. Why do we expect that poor cities can become livable communities without national government intervention? How can poor people do what middle-class people were not able to do alone? To rebuild cities and to improve the life of poor residents, we need a combination of local, regional, and national development policies.

In the public debate, this view is gaining recognition and acceptance. But there is no consensus about how to do it. One position is that, in order to become more influential, local governments, businesses, and community-based organizations need to develop coalitions on the regional, state, and national level. Multilocal coalition tasks become "to press for reallocation of federal resources in favor of domestic needs and for redirection of the national economy in favor of workers and common citizens" (Goldsmith and Blakely 1992:12). Larger redevelopment policies, such as improving urban infrastructure, education, and health care, will help create livable communities in cities that in turn will have positive implications for urban economic development.

Another view is that declining industrial cities can benefit by being part of an integrated regional economy. In global terms regional economies are more important than the economy of a single city, just as regional clusters—companies that are in the same industry or linked through customer-supplier relationships—are more important than single companies. "The increasing importance of these regional clusters and of such concepts as just-in-time delivery, superior customer service, and close partnerships between customers and suppliers, are making location more critical than ever before" (Porter 1995:58).

This new regional-development orientation calls for more cooperation instead of competition among the cities. It also gives the states a more active role in articulating the direction of economic development and in bringing different actors together to address urban problems. Some declining industrial cities may become residential communities, while others can rebuild themselves as postindustrial production centers (see Porter 1995).

We cannot expect that every local government will have an entrepreneurial local government, but "it can pick up the garbage, control traffic, maintain the capital plan, and make the streets safer and more orderly" (Vitullo-Martin 1993:28). Residents who can find employment in a regional economy are looking for such communities. This is a niche declining industrial cities can fill. The investment in local services will pay off, because the city's face can become its fortune (cited in Vitullo-Martin 1993:34).

Even though the decentralization and fragmentation of the United States limits the role of national government now, it is clear that in the past national policies helped cities and their residents, especially those policies that targeted specific problems. The supply of affordable housing increases if resources for its construction are provided; welfare mothers find jobs and become economically independent when they are provided with child care, health benefits, education, and job training; social security is containing poverty among the elderly. Some of these policies apply to all cities; others depend more on the particular city's circumstances. The role of national government is not so much to come up with specific solutions for each city's problems, but rather to provide cities with resources that will make designing solutions possible.

To address city-specific problems, the federal government already provides resources to a broad range of organizations. Some academic institutions are already working with community-based organizations and agencies to generate more knowledge about urban problems. The synergy among these organizations is based on their strengths: Researchers have more broad-based knowledge and, because they are connected nationally and internationally, have information about successful actions and innovation at other places. Community agencies deal more with specific social problems. Their work is influenced by their direct contact with clients and their relationships with other organizations that provide fiscal resources, legitimization, and supplementary services. By combining knowledge, expertise, and skills, academic institutions and community agencies sponsor collaborative projects that bring together people who share the common goals of improving residential life and business opportunities in the cities.

Building a City for Everyone

Patterns of neighborhood mobilization show that urban spaces are important to people. Policies that improve life in a city can have long-lasting effects upon individual and group well-being. In looking for solutions to urban problems we have to start with specific characteristics of cities—the city context. Service-sector cities have solid economies, provide jobs and services, and have resources. By being part of decision making, low-income neighborhoods can gain resources for their neighborhood development. Community development creates safe neighborhoods and provides decent housing. It improves health care and education. It creates collective benefits that compensate for the lack of individual resources due. Community development in itself becomes a source of employment and brings money into the community.

The destiny of low-income neighborhoods is connected to the economic, political, and social development of whole cities. However, their organizations have to play a much more active role in city development than they do now. To save their neighborhoods, residents have to save the city as well. And to do that, they have to gain support from middle-class neighborhoods.

Declining industrial cities are like Third World countries. Their problems are caused by economic changes that they do not control. This is why residents have to take active roles in decision making and service provision if they are to help themselves. Declining industrial cities cannot compete for existing manufacturing and service-sector jobs. For the former, labor costs are too high; for latter, there are not enough well-educated residents. Instead, they have to start from their strengths and rebuild the cities around them.

Poor residents need the help of middle-class residents and entrepreneurial city administrations. Poor neighborhoods and declining cities will also need external, public financial support because they cannot maintain services and support communities on their own. To rebuild the public sector in the city they will need resources from state and national governments, foundations, nonprofit organizations, and corporations.

What if these solutions are not implemented? Cities will become more segregated and more stratified. Immigrants create ethnic enclaves and use ethnic solidarity to address collective problems. Middle-class residents create elite enclaves in cities, protected by walls and private security guards. But is it possible to have "safe" neighborhoods in an "unsafe" city? This is why residents also continue to choose the exit the cities. Black and Latino migration to suburbs exceeds that of Whites. However, the move is not always successful. Minority residents who move to the suburbs find out that it is not much better there. They often move to older suburbs, pay higher taxes than before, and still have inadequate services.

Some of these solutions also depend on how we define work, welfare, education, family needs, and crime prevention. If we are really serious about finding solutions for urban problems, we have to look at their causes. Policies that stress human development and provide resources for it also make it possible for cities to prosper. Policies that try to reduce and prevent crime by focusing on punishment are expensive and doomed to fail.

We need the public sector in the city because it facilitates a democratic way of delivering local services. It provides us with opportunities to participate in decision making, and to protect our rights as individuals. To balance a need for economic development with the need for social services, it is necessary to coordinate local, regional, and national development, to promote a civil society, to fight against racism, discrimination, and exclusion. These are not easy tasks: It is difficult to crack the entrenched interests of public workers or political machines. Not all neighborhoods and cities will succeed. But in some places, the public sector is changing. It is less bureaucratic, more flexible, and more oriented toward innovation and entrepreneurship. Together with resources provided by federal and state governments, and with participation from community residents, cities not only can achieve economic development but also can become livable communities for all their residents.

REFERENCES

Ackelsberg, Martha A. 1988. "Communities, Resistance, and Women's Activism: Some Implications for a Democratic Polity." In *Women and the Politics of Empowerment,* ed. Ann Bookman and Sandra Morgen, pp. 297–313. Philadelphia: Temple University Press.

Agnew, John A. 1978. "Market Relations and Locational Conflict in Cross-National Perspective." In *Urbanization and Conflict in Market Societies,* ed. Kevin Cox, pp. 128–143. New York: Methuen.

Albany County Planning Board. 1986. *Albany: New York's Capital Community.* Albany, N.Y.: Albany County Planning Board.

Albany Strategic Planning Committee. 1985. *Business Opportunities and Employment.* Albany, N.Y.: Nelson A. Rockefeller Institute of Government.

Aldrich, Howard E., and Jeffrey Pfeffer. 1976. *Environments of Organizations.* Annual Review of Sociology 2. Palo Alto, Calif.: Sage.

Alinsky, Saul D. 1946. *Reveille for Radicals.* Chicago: University of Chicago Press.

Arensberg, Conrad W. 1942. "Industry and Community." *American Journal of Sociology* 48:1–12.

Arnold, Joseph L. 1979. "The Neighborhood and City Hall: The Origin of Neighborhood Associations in Baltimore, 1880–1910." *Journal of Urban History* 6:3–30.

Austin, Michael J., and Neil Betten. 1990. "The Intellectual Origin of Community Organizing." In *The Roots of Community Organizing, 1917–1939,* ed. Neil Betten and Michael J. Austin, pp. 16–31. Philadelphia: Temple University Press.

Bachrach, Peter, and Morton S. Baratz. 1962. "Two Faces of Power." *American Political Science Review* 56, 4:947–952.

Banfield, Edward. 1974. *The Unheavenly City Revisited.* Boston, Mass.: Little, Brown.

Barber, Bernard. 1950. "Participation and Mass Apathy in Associations." In *Studies in Leadership,* ed. Alvin W. Gouldner, pp. 477–504. New York: Harper.

Bell, Daniel. 1976. *The Coming of Post-Industrial Society.* New York: Basic Books.

Bendick, Mark, and David Rasmussen. 1986. "Enterprise Zones and Inner-City Economic Revitalization." In *Reagan and the Cities,* ed. George E. Peterson and Carol W. Lewis, pp. 98–129. Washington, D.C.: Urban Institute.

Berry, Jeffrey M., Kent E. Portney, and Ken Thomson. 1993. *The Rebirth of Urban Democracy.* Washington, D.C.: Brookings Institution.

Biggs, John. 1994. "How to Choose from the CREF Menu for Common Stock Investments." *The Participant,* August, 6–7.

Birch, John J. 1955. *The Pioneering Church of the Mohawk Valley.* Schenectady, N.Y.: Consistory of the First Reformed Church.

Black, Thomas J. 1975. "Private-Market Housing Renovation in Central Cities: A ULI Survey." *Urban Land* 34:6.

Blakely, Edward, and Armando Aparicio. 1990. "Balancing Social and Economic Objectives: The Case of California's Community Development Corporations." *Journal of the Community Development Society* 21:115–128.

Bluestone, Barry, and Bennett Harrison. 1982. *The Deindustrialization of America.* New York: Basic Books.

Bogert, Van Der Giles. 1966. *Walls Have Ears.* Schenectady, N.Y.: Stockade Association.

Bookman, Ann. 1988. "Unionization in an Electronics Factory: The Interplay of Gender, Ethnicity, and Class." In *Women and the Politics of Empowerment,* ed. Ann Bookman and Sandra Morgen, pp. 159–179. Philadelphia: Temple University Press.

Bookman, Ann, and Sandra Morgen. 1988. "Rethinking Women and Politics." In *Women and the Politics of Empowerment,* ed. Ann Bookman and Sandra Morgen, pp. 3–32. Philadelphia: Temple University Press.

Boyer, Richard O., and Herbert M. Morais. 1955. *Labor's Untold Story.* New York: United Electrical, Radio, and Machine Workers of America.

Boyte, Harry, Heather Booth, and Steve Max. 1986. *Citizen Action and the New American Populism.* Philadelphia: Temple University Press.

Brown, Craig. 1986. "Machine Politics." In *Experiencing Albany: Perspectives on a Grand City's Past,* ed. Anne F. Roberts and J. A. Van Dyk, pp. 67–73. Albany, N.Y.: Nelson A. Rockefeller Institute of Government.

Bruce, Willard, and Todd Swanstrom. 1986. "The Albany Strategic Planning Task Force on Downtown Albany: The Present Conditions of Downtown Albany." Albany, N.Y.: City of Albany.

Bruyn, Severyn. 1987. "Beyond the Market and the State." In *Beyond the Market and the State,* ed. Severyn T. Bruyn and James Meehan, pp. 3–27. Philadelphia: Temple University Press.

Burgess, Ernest E. W. 1929. *Urban Areas of Chicago: An Experiment in Social Science Research.* Edited by T. Smith and J. White. Chicago.: University of Chicago Press.

Burnett, Alan. 1983. "Neighborhood Participation, Political Demand Making, and Local Outputs in British and North American Cities." In *Public Service Provision and Urban Development,* ed. Andrew Kirby, Paul Knox, and Steven Pinch, pp. 316–362 New York: St. Martin's.

Bursik, Robert J., and Harold G. Grasmick. 1993. *Neighborhoods and Crime: The Dimensions of Effective Community Control.* New York: Lexington.

Callaghan, Polly, and Heidi Hartmann. 1991. *Contingent Work: A Chart Book on Part-Time and Temporary Employment.* Washington, D.C.: Institute for Women's Policy Research, Economic Policy Institute.

Čapek, Stella M., and John I. Gilderbloom. 1992. *Community versus Commodity: Tenants and the American City.* Albany, N.Y.: State University of New York Press.

Castells, Manuel. 1983. *The City and the Grassroots.* Berkeley and Los Angeles: University of California Press.

Chafetz, Janet S., and Anthony G. Dworkin. 1986. *Female Revolt: Women's Movements in World and Historical Perspective.* Totowa, N.J.: Rowman and Allanheld.

Clarke, Susan E., and Gary L. Gaile. 1994. "Globalism and the New Work of Cities." Paper presented at *Shaping the Urban Future. International Perspectives and Exchanges 10–13 July 1994*, Bristol, England.

Clarke, Susan E., Gary L. Gaile, and Martin Saiz. 1994. "State and Local Developmental Strategies in Economically Depressed Areas in the USA." Paper presented at the Thirteenth World Congress of the International Sociological Association, Bielefeld, Germany, July.

Clavel, Pierre. 1986. *The Progressive City: Planning and Participation, 1969–1984.* New Brunswick, N.J.: Rutgers University Press.

Clavel, Pierre, and Nancy Kleniewski. 1990. "Space for Progressive Local Policy: Examples from the United States and the United Kingdom." In *Beyond the City Limits,* ed. John R. Logan, and Todd Swanstrom, pp. 199–234. Philadelphia: Temple University Press.

Clay, Phillip L. 1979. *Neighborhood Renewal: Middle Class Resettlement and Incumbent Upgrading in American Neighborhoods.* Lexington, Mass: Lexington Books.

Cohen, Jonathan. 1983. "Albany's Proposed Mid-Cross-town and South Mall Arterials." Report.

Coleman, James S., and Thomas Hoffer. 1987. *Public and Private High Schools: The Impact of Communities.* New York: Basic Books.

Conant, Ralph W. 1973. "Patterns of Civil Protest: Ghetto Riots." In *Political Power and the Urban Crisis,* ed. Alan Shank, pp. 445–459. Boston: Holbrook.

Conroy, Diane C. 1987. "The Fight for Civil Rights in Our Backyard." Albany: Oral History Project, State University of New York.

Coontz, Stephanie. 1992. *The Way We Never Were: American Families and the Nostalgia Trap.* New York: Basic Books.

Corning, Erastus. Papers. Box 5, Albany Hall of Records, Albany, N.Y.

Cox, Kevin R. 1973. *Conflicts, Power, and Politics in the City.* New York: McGraw Hill.

———. 1981. "Capitalism and Conflict around the Communal Living Space." In *Urbanization and Urban Planning in Capitalist Society,* ed. Michael Dear and Allen J. Scott, pp. 431–456. New York: Methuen.

Cox, Kevin R., and Jeffrey M. McCarthy. 1980. "Neighborhood Activism in the American City." *Urban Geography* 1:22–28.

Craypo, Charles, and Bruce Nissen. 1993a. "The Impact of Corporate Strategies," in *Grand Designs: The Impact of Corporate Strategies on Workers, Unions, and Communities,* ed. Charles Craypo and Bruce Nissen, pp. 224–250. Ithaca, N.Y.: ILR Press.

———. 1993b. "Introduction," in *Grand Designs: The Impact of Corporate Strategies on Workers, Unions, and Communities,* ed. Charles Craypo and Bruce Nissen, pp. 3–17. Ithaca, N.Y.: ILR Press.

Crenson, Matthew. 1983. *Neighborhood Politics.* Cambridge: Harvard University Press.

Crowe, Kenneth C., II. 1988. "Albany GOP Seeks to Revive Police Unit." *Albany Times Union,* May 28.

Cumbler, John T. 1979. *Working Class Community in Industrial America; Work, Leisure, and Struggle in Two Industrial Cities, 1880–1930.* Westport, Conn.: Greenwood.

Curtis, Lynn A. 1985. *American Violence and Public Policy: An Update of the National Commission on the Causes and Prevention of Violence.* New Haven, Conn.: Yale University Press.

Dahl, Robert Alan. 1961. *Who Governs?* New Haven, Conn.: Yale University Press.

Davidson, Jeffrey. 1979. *Political Partnerships: Neighborhood Residents and their Council Members.* Beverly Hills, Calif.: Sage.

Davis, John E. 1991. *Contested Ground: Collective Action and the Urban Neighborhoods.* Ithaca, N.Y.: Cornell University Press.

Davis, Thomas J. 1983. "Three Dark Centuries around Albany: A Survey of Black Life in New York's Capital City Area before World War I." *Afro-Americans in New York Life and History* 7 (1).

DeGiovanni, Frank F., and N. Paulson. 1984. "Housing Diversity in Revitalizing Neighborhoods." *Urban Affairs Quarterly* 202:211–232.

Delgado, Gary. 1993. "Building Multiracial Alliances: The Case of People United for a Better Oakland." In *Mobilizing the Community: Local Politics in the Era of the Global City,* ed. Robert Fisher and Joseph Kling, pp. 103–127. Urban Affairs Annual Review 41. Newbury Park, Calif.: Sage.

DiMaggio, Paul J., and Walter W. Powell. 1983. "The Iron Cage Revisited: Institutional Isomorphism and Collective Rationality in Organizational Fields." *American Sociological Review* 48:147–160.

Dougherty, Laurie. 1993. "Jack and Me." *Dollars and Sense.* September 12–15.

Downs, Anthony. 1976. *Urban Problems and Prospects.* Chicago: Rand McNally

———. 1981. *Neighborhood and Urban Development.* Washington, D.C.: Brookings Institution.

DuBow, Fred, and David Emmons. 1981. "The Community Hypothesis." In *Reactions to Crime,* ed. Dan A. Lewis, pp. 167–182. Beverly Hills, Calif.: Sage.

Dunn, Robert. 1986. "Hamilton Hill Street Blues: Straight Talk from a Schenectady Cop." *Capitol Region Magazine,* November,: 28–32.

Egan Timothy. 1995. "Many Seek Security in Private Communities." *New York Times.* September 3,1.

Eisinger, K. Peter. 1988. *The Rise of the Entrepreneurial State: State and Local Development Policy in the United States.* Madison: University of Wisconsin Press.

Elkin, Stephen L. 1985. "Twentieth Century Urban Regimes." *Journal of Urban Affairs* 7(3):11–28.

———. 1987. "State and Market in City Politics: Or, the 'Real' Dallas." In *The Politics of Urban Development,* ed. Clarence Stone and Heywood T. Sanders, pp. 25–51. Lawrence: University Press of Kansas.

Etzioni, Amitai. 1991. *A Responsive Society: Collected Essays on Guiding Deliberate Social Change.* San Francisco, Calif.: Jossey-Bass.

Fainstein, Norman, and Susan Fainstein. 1986a. "Economic Change, National Policy, and the System of Cities." In *Restructuring the City: The Political Economy of Urban Redevelopment,* ed. Norman Fainstein and Susan Fainstein, pp. 1–26. White Plains, N.Y.: Longman.

———. 1986b. "Regime Strategies, Communal Resistance, and Economic Forces." In *Restructuring the City: The Political Economy of Urban Redevelopment,* ed. Norman Fainstein and Susan Fainstein, pp. 245–282. White Plains, N.Y.: Longman.

Fasenfest, David. 1993. "Cui Bono?" In *Grand Designs; The Impact of Corporate Strategies on Workers, Unions, and Communities,* ed. Charles Craypo and Bruce Nissen, pp. 119–137. Ithaca, N.Y.: ILR Press.

Feagin, Joe R. 1985. "The Socioeconomic Base of Urban Growth: The Case of Houston and the Oil Industry." *American Journal of Sociology* 90(6):1204–1230.

Fischer, Claude S. 1982. *To Dwell among Friends: Personal Networks in Town and City.* Chicago: University of Chicago Press.

Fisher, Robert. 1984. *Let the People Decide: Neighborhood Organizing in America.* Boston: Twayne.

Fosler, Scott R. 1991. "Human Capital Investment and Federalism." In *Human Capital and the American Future,* ed. David W. Hornbeck and Lester M. Salamon, pp. 297–327. Baltimore: Johns Hopkins University Press.

Galaskiewicz, Joseph. 1979. *Exchange Networks and Community Politics.* Beverly Hills, Calif.: Sage.

Gamson, William. 1968. *Power and Discontent.* Homewood, Ill.: Dorsey.

———. 1975. *The Strategy of Social Protest.* Homewood, Ill.: Dorsey.

Gans, Herbert. 1962. *The Urban Villagers.* New York: Free Press.

Gesensway, Deborah. 1988. "Money Pinch." *Schenectady Times Union,* November 6, B5.

Gilkes, Cheryl Townsend. 1988. "Building in Many Places: Multiple Commitments and Ideologies in Black Women's Community Work." In *Women and the Politics of Empowerment,* ed. Ann Bookman and Sandra Morgen, pp. 53–76. Philadelphia: Temple University Press.

Gittell, Marilyn. 1980. *Limits to Citizen Participation: The Decline of Community Organizations.* Beverly Hills, Calif.: Sage.

Gittell, Ross. 1992. *Renewing Cities.* Princeton, N.J.: Princeton University Press.

Glyn, Andrew, Alan Hughes, Alain Lipietz, and Ajit Singh. 1990. "The Rise and Fall of the Golden Age." In *The Golden Age of Capitalism,* ed. Stephen Marglin and Juliet Schor, pp. 39–125. Oxford, Eng.: Clarendon.

Goering, John M. 1979. "The National Neighborhood Movement: A Preliminary Analysis and Critique." *American Planners Association Journal* 45: 506–514.

Goetz, Edward. 1993. *Shelter Burden.* Philadelphia: Temple University Press.

Gold, Daniel. 1987. "Arbor Hill: A Political Battleground." *Albany Times Union,* July 5.

Goldsmith, William W., and Edward J. Blakely. 1992. *Separate Societies: Poverty and Inequality in U.S. Cities.* Philadelphia: Temple University Press.

Goode, Judith G., Jo Anne Schneider, and Suzanne Blanc. 1992. "Transcending Boundaries and Closing Ranks: How Schools Shape Interrelations." In *Structuring Diversity: Ethnographic Perspectives on the New Immigration,* ed. Louise Lamphere, pp. 173–214. Chicago: University of Chicago Press.

Gottdiener, Mark. 1985. *The Social Production of Urban Space.* Austin: University of Texas Press.

Gottlieb, Naomi. 1992. "Empowerment, Political Analyses, and Services for Women." In *Human Services as Complex Organizations,* ed. Yeheskell Hasenfeld, pp. 301–319. Beverly Hills, Calif.: Sage.

Granovetter, Mark. 1973. "The Strength of Weak Ties." *American Journal of Sociology* 78:1360–1380.

———. 1992. *Sociology of Economic Life.* Boulder, Colo.: Westview.

Greenberg, Stephanie. 1985. *Informal Citizen Action and Crime Prevention at the Neighborhood Level.* Washington, D.C.: National Institute of Justice.

Greenhouse, Linda. 1974. "Mall Neighborhood in Fight to Preserve Charm." *New York Times,* February 20, M/33.

Greer, Scott. 1962. *The Emerging City: Myth and Reality.* New York: Free Press.

Guest, Avery M. 1985. "The Mediate Community: The Nature of Local and Extra-Local Ties within the Metropolis." Paper presented at the American Sociological Association Annual Meeting, Washington D.C., August 29.

Guest, Avery M., and Sol R. Oropesa. 1984. "Problem-Solving Strategies of Local Areas in the Metropolis." *American Sociological Review* 49:828–840

Gutiérrez, Lorraine M. 1992. "Empowering Ethnic Minorities in the Twenty-First Century: The Role of Human Service Organizations." In *Human Services as Complex Organizations,* ed. Yeheskell Hasenfeld, pp. 320–338. Beverly Hills, Calif.: Sage.

Gutman, Herbert G. 1976. *Work, Culture, and Society in Industrializing America: Essays in American Working-Class and Social History.* New York: Knopf.

Hallman, Howard W. 1984. *Neighborhoods: Their Place in Urban Life.* Beverly Hills, Calif.: Sage.

Haraven, Tamara K. 1982. *Family and Industry in New England.* New York: Cambridge University Press.

Hardy-Fanta, Carol. 1993. *Latina Politics, Latino Politics: Gender, Culture, and Political Participation in Boston.* Philadelphia: Temple University Press.

Hart, Larry. 1975. *Tales of Old Schenectady.* Scotia, N.Y.: Old Dorp Books.

———. 1984. *Schenectady: A Pictorial History.* Scotia:, N.Y. Old Dorp Books.

Harvey, David. 1973. *Social Justice and the City.* Baltimore: John Hopkins University Press.

Hasenfeld, Yeheskell. 1983. *Human Service Organizations.* Englewood Cliffs, N.J.: Prentice-Hall.

Henig, Jeffrey R. 1982. *Neighborhood Mobilization: Redevelopment and Response.* New Brunswick, N.J.: Rutgers University Press.

Heskin, Allan David. 1991. *The Struggle for Community.* Boulder, Colo.: Westview.

Hirschman, Albert. 1970. *Exit, Voice, and Loyalty: Response to Decline in Firms, Organizations, and States.* Cambridge: Harvard University Press.

Huey, John. 1991. "The Best Cities for Business." *Fortune Magazine,* November 4, 52–84.

Hunter, Albert. 1974. *Symbolic Communities: The Persistence and Change of Chicago's Local Communities.* Chicago: University of Chicago Press.

Jackson, Kenneth T. 1985. *Crabgrass Frontier: The Suburbanization of the United States.* New York: Oxford University Press.

Janelle, Donald G. 1977. "Structural Dimension in the Geography of Locational Conflicts." *Canadian Geographer* 21:311–328.

Janowitz, Morris. 1952. *The Community Press in an Urban Setting.* Glencoe, Ill.: Free Press.

Jochnowitz, Jay. 1988. "Whalen Spurns Meeting on Arbor Hill with Republican Leader." *Albany Times Union.* September 13.

Judd, Dennis R, and Todd Swanstrom. 1994. *City Politics: Private Power and Public Policy.* New York: Harper Collins.

Kantor, Paul, with Stephen David. 1987. *The Dependent City: The Changing Political Economy of Urban America.* Glenview, Ill.: Scott, Foresman.

Kasarda, John. 1983. "Entry Level Jobs, Mobility, and Minority Unemployment." *Urban Affairs Quarterly* 19(1):21–40

Kasarda, John D., and Morris Janowitz. 1977. "Community Attachment in Mass Society." *American Sociological Review* 39: 328–340.

———. 1993. "Urban Industrial Transition and the Underclass." In *The Ghetto Underclass: Social Science Perspectives*, ed. William J. Wilson, pp. 43–64. Newbury Park, Calif.: Sage.

Kava, Janine. 1994. "City Reduces Drug Violence, Still Sees Threat." *Schenectady Daily Gazette*, December 21.

Kendall, Richard. 1986. "Making a Living: Merchants, Manufacturers, and Bureaucrats." In *Experiencing Albany: Perspectives on a Grand City's Past* ed. Anne F. Roberts and J. A. Van Dyk, pp. 43–49. Albany, N.Y.: Nelson A. Rockefeller Institute of Government.

Kennedy, William O. 1983. *O Albany.* Harrisonburg, Va.: Viking-Penguin.

Kenney, Alice P. 1985. "Crossroads of Centuries." In *Albany Tercentennial Guidebook*, ed. Duane LaFleche, pp. 143–164. Albany, N.Y.: Matthew Bender.

Knoke, David and James R. Wood. 1981. *Organized for Action: Commitment in Voluntary Associations.* New Brunswick, N.J.: Rutgers University Press.

Kurp, Patrick. 1986. "The Hill." *Albany Knickerbocker News*, December 17.

Lamphere, Louise. 1992. "Introduction." In *Structuring Diversity: Ethnographic Perspectives on the New Immigration*, ed. Louise Lamphere, pp. 1–34. Chicago: University of Chicago Press.

Lamphere, Louise, Patricia Zavella, and Felipe Gonzales, with Peter B. Evans. 1993. *Sunbelt Working Mothers: Reconciling Family and Factory.* Ithaca, N.Y.: Cornell University Press.

Lavrakas, Paul J. 1985. "Citizen Self-Help and Neighborhood Crime Prevention Policy." In *American Violence and Public Policy*, ed. Lynn A. Curtis, pp. 87–116. New Haven, Conn.: Yale University Press.

Lawson, Ronald, and Stephen E. Barton. 1990. "Sex Roles in Social Movements: A Case Study of the Tenant Movement in New York City." In *Women and Social Protest*, ed. Guida West and Rhoda L. Blumberg, pp. 41–56. New York: Oxford University Press.

Leavitt, Jacqueline, and Susan Seagert. 1988. "The Community-household: Responding to Housing Abandonment in New York City." *Journal of the American Planning Association* 54 (4):489–500.

Lee, Barnett A., S. R. Oropesa, B. J. Metch, and A. M. Guest. 1984. "Testing the Decline-of-Community Thesis." *American Journal of Sociology* 89:1161–1181.

Lemann, Nicholas. 1994. "The Myth of Community Development." *New York Times Magazine*, January 9.

Ley, David, and John Mercer. 1980. "Locational Conflict and the Politics of Consumption." *Economic Geography* 56:89–109.

Lin, Nan. 1982. "Social Resources and Instrumental Action." In *Social Structure and Network Analysis*, ed. Peter V. Marsden and Nan Lin, pp. 131–146. Beverly Hills, Calif.: Sage.

Lin, Nan, Paul W. Dayton, and Peter Greenwald. 1978. "Analyzing the Instrumental Use of Relations in the Context of Social Structure." *Sociological Methods and Research* 7: 149–166.

Lin, Nan, Walter M. Ensel, and John C. Vaughn. 1981. "Social Resources and the Strength of Ties: Structural Factors in Occupational Status Attainment." *American Sociological Review* 46:393–405.

Lind, Amy C. 1992. "Power, Gender, and Development: Popular Women's Organizations and the Politics of Needs in Ecuador." In *The Making of Social Movements in Latin America: Identity, Strategy, and Democracy*, ed. Arturo Escobar and Sonia Alvarez, pp. 134–149. Boulder, Colo.: Westview.

Lipsky, Michael. 1980. *Street-Level Bureaucracy.* New York: Russell Sage Foundation.

Logan, John R. 1988. "Fiscal and Developmental Crisis in Black Suburbs: The Case of Philadelphia." In *Business Elites and Urban Development: Case Studies and Critical Perspectives*, ed. Scott Cummings, pp. 333–356. Albany: State of New York University Press.

Logan, John R., and Harvey Molotch. 1987. *Urban Fortunes: The Political Economy of Place.* Berkeley and Los Angeles: University of California Press.

Logan, John R., and Gordana Rabrenovic. 1990. "Neighborhood Associations: Their Issues, Allies, and Opponents." *Urban Affairs Quarterly* 26(1):68–94.

Long, Norman. 1973. "Have Cities a Future?" *Public Administration Review* 33(6):543–552.

Lowe, P. D. 1977. "Amenity and Equity: A Review of Local Environmental Pressure Groups in Britain." *Environment and Planning* 9:35–58.

Mansbridge, Jane J. 1980. *Beyond Adversary Democracy.* New York: Basic Books.

Marglin, Stephen A., and Juliet B. Schore, eds. 1990. *The Golden Age of Capitalism: Reinterpreting the Post War Experience.* Oxford, Eng.: Clarendon.

Marsden, Peter V., and Jeanne S. Hurbert. 1988. "Social Resources and Mobility Outcomes: A Replication and Extension." *Social Forces* 66(4):1038–1059.

Marx, Karl. 1967. *Capital.* 3 vols. New York: International Publishers.

Massey, Douglas S. 1990. "American Apartheid: Segregation and the Making of the Underclass." *American Journal of Sociology* 96:329–357.

Massey, Douglas S., and Nancy A. Denton. 1988. "Suburbanization and Segregation in U.S. Metropolitan Areas." *American Journal of Sociology* 94:592–626.

Mayer, Neil S. 1984. *Neighborhood Organizations and Community Development: Making Revitalization Work.* Washington D.C.: Urban Institute.

Mayfield, Lorraine P. 1991. "Early Parenthood among Low-Income Adolescent Girls." In *The Black Family*, ed. Robert Staples, pp. 227–239. Belmont, Calif.: Wadsworth.

McCarthy, John, and Mayer Zald. 1977. "Resource Mobilization and Social Movements: A Partial Theory." *American Journal of Sociology* 82:1212–1241.

McCourt, Kathleen. 1977. *Working-Class Women and Grass-Roots Politics.* Bloomington: Indiana University Press.

McDonald, S. C. 1983. Human and Market Dynamics in the Gentrification of a Boston Neighborhood. Ph.D. diss., Harvard University.

McEneny, John J. 1981. *Albany: Capital City on the Hudson.* Woodland Hills, N.Y.: Windsor.

McKenzie, Richard B. 1984. *Fugitive Industry: The Economics and Politics of Deindustrialization.* San Francisco: Pacific Institute for Public Policy Research.

McKenzie, Roderick Duncan. 1923. *The Neighborhoods: A Study of Local Life in the City of Columbus, Ohio.* Chicago: University of Chicago Press.

Merton, Robert K. 1957. *Social Theory and Social Structure.* Glencoe, Ill.: Free Press.

Meyer, John W., and Brian Rowan. 1977. "Institutionalized Organizations: Formal Structure as Myth and Ceremony." *American Journal of Sociology* 83:340–363.

———. 1983. "The Structure of Educational Organizations." In *Organizational Environments: Rituals and Rationality,* ed. John W. Meyer and Brian Rowan, pp. 71–99. Beverly Hills, Calif.: Sage.

Milofsky, Karl. 1987. "Neighborhood-Based Organizations: A Market Analogy." In *The Nonprofit Sector: A Research Handbook,* ed. Walter W. Powell, pp. 277–296. New Haven, Conn.: Yale University Press.

Mollenkopf, John H. 1983. *The Contested City.* Princeton, N.J.: Princeton University Press.

Mollenkopf, John H., and Manuel Castells. 1991. *Dual City: Restructuring New York.* New York: Russell Sage Foundation.

Molotch, Harvey. 1976. "The City as a Growth Machine." *American Journal of Sociology* 82:309–330.

Monroe, Joel Henry. 1914. *Schenectady: Ancient and Modern.* Geneva, N.Y.: W. F. Humphrey.

Morgen, Sandra. 1988. "It's the Whole Power of the City against Us: The Development of Political Consciousness in a Women's Health Care Coalition." In *Women and the Politics of Empowerment,* ed. Ann Bookman and Sandra Morgen, pp. 97–115. Philadelphia: Temple University Press.

Naples, Nancy. 1991. "Contradictions in the Gender Subtext of the War on Poverty: The Community Work and Resistance of Women from Low Income Communities." *Social Problems* 38:316–332.

Nash, June C. 1989. *From Tank Town to High Tech: The Clash of Community and Industrial Cycles.* Albany: State University of New York Press.

Newman, Oscar. 1981. *Community of Interest.* Garden City, N.Y.: Anchor.

Nilsson, B. A. 1988. "Shedding Light on General Electric's Past." *Metroland,* November 17–23, 10–16.

Nissen, Bruce. 1993. "Successful Labor-Community Coalition Building." In *Grand Designs: The Impact of Corporate Strategies on Workers, Unions, and Communities,* ed. Charles Craypo and Bruce Nissen, pp. 209–223. Ithaca, N.Y.: ILR Press.

Oberschall, Anthony. 1973. *Social Conflict and Social Movements.* Englewood Cliffs, N.J.: Prentice-Hall.

O'Brien, David. 1975. *Neighborhood Organization and Interest-Group Processes.* Princeton, N.J.: Princeton University Press.

Osborne, David, and Ted Gaebler. 1992. *Reinventing Government: How the Entrepreneurial Spirit Is Transforming the Public Sector.* Reading, Mass.: Addison-Wesley.

Osterman, Paul. 1989. *In the Midst of Plenty: A Profile of Boston and Its Poor.* Boston: Persistent Poverty Project, Boston Foundation.

Pare, Terence P. 1994. "Jack Welch's Nightmare on Wall Street." *Fortune Magazine,* September 5, 40–48.

Park, Robert E., and Ernest E. W. Burgess. 1925. *The City.* Chicago: University of Chicago Press.

Pascucci, Robert R. 1984. "Electric City Immigrants: Italians and Poles in Schenectady, N.Y., 1880–1930. Ph.D. diss., State University of New York at Albany.

Paterson, Thomas. 1973. *Soviet-American Confrontation: Post-War Reconstruction and the Origins of the Cold War.* Baltimore: Johns Hopkins University Press.

Perrucci, Carolyn C., Robert Perrucci, Dena B. Targ, and Harry R. Targ. 1988. *Plant Closings: International Context and Social Costs.* New York: Aldine De Gruyter.

Peterson, Paul E. 1981. *City Limits.* Chicago: University of Chicago Press.

Pfeffer, Jeffrey, and Gerald R. Salancik. 1978. *The External Control of Organizations: A Resource Dependence Perspective.* New York: Harper and Row.

Piven, Frances Fox, and Richard A. Cloward. 1979. *Poor People's Movements: Why They Succeed, How They Fail.* New York: Vintage.

Podolefsky, Aaron M., and Fred DuBow. 1981. *Strategies for Community Crime Prevention.* Springfield, Ill.: Thomas.

Pope, Jackie. 1990. "Women in the Welfare Rights Struggle: The Brooklyn Welfare Action Council." In *Women and Social Protest,* ed. Guida West and Rhoda L. Blumberg, pp. 57–74. New York: Oxford University Press.

Porter, Michael. 1995. "The Competitive Advantage of the Inner City." *Harvard Business Review* 73:55–71

Portz, John. 1990. *The Politics of Plant Closings.* Lawrence: University Press of Kansas.

Rabrenovic, Gordana. 1995. "Women and Collective Action in Urban Neighborhoods." In *Gender in Urban Research,* ed. Judith A. Garber and Robyne S. Turner, pp. 77–96. Urban Affairs Annual Review 42. Thousand Oaks, Calif.: Sage.

Rachleff, Peter. 1994. "A Page from History? Seeds of a Labor Resurgency." *Nation* February 21, 226–229.

Reich, Robert. 1991. *The Work of Nations.* New York: Knopf.

Reidy, Daniel F. 1975. *Urban Ethnic Organizing.* Working Paper Series #6. New York: Institute on Pluralism and Group Identity.

Rich, Kathryn. 1966. "George R. Lunn: Socialist Mayor of Schenectady." Available at the Schenectady Country Public Library. Report.

Rich, Richard. 1980a. "The Dynamics of Leadership in Neighborhood Organizations." *Social Science Quarterly* 60:570–587.

———. 1980b. "A Political-Economy Approach to the Study of Neighborhood Organizations." *American Journal of Political Science* 24:559–592.

Robinson, Frank. 1973. *Albany's O'Connell Machine: An American Political Relic.* Albany: Washington Park Spirit.

Roseberry, Cecil R. 1964. *Capitol Story.* Albany: State of New York.

Rosenbaum, Dennis P. 1987. "The Theory and Research behind Neighborhood Watch: Is It a Sound Fear and Crime Reduction Strategy?" *Crime and Delinquency* 33: 103–134.

Rowley, William E. 1959. "Albany Slow in Fight on Urban Blight." *Albany Knickerbocker News,* August 19, A16.

Rubin, J. Herbert. 1994. "There Ain't Going to Be Any Bakeries Here If There Is No Money to Afford Jelly Rolls: The Organic Theory of Community Based Development." *Social Problems* 41:401–424.

Sacks, Karen. 1988. *Caring by the Hour: Women, Work, and Organizing at Duke Medical Center.* Urbana: University of Illinois Press.

Sampson, Robert J. 1988. "Local Friendship Ties and Community Attachment in Mass Society: A Multilevel Systemic Model." *American Sociological Review* 53:766–779.

Saunders, Peter. 1981. *Social Theory and the Urban Question.* London: Hutchinson.

Schnectady City Directory. 1912. Schnectady, N.Y.: H. A. Manning.

Schoenberg, Sandra, and Patricia Rosenbaum. 1980. *Neighborhoods That Work: Sources for Viability in the Inner City.* New Brunswick, N.J.: Rutgers University Press.

Schumpeter, Joseph A. 1950. *Capitalism, Socialism, and Democracy.* New York: Free Press.

Scott, Richard W. 1987. *Organizations: Rational, Natural, and Open Systems.* Englewood Cliffs, N.J.: Prentice-Hall.

Sears, David, and John McConahay. 1973. *The Politics of Violence: The New Urban Blacks and Watts Riot.* Boston: Houghton Mifflin.

Seyse, J. 1987. "Arbor Hill Urban Renewal Project." Unpublished paper.

Skogan, Wesley G. 1990. *Disorder and Decline: Crime and the Spiral of Decay in American Neighborhoods.* New York: Free Press.

Skolnick, Jerome H., and David H. Bayley. 1986. *The New Blue Line: Police Innovation in Six American Cities.* New York: Free Press.

Smith, Christopher. 1988. *Public Problems: The Management of Urban Distress.* New York: Guilford.

Smith, Michael Peter, and Marlene Keller. 1983. "Managed Growth and the Politics of Uneven Development in New Orleans." In *Restructuring the City: The Political Economy of Urban Redevelopment,* ed. Norman Fainstein and Susan Fainstein, pp. 126–166. White Plains, N.Y.: Longman.

Sorin, S. Gretchen, Bruce Buckley, and Beth Kloppot. 1989. *New Audiences for the Year 2000—Phase II. Final Report.* Albany, N.Y.: Albany Institute of History and Art.

Sparrow, Malcolm K. 1988. *Implementing Community Policing.* Washington, D.C.: National Institute for Justice.

Stack, Carol B. 1974. *All Our Kin: Strategies for Survival in a Black Community.* New York: Harper and Row.

Stanback, Thomas M., and Thierry J. Noyelle. 1982. *Cities in Transition.* Totowa, N.J.: Alanheld, Osmun.

Stephen, Lynn. 1992. "Women in Mexico's Popular Movements: Survival Strategies against Ecological and Economic Impoverishment." *Latin American Perspectives* 19(1): 73–96.

Stockade Spy. Stockade Historical Society, Schenectady, N.Y.

Stoecker, Randy. 1991. *Community Organizing and Community Development in Cedar-Riverside and East Toledo: A Comparative Study.* Toledo, Ohio: Urban Affairs Center, University of Toledo.

———. 1994. *Defending Community: The Struggle for Alternative Redevelopment in Cedar-Riverside.* Philadelphia: Temple University Press.

Stone, Clarence N. 1987. "The Study of the Politics of Urban Development." In *The Politics of Urban Development,* ed. Clarence N. Stone and Heywood T. Sanders, pp. 3–22. Lawrence: University Press of Kansas

———. 1989. *Regime Politics.* Lawrence: University Press of Kansas.

Susser, Ida. 1982. *Norman Street: Poverty and Politics in an Urban Neighborhood.* New York: Oxford University Press.

———. 1988. "Working-Class Women, Social Protest, and Changing Ideologies. In *Women and the Politics of Empowerment,* ed. Ann Bookman and Sandra Morgen, pp. 257–271. Philadelphia: Temple University Press.

Suttles, Gerald. 1972. *The Social Construction of Communities.* Chicago: University of Chicago Press.

Swanstrom, Todd. 1985. *The Crisis of Growth Politics: Cleveland, Kucinich, and the Challenge of Urban Populism.* Philadelphia: Temple University Press.

Swanstrom, Todd, and Sharon Ward. 1987. "Albany's O'Connell Organization: The Survival of an Entrenched Machine." Paper presented at the Annual Meeting of the American Political Science Association, Chicago, September.

Taub, Richard P., and George P. Surgeon. 1977. "Urban Voluntary Associations, Locality Based and Externally Induced." *American Journal of Sociology* 83:425–442.

Thomas, Clayton John. 1986. *Between Citizen and City: Neighborhood Organizations and Urban Politics in Cincinnati.* Lawrence: University Press of Kansas.

Tichy, Noel, and Stratford Sherman. 1993. *Control Your Destiny or Someone Else Will: How Jack Welch Is Making GE the World's Most Competitive Corporation.* New York: Doubleday.

Tiebout, Charles M. 1956. "A Pure Theory of Local Expenditures." *Journal of Political Economy* 64:416–424.

Tilly, Charles. 1973. "Does Modernization Breed Revolution?" *Comparative Politics* 5:425–447.

Titterton, Pat. 1988. "Electric City Limits." *Metroland,* November 17–23, 10–16.

Tönnies, Ferdinand. 1963. *Community and Society.* Translated and edited by Charles P. Loomis. New York: Harper.

Touraine, Alain. 1981. *The Voice and the Eye: An Analysis of Social Movements.* Cambridge: Cambridge University Press.

U.S. Department of Commerce, Bureau of the Census. 1981. *Census of Population and Housing.* Washington, D.C.: U.S. Government Printing Office.

———. 1988. *Statistical Abstract of the United States.* Washington D.C.:U.S. Government Printing Office.

Uriarte, Miren B., and Nelson Merced. 1985. "Social Service Agencies in Boston's Latino Community: Notes on Institutionalization." *Catalyst* 5, (17/18): 21–33.

Verba, Sidney, and Norman H. Nie. 1972. *Participation in America.* New York: Harper and Row.

Vitullo-Martin, Julia. 1993. "The Livable City." *City Journal,* Autumn, 27–34.

Vogel, Ronald. 1992. *Urban Political Economy.* Gainesville: University Press of Florida.

Walkowitz, Daniel J. 1978. *Worker City, Company Town.* Urbana: University of Illinois Press.

Wamsley, Gary L., and Mayer N. Zald. 1973. *The Political Economy of Public Organizations.* Lexington, Mass.: Heath.

Warner, Sam Bass, Jr. 1968. *The Private City: Philadelphia in Three Periods of Its Growth.* Philadelphia: University of Pennsylvania Press.

Weiher, R. Gregory. 1991. *The Fractured Metropolis. Political Fragmentation and Metropolitan Segregation.* Albany: State University of New York Press.

Weise, Arthur James. 1884. *The History of the City of Albany, New York.* Albany, N.Y.: E. H. Bender.

Wellman, Barry. 1979. "The Community Question: The Intimate Network of East Yorkers." *American Journal of Sociology* 84:1201–1231.

West, Guida, and Rhoda L. Blumberg. 1990. "Reconstructing Social Protest from a Feminist Perspective." In *Women and Social Protest,* ed. Guida West and Rhoda L. Blumberg, pp. 3–35. New York: Oxford University Press.

Williams, Michael R. 1985. *Neighborhood Organizations: Seeds of a New Urban Life.* Westport, Conn.: Greenwood.

Wilson, William Julius. 1987. *The Truly Disadvantaged: The Inner City, the Underclass, and Public Policy.* Chicago: University of Chicago Press.

Wolfe, Jeanne M., and Grace Stracham. 1988. "Practical Idealism: Women in Urban Reform, Julia Drummond and the Montreal Park and Playground Association." In *Life Spaces: Gender, Household, Employment,* ed. Caroline Andrew and Beth Moore Milroy, pp. 65–80. Vancouver, University of British Columbia Press.

Wood, James R. 1981. *Leadership in Voluntary Organizations.* New Brunswick, N.J.: Rutgers University Press.

Zald, Mayer. 1970. *Organizational Change: The Political Economy of the YMCA.* Chicago: University of Chicago Press.

———. 1987. "The Future of Social Movements." In *Social Movements in an Organizational Society,* ed. Mayer Zald and John McCarthy. New Brunswick, N.J.: Transaction.

Zavella, Patricia. 1987. *Women's Work and Chicano Families: Cannery Workers of the Santa Clara Valley.* Ithaca, N.Y.: Cornell University Press.

Zdenek, Robert. 1987. "Community Development Corporations." In *Beyond the Market and the State,* ed. Severyn T. Bruyn and James Meehan, pp. 112–130. Philadelphia: Temple University Press.

Zukin, Sharon. 1987. "Gentrification: Culture and Capital in the Urban Core." *Annual Review in Sociology* 13:129–147.

INDEX